WRITING FOR
EMERGING
SOCIOLOGISTS

Because we believe that anyone can write and everyone should

Angelique Harris | Alia R. Tyner-Mullings
Marquette University *The New Community College at CUNY*

WRITING FOR EMERGING SOCIOLOGISTS

Los Angeles | London | New Delhi
Singapore | Washington DC

Los Angeles | London | New Delhi
Singapore | Washington DC

FOR INFORMATION:

SAGE Publications, Inc.
2455 Teller Road
Thousand Oaks, California 91320
E-mail: order@sagepub.com

SAGE Publications Ltd.
1 Oliver's Yard
55 City Road
London EC1Y 1SP
United Kingdom

SAGE Publications India Pvt. Ltd.
B 1/I 1 Mohan Cooperative Industrial Area
Mathura Road, New Delhi 110 044
India

SAGE Publications Asia-Pacific Pte. Ltd.
3 Church Street
#10-04 Samsung Hub
Singapore 049483

Acquisitions Editor: David Repetto
Editorial Assistant: Lauren Johnson
Production Editor: Brittany Bauhaus
Copy Editor: Megan Granger
Typesetter: C&M Digitals (P) Ltd.
Proofreader: Sally Jaskold
Cover Designer: Karine Hovsepian
Marketing Manager: Erica DeLuca
Permissions Editor: Karen Ehrmann

Copyright © 2013 by SAGE Publications, Inc.

Printed in the United States of America

Library of Congress Cataloging-in-Publication Data

Harris, Angelique.
Writing for emerging sociologists / Angelique Harris, Marquette University, USA, Alia Tyner-Mullings, The New Community College, City University of New York.

pages cm
ISBN 978-1-4129-9179-7 (pbk. : alk. paper)

1. Sociology—Authorship. 2. Sociology—Research. I. Tyner-Mullings, Alia. II. Title.

HM569.H37 2013
301.072—dc23   2012040731

This book is printed on acid-free paper.

SUSTAINABLE FORESTRY INITIATIVE
Certified Chain of Custody
Promoting Sustainable Forestry
www.sfiprogram.org
SFI-01268

SFI label applies to text stock

12 13 14 15 16 10 9 8 7 6 5 4 3 2 1

BRIEF CONTENTS

DETAILED CONTENTS

ACKNOWLEDGMENTS

The writers of this fully coauthored volume would first like to acknowledge the contributors to the "Writing in Practice" sections that appear in every chapter (starting with Chapter 2). We greatly appreciate the work they put into their writing and the advice they provided to us and will provide to the students and professionals reading this book. The authors would also like to thank research assistants from California State University, Fullerton, and Marquette University—Omar Mushtaq, Burrel Vann, Jr., and Nikhita Navani—who helped us conduct research and gather material, as well as assisting with the editing and organization of this project. Additionally, we send thanks to the many college and university professors who reviewed an early version of this text and provided us with valuable feedback. Finally, we are extremely grateful to our editors at SAGE for their interest in this project and their dedication to working with us during its creation.

Individual Acknowledgments

First and foremost, I'd like to thank my coauthor, Alia Tyner-Mullings, whose insight and partnership were vital to the production of this text. I owe much gratitude to my undergraduate and graduate school professors, who are far too many to name, for their help and encouragement. I thank my past and current professional colleagues for the advice and motivation they have provided me. I'd also like to thank my family and friends for their support through the process of writing this text.

—Angelique Harris

I would first like to thank all my students and colleagues, whose struggles with writing inspired me to embark on this project. I also greatly appreciate the teachers at Central Park East Secondary School, Oberlin College, and the Graduate School and University Center, City University of New York, whose patience, knowledge, and mentorship gave me the opportunity to become the writer I am today. I would also like to thank my friends and family for their patience—especially my mother, who has spent years dissecting my writing with me and whose advice has allowed me to improve. Finally, I give great thanks to my coauthor, Angelique Harris, for the idea that blossomed into this joint intellectual venture, as well as for the pleasure of her collaboration.

—Alia R. Tyner-Mullings

CHAPTER 1

INTRODUCTION TO WRITING IN SOCIOLOGY

Sociologists can emerge from anywhere. On a basic level, we can all say we are sociologists. Put simply, sociology is the study of society. Sociology is the study of social interactions, institutions, and how social forces shape our everyday lives. Sociologists observe the behavior of people as they interact with others. The true marker of a sociologist, however, is how she observes and what she does with those observations. The sociologist is not simply looking for the existence of these behaviors. The sociologist is seeking to understand why these behaviors happen, what they mean, and how they come to be.

If you have been an emerging sociologist for some time, none of this is new to you. You have likely spent some time learning about sociology while learning about society. As a sociologist, you translate society, just as you might translate something from one language to another. Your goal is to view social interactions through the lens of sociology, using what sociologist C. Wright Mills refers to as the "sociological imagination"[1]—the ability to make a connection between your private life and public issues. A conversation between a woman and a man at the snack table at a party becomes the interaction of gender, race, class, and education. How do her status symbols emphasize her positioning in society? How does he "do gender"[2] and emphasize his masculinity? How might their conversation be different in a different time or place?

Sociologists do more than simply describe society as they see it. Sociology is the *scientific* study of society. Sociologists follow the scientific method in their research and incorporate data analysis and tests of theories from research conducted by others. The ability to translate that research into language for diverse audiences is what makes sociologists sought after by employers in so many occupations. Sociologists work in government, human and social services, public relations, advertising, marketing, finance, and entertainment, as well as in many other fields. These fields regularly employ sociologists because people who can read, understand, and, most important, explain society are often needed.

To translate society properly, sociologists must be able to communicate with others, and one of the primary ways sociologists communicate is through writing. Writing is how sociology is shared; it is how we are able to learn from the work of others and how we share our own work with others.

This does not mean sociological writing—or any writing—comes naturally. Most of us come from backgrounds where we wrote a paper or two in high school or college but did not necessarily feel we had enough instruction on how to do so. A teacher might have told you to write a paper about pirates, or an assignment may have prompted you to write an essay about *Romeo and Juliet*. It was not until you tried to write it that you were penalized for not having an introduction, conclusion, or enough supporting evidence. When professors tell students, "You need a literature review," students often struggle to find out what that is, and it may be only through trial and error that students discover what their professors meant. For too many people, this process leads to frustration and the belief that they are not good writers. It is important to remember, however, that no one is born a good writer. We all have to work at writing, and we all can strive to become good writers.

During the process of writing, you will come to realize how it can also help you think. By putting our ideas down on paper or on a computer screen, we can more fully understand and organize them. Writing up our work can give it form. Even if that form needs to be changed through editing and revising, once we have written down our thoughts, the ability to manipulate and make ideas more concrete becomes possible.

In addition to facilitating thinking, writing contributes to other parts of the research and learning process. Much of the work we do in collecting our data involves writing, and whether research is qualitative (dealing with nonmeasureable data) or quantitative (dealing with numerical data), poorly written instruments and fieldnotes can lead to poorly collected data. We use the writing in our research methods and data collection both to communicate with our respondents and informants and to understand them. It is through clear and informational writing that we accomplish this. Without the quality work we collect, produce, and distribute, we are not able to interpret the world of others or translate our world for them.

In our translation, we are able to complete the most important aspect of academic research—the sharing of our work. Once our research is complete (and sometimes before that), we use our writing to share it with our colleagues, students, professors, and sometimes the public. We write journal articles and encyclopedia entries. We write book reviews and research proposals. We do this because, as sociologists, our work lacks purpose if it is not shared. We do it for the mission, the grade, the recognition, or the money. If we're lucky, we also get to do it for ourselves. Whether it is torn apart, revised, or accepted as it is, our goal is for our work to be effective—to be seen and understood. The purpose of this book is to help you reach those and all your writing goals.

HOW TO USE THIS BOOK

This book was created as a response to our experiences as students, sociologists, and professors who emphasize writing in our classrooms. The fundamental goal of this book is to introduce emerging sociologists to the breadth of writing a sociologist does while increasing the quality of writing within the field of sociology. The types of writing we describe in the book, however, can also be found in psychology, anthropology, political science, other social sciences, and even the humanities. When you finish this book, you should be able to meet any writing challenge within sociology and share your thoughts and ideas with the social world you strive to study.

The conceptual and organizational approach of *Writing for Emerging Sociologists* explores the styles of sociological writing at various stages, from conducting library research and avoiding plagiarism to writing a research proposal, book review, grant proposal, fieldnotes, or a scholarly journal article. The text also includes a discussion of the writing required in graduate school and using writing in your career, as well as writing outside of the traditional academic sphere. In addition to instruction on writing for newspapers and magazines, we also include information on writing for new media such as websites, blogs, and e-mails.

For Students

Writing for Emerging Sociologists is both a reference book and a course book. For a student, the chapters in this book provide a guide for actively participating in the discipline. Students can find instruction on most of the writing they will be asked to complete for courses or for their own professional development.

This book also spans the spectrum for writers at different levels. Writers at the beginning of their educational journeys may find the sections on writing letters and e-mails in the next chapter to be extremely useful. More advanced students will benefit from our discussion of graduate-level writing such as grants and journal articles.

For Professors

Writing for Emerging Sociologists can be used as a course text in a sociology writing class. In this case, students can work their way through each type of writing collected in these pages and complete the suggested assignments. Professors might also create their own assignments and use our book to supplement additional course readings.

This book can also be on a suggested reading list for any social science course. If your course requires students to write a final paper, create a survey, or write fieldnotes, this book provides that instruction. *Writing for Emerging Sociologists* will allow you to focus your course time on other learning, as it will help your students break down, understand, and create the writing you would like them to produce.

For Professionals

This book can also be used as a reference guide for professionals early in their careers as sociologists. It provides a detailed breakdown of many of the types of writing sociologists participate in and can give early professionals the direction they need to understand and complete different categories of writing. This book also addresses writing that can satisfy both academic and professional requirements, such as writing for journal submission, promotion, tenure, and grant writing.

THE STRUCTURE OF THE BOOK

Each chapter in this book describes one or several different types of writing in detail. Also featured in each chapter is a section called "Writing in Practice," written by a sociologist explaining her or his approach to the style of writing addressed in that chapter. We include this to help students understand how professional sociologists approach writing and to offer them insight and encouragement in their own process.

Chapter 2, "The Bricks and Mortar of Writing," covers some of the basics. The chapter does not go into detail on aspects of writing such as grammar and spelling, but it describes how a paper is organized and the elements needed to create a document. The chapter begins with a general discussion about building a paper. This includes an examination of subsections, sentences, and paragraphs. Additionally, the chapter also includes an overview of voice, which is also explored in Chapter 9, "Editing and Revising."

Chapter 2 ends with a review of letter writing, which will be valuable to students, especially those who do not have much experience with writing professional letters or e-mails. More advanced writers could also benefit from a refresher on the information provided in this chapter. The "Writing in Practice" section is written by Dr. Barbara Katz Rothman, professor of sociology at Baruch College and the Graduate School and University Center, City University of New York (CUNY).

Chapter 3, "Writing and the Search for Literature: Proposals, Library Research, and the Preparation of Literature," explores the writing that occurs as you conduct your research. This chapter describes the process of selecting a research topic and beginning to research that topic. It also describes how to write an annotated bibliography as part of the writing process and how to write a research proposal. Cynthia Bruns, an instruction and reference librarian at the Pollak Library at California State University, Fullerton, wrote the "Writing in Practice" section for this chapter.

Chapter 4, "Writing Textual Analyses: Literature Reviews, Book Reviews, Annotated Bibliographies, and Encyclopedia Entries," examines the writing developed directly from analysis of one or more pieces of literature. This chapter includes further detail on the writing of annotated bibliographies, with a specific focus on how they are written for publication. Textual documents, such as book reviews and encyclopedia entries, are also reviewed in this chapter. Dr. Richard E. Ocejo, assistant professor of sociology at John Jay College of Criminal Justice, CUNY, completes the chapter with a "Writing in Practice" section describing his experiences writing book reviews and encyclopedia entries.

Chapter 5, "Writing for the Institutional Review Board," is an overview of the process of applying for permission to conduct your research. The chapter begins with a short summary of the historical justification for institutional review boards. It describes in detail the process of writing up each section of the application, including consent forms. The "Writing in Practice" section for this chapter is written by Dr. Carter Rakovski, associate professor of sociology at California State University, Fullerton, and former member of the university's institutional review board committee.

Chapter 6, "Writing and the Research Grant Application Process" breaks down the application process into its individual components, and each is described in detail. The focus of the chapter is on grant applications for research funding; however, many of the sections are also applicable for other types of research proposals, building on the instruction from Chapter 2. Dr. Juan Battle, professor of sociology, public health, and urban education at the Graduate School and University Center, CUNY, and author of numerous grants, composed the "Writing in Practice" section for this chapter.

Chapter 7, "Writing and the Data Collection Process," examines the selection and use of research methods through the writing one must create within them. This chapter is not intended to replace or replicate the information one might find in a research methods text or course. Rather, it is meant to supplement such information by emphasizing the different types of writing involved. Here we provide a brief overview of research methods before explaining the preparation and process of creating qualitative and quantitative instruments, scripts, fieldnotes, and transcripts. This chapter is one of two in the book that include two "Writing in Practice" sections. For Chapter 7, they cover qualitative and quantitative research. Dr. Randol Contreras, assistant professor of sociology at California State University, Fullerton, wrote the qualitative piece, and Dr. Thurston Domina, assistant professor of education and sociology at the University of California, Irvine, wrote the quantitative piece.

Chapter 8, "Writing Empirical Papers for Journal Submission," addresses the writing of a journal article for those conducting qualitative, quantitative, or mixed-methods research. This chapter describes each section of a paper manuscript, the process of writing and submitting it, as well as the peer-review process. In the "Writing in Practice" section, Dr. Colin Jerolmack, assistant professor of sociology and environmental studies at New York University, discusses his experiences submitting manuscripts for review in scholarly journals.

How we revise and edit our work is the focus of Chapter 9, "Editing and Revising." Important for all students and professionals, this chapter provides strategies for quick edits as well as for more extensive ones. The chapter also describes the process in which we all participate to create a first draft, then form and rewrite subsequent versions. Dr. James A. Holstein, professor of sociology at Marquette University and former editor of the scholarly journal *Social Problems,* provides the "Writing in Practice" section for this chapter. Dr. Holstein gives advice for approaching the revision process.

Chapter 10, "Writing for the Public," describes sociological writing intended for a nonsociological audience. Debates continue over whether sociologists should participate in writing for the public, and this issue will be discussed briefly in Chapter 10. The chapter dissects the process of writing for a newspaper or blog or creating a policy document. Some advice on the writing of talking points is also included. Dr. R. L'Heureux Lewis-McCoy, assistant professor of sociology and Black studies at The City College of New York, CUNY, concludes the chapter with his "Writing in Practice" piece, discussing his views on writing for the public.

The final chapter in this book provides advice for those transitioning from one educational situation into another or into a career. Chapter 11, "Writing in Graduate School and Beyond," describes the writing involved in applying for graduate school and the types of writing one can expect upon acceptance into a program. The chapter does not go into detail on the types of writing used in different careers but does address the writing of résumés and curriculum vitae, or academic resumes. In the "Writing in Practice" pieces for this chapter, Shatima Jones, a sociology doctoral student at Rutgers University, writes about the experiences of being a graduate student, and Dr. Martine Hackett, special assistant professor at Hofstra University in Long Island, New York, discusses her process of translating sociology as the deputy director of the Office of the Medical Director at the New York City Health Department's Bureau of Maternal, Infant, and Reproductive Health.

Writing for Emerging Sociologists provides the resources needed to enhance the skills of emerging sociologists at varying levels. Readers should be able to find a chapter that addresses any kind of writing they might encounter during college, graduate school, and their early careers. Through the use of this book, we hope your understanding of writing and confidence in your own writing ability will be enhanced and expanded.

NOTES

1. Mills, C. Wright. 1959. *The Sociological Imagination.* New York: Oxford University Press.
2. West, Candace and Don H. Zimmerman. 1987. "Doing Gender." *Gender and Society* 1(2): 125–51.

CHAPTER 2

THE BRICKS AND MORTAR OF WRITING

Writing is more than just organizing words on a piece of paper. It is a process of creating and revising. It is a way to think through ideas as well as a way to express them. Unfortunately, what is in your head does not always reach the paper intact. This can have a dramatic effect on how we understand the thoughts of others and the ways others understand us. This chapter will provide guidance on writing at the level of organization and presentation, ensuring that the final writing product is received as intended.

THE STRUCTURE OF WRITING

For most of us, our first experience with significant writing was the five-paragraph essay. It begins with an introduction, is supported by three paragraphs within the body, and ends with a conclusion. While it often feels as though we are starting from scratch when we write papers at the postsecondary or even graduate level, that basic structure does not change as we advance through our education. What does change when writing becomes more complex are the details within the body of the work, which will vary depending on the type of writing. Those details will be discussed thoroughly over the remaining chapters of this book. Here, we will examine the general structure of writing with an overview of its basic building blocks.

The Foundation of Your House

Building a paper is similar to building a house with a particular budget. Each piece has a purpose, and extraneous pieces should be avoided. The paper is built on propositions—research questions, a hypothesis, and/or a thesis. A research question is the question that guides your research. A hypothesis is the potential answer to the research question based on little research or knowledge. Similarly, a thesis is the potential answer to the research question based on significant research or knowledge. Regardless of how you structure your research question, hypothesis, and thesis, they act as the mortar that holds the paper together. Every so often a paper will have to return to the propositions and connect that particular brick (a word), row (a sentence), or wall (a paragraph) to the rest of the house.

This means that each paragraph must be properly justified or supported. There should be a reason for each paragraph that is evident within the paragraph itself or in those that surround it. It should be possible to pick out a few paragraphs, or an entire section in a paper, and understand how it connects to the propositions. The length of the paper determines how long you can go without directly referring to your propositions. In a short paper, each paragraph should have a direct justification. For longer works, the document is likely to be divided into sections. In this case, each section should refer back to the propositions. Many writers rely on headings to distinguish between sections. However, headings should not be used as a replacement for transitions—the indicators of change from one thought to the next. It is still necessary both to introduce a section (and its connection to the topic as a whole) and to conclude the section before transitioning into the next one.

Figure 2.1

The Walls of Your Room

In any long piece, some paragraphs will not refer directly to the propositions. These can be characterized into four types—introductory, main point, elaboration, and concluding paragraphs. An introductory paragraph explains the importance of that section to the overall propositions. The main point paragraph provides and explains the most important point in the section. Elaboration paragraphs provide the evidence and examples that prove that connection. The section ends with the conclusion paragraphs, which restate the connection and the evidence and connect that section to the section that follows.

Additionally, elaboration paragraphs will likely fall into two categories: affirmation or contradiction. You can use these paragraphs to develop or support your point further or to present the opposing perspective. To affirm or confirm a point, you should include evidence or expound on previous evidence. In presenting an opposing viewpoint, you should present evidence from other research and explain why your perspective should be considered over the perspectives of others.

The Lines That Form the Walls

Similar to how you write each section of the paper as though it is a paper in itself, each individual paragraph should be written in the same manner. Each paragraph should have an <u>introduction</u>, an <u>elaboration</u>, and a <u>conclusion and/ or transition</u> into the next paragraph. In theory, someone should be able to follow a paper at a very basic level by simply reading the first and last sentences (the introductions and conclusions) in the paragraphs.

<u>Most of the students' complaints about their CPESS (Central Park East Secondary School) experience can be placed in [the college category]. According to the data collected here, 95.8% of former CPESS students applied to college, nearly all were accepted and 89% of survey participants began college.</u> However, sustainability in college proved to be more of a challenge than may have been expected. <u>One of the most significant problems, as discussed earlier in this chapter, is that after spending between two and 14 years in an alternative educational program, students had to return to or for many students enter for the first time, the type of traditional educational institution that CPESS had socialized them to resist.</u> Similar to findings in other chapters in this volume (see

Hantzopoulos; Bloom), many former students and teachers from the first five graduating classes referred to a culture shock in the process of moving from the sheltered, nurturing CPESS environment into college.[1]

In this example, the reader can gain an understanding of the context of this paragraph and the next one by simply examining the introductory and concluding sentences. However, the elaboration is important for a more complete understanding of the writer's point.

As illustrated in the previous example, sentences line up to build the "walls" of the paragraph. While many of the serious edits you make to a sentence often happen during the revising phase (which will be examined more fully in Chapter 9), there are guidelines that you can consider while writing an early draft. Remember that every sentence tells a particular story. If words are missing from a sentence, pieces are missing from the story. If something is unclear in a sentence, the story being told is unclear to the reader. You should keep in mind the story you are trying to tell when you write and check to make sure it has been told (see the Appendix for more information on sentences).

Clarity can often come from finding the proper balance of information to place within a sentence. If there is not enough information in a sentence, the reader's picture is incomplete. Some of the information may be included in the sentence(s) that precedes or follows. However, there should be enough information in the sentence that it does not leave the reader with too many questions about what he has just read. For example:

The relationship between family structure and education has been researched a lot.

If a reader is presented with this sentence, she will have several questions that can easily be answered by elaborating on the provided information: What is a lot? What time period is being referred to? What kinds of results have been found? A lack of answers to these questions will not necessarily encourage the reader to move on and might, instead, allow her interest to wane. Here are a few possible revisions to this sentence:

The relationship between family structure and education has been well researched over the past 50 years.

There are more than 1,000 articles that examine the potential effects of family structure on educational attainment, and the results have varied.

The results of studies on the relationship between family structure and education have been inconclusive over the past 50 years.

A sentence can also contain too much information and become what many teachers and professors refer to as a run-on sentence. You should try to make only one or two points in a sentence. When you make multiple points within a sentence, you are likely weakening your paper. It is very possible that each piece of the sentence is more powerful on its own. Also, you should watch for multiple independent clauses within one sentence. If another sentence can be made, it probably should be.

The formation of the United States began in 1776 with the signing of the Declaration of Independence, but the ideals of democracy for all citizens were delayed because African Americans were not officially able to act as citizens until 1965 with the ratification of the Civil Rights Act, even though the Fourteenth Amendment to the Bill of Rights stated that "all persons born or naturalized in the United States . . . are citizens of the United States" (Bill of Rights 1965), many people were prevented from taking full advantage of their rights.

This is an extreme example, but this type of sentence is not unheard of. One cannot expect to explain the history of American democracy and civil rights in one sentence. There are several places within the sentence where the writer could have added a period to create a paragraph composed of more than one sentence. If the reader has to take several breaths to get through a sentence, it is too long.

The formation of the United States legally began in 1776 with the signing of the Declaration of Independence. However, even though the Fourteenth Amendment to the Bill of Rights in 1868 stated that "all persons born or naturalized in the United States . . . are citizens of the United States" (Bill of Rights 1965), the ideals of democracy for all citizens were delayed. African Americans, for example, were not officially able to act as citizens until 1965, with the ratification of the Civil Rights Act.

The Bricks That Build the Walls

The other problems within sentences can come from the words used to build them. To ensure that the meaning a reader receives from a work is the meaning intended, it is important to examine each piece and its interaction with every other piece. One common mistake in creating sentences is use of the wrong words. When writing, and especially when revising, it is important to double-check which words have been used and whether there is a better choice or, if you have misused a word, a correct choice. Many words are easily mistaken for others. *Then* and *than*, for example, are often misused; *then* means following after, while *than* indicates a comparison (see the Appendix for additional examples).

Words can also be misused because of an uncertainty of the audience you are serving and how to speak to them. Some writers will use every word they know to make their point because they believe that having a large vocabulary makes them appear intelligent. However, you must also know how to use the words properly for them to be effective. If you truly know the vocabulary of sociology, or of the specific area in which you have interest in the discipline, you will be able to use the words economically and not overburden your paper with attempts to display your vocabulary. If you do not yet know the language of your discipline, reading is the best way to learn it. Study scholarly journal articles and read books within sociology to grow your familiarity with the discipline, and its language will eventually become yours.

Features of Academic Writing

In addition to the more general structure of a paper, particular attributes are important in the creation of an academic paper.

Formality

Some refer to academic writing as formal, others as semiformal. What this generally means is that the informality that is a part of other types of writing you might do is not present in academic writing. We elaborate on this a little more in our section on letters, but your writing should generally avoid slang, most abbreviations, colloquialisms (informal words or phrases found in casual speech), and contractions.

Objectivity

While writing in academia usually means presenting a particular perspective, objectivity is still important to maintain. You should always avoid any indications of bias by presenting multiple sides to your arguments. In many cases, the opposing arguments are the foundation of your perspective and you write your piece in response to them. In these situations, an overview of the opposing ideas is integrated into your literature review (see Chapter 8) or the context section of your paper. However, even when such an overview does not flow organically from your viewpoint, an objective presentation is important to the legitimacy of your paper.

Caution

Regardless of whether or not your data are qualitative or quantitative, they are usually indefinite. Generally, you can say that "the evidence demonstrates" or that the "data appear to show." It is unlikely that you will come across any information that provides you with something definite. Therefore, your language should reflect that. If you do have some evidence that shows a firm result, you should share that. More likely, however, you will find a suggested relationship, and you should write it up as such. Words such as *should, may, could,* and *potentially* may be important in your writing.

Clarity

You should be clear and precise with your language in academic writing. If you are explaining a relationship in your data, your language should reflect that particular relationship. If you want to lead your reader in a particular direction in your paper, use indicators such as transitions to let them know where the story will be taking them. Your vocabulary should also be accurate and representative of what you actually intend to say. We speak more about this when we discuss voice below.

Evidence

Any points you make in academic writing will have to be supported by evidence. This evidence may be data you collected, information you read from what others have examined, or conclusions drawn from analysis of the data of other researchers. All evidence that you include must be properly cited (see Chapter 3) and should be well integrated into your document. This includes both introducing the quote and explaining its place in your work.

Third Person

Academic writing is generally written in the third person. This means that work is done by her or him, rarely by I (first person) and never by you (second person). This can often lead to passive sentences (see below), but it can also add a level of objectivity (see above), which is important for scientific writing in academia. There is still discussion about the use of the first person in academic writing, and where this perspective is most likely to be seen is in a methods section (see Chapter 8), but it is important to ask or to examine the work of others to find out if and how first person is used.

The construction of your paper with the proper words, academic structure, fully formed sentences, and well-structured paragraphs can help you build your paper and express your ideas. This enables you not only to be understood but also to share your writing persona or personality with the reader. We refer to this representation of yourself—the personality of your writing—as its voice.

THE VOICE ON THE PAPER

What a professor refers to as "voice" comes down to two general ideas. The first is when a professor tells you that *you* are missing from the work. This form of voice is about understanding the research and the writer's contribution to his work. The way this type of voice is emphasized in writing varies depending on the type of writing that is created. We will examine it further as we work our way through this volume and the different types of writing. The type of voice we will examine in this section, as well as in the chapter on editing and revising, is more general. Here, we will explore the ways a written piece can be imbued with a voice to make it both interesting and clear—what we will refer to as aesthetic voice.

Aesthetic voice is also about the audience to whom you are speaking. As you will read about in other chapters in this volume, your voice will be dictated to some extent by your intended audience. Writing a paper for an academic journal requires a certain type of formal, semiformal, or academic voice, while an entry on a webpage or blog might use a different voice. You will hear much more about this as we work our way through the book, but most of the types of writing you will find here will be academic. However, our own writing in this text will be less formal, as our goal here is to interest our broad audience of both current and emerging sociologists in the types of writing in which sociologists participate.

Providing an interesting and clear voice is not easy. While some may be born with the ability to speak beautifully and translate it perfectly to paper, for most of us, it takes some work to create a masterpiece. After much practice, you can reach a point where a first draft will contain a level of aesthetic voice, but until you reach that point, much of the insertion of voice may happen during the editing stage (see Chapter 9).

The first part of including aesthetic voice in a written piece is knowing the audience. Understanding who the audience is, as well as what they expect, allows the writer to speak in a way that resonates with those who are reading. If the audience is other academics, using the vocabulary and formal structure of the relevant field of sociology will be important. If the writing is for a blog or a magazine, sociological language can quickly become jargon to the audience.

The first step to adding voice is reading the piece aloud. While writing for a presentation and for written formats is different, voice is heard in the minds of the individuals reading the work. If it flows when the writer speaks it out loud, it will probably sound similar to the reader. Several voice edits may happen during your first and subsequent read-throughs, as you may struggle somewhere in your piece or become out of breath and will therefore know it is necessary to change some words or add periods or commas.

If the problem is not immediately evident, there are several places to look to make changes. Many of the structural aspects mentioned above can add to voice when utilized properly. Check your sentences for run-ons or vagueness. Another common problem in papers without a strong voice is a lack of variation in sentences. Writing is very much about flow. Sentences with the same or very similar lengths give the writer's voice an automated tone. Changing the length of sentences might include combining a couple of sentences, inserting a new sentence between existing ones, or adding additional words to refine the sentences.

Example:

The researchers did not agree. One study found positive effects. The other study found negative effects. More research needs to be conducted.

Possible revision:

More research needs to be conducted to explore the topic more fully. The two studies differed in their findings, as one found positive effects and the other, negative.

Another way to add variation to sentences is to ensure that the words used to begin or conclude a sentence vary throughout a paragraph or section. *The*, for example, is an easy word to begin a sentence with, and it is just as easy to be unaware of using it repeatedly. If the same word, group of words, or type of word is being used to start every sentence, the sentence should be restructured or, if possible, the structure of the paragraph should be changed. A thesaurus can be extremely useful in dealing with variation at the beginning of sentences.

Example:

The school used alternative pedagogical methods. The students in the classes did much of their work in groups. The teachers emphasized student-centered pedagogy. The administrators protected the teachers from outside influences that might have a negative effect on what occurred within their classrooms.

Possible revision:

The school used alternative methods, which included group work and student-centered pedagogy. Administrators at the school also protected the teachers from outside influences that might have a negative effect on what occurred within their classrooms.

A thesaurus can also be useful in creating variation in the words used. Clichés, for example, are considered too casual for most academic papers and should be replaced by words that do a better job of making the same point. Clichés are phrases that use a well-known illustration of an idea, such as "sharp as a tack." Instead of clichés, you should use a selection of accurate and precise words to describe what you are trying to say.

You should also check your sentences for words that are repeated, places where several words have been used when one might work better, and words that may not have been used properly. These modifications will all assist in changing the voice of a paper. Additionally, once you have revised the work by reading aloud, you should look for another person to read it. If that other person can read it aloud, that is even better. Listening to it read by someone else will certainly help illuminate for you any problems in voice.

Recognizing the difference between active and passive sentences can also change the voice of a piece. Passive sentences can make a piece sound flat, while active sentences can add interest or action to your writing. In a passive sentence, the subject of the sentence is being acted on rather than initiating the action. Academic writing is often written with a more passive voice because sometimes there is no subject, the subject is unknown, or the use of a subject comes off as too casual. The third-person perspective that dominates academic writing can also lead a paper to more passive than active sentences. For example, "Research was conducted on the subjects" is a passive sentence often used in a methods section. While, technically, you conducted the research, some academics believe it is poor form to refer to yourself in an academic paper. Most individuals will accept it either way, but some journals may prefer the more passive version.

A sentence can usually be changed from passive to active by finding the active subject and making sure it is doing the work. Often, in a passive sentence, the subject is missing and/or only implied. If you add the word *by* to the end of a passive sentence, the subject implied after the *by* should be the focus of the sentence to make it active. In the passive sentence, "The test was taken," the invisible subject might be students, professionals, or teachers. To turn the sentence active, make sure the "students took the test."

Most of this book will focus on writing with a formal voice, but we begin our instruction on specific types of writing with something that is often a little less formal—the letter. Even though the letter is one of the shortest types of writing involved in sociology, when written properly, the structure of a letter still mirrors many of the other types of writing in this book. We begin with this because it is something we are all familiar with yet still often have trouble completing in an academic, formal, or professional manner.

LETTERS

Letter writing is a very specific type of writing and an art that was once valued and is now, for the most part, lost. It is not the first thing that comes to mind when you think of writing for emerging sociologists. However, as a sociologist, emerging or otherwise, you will have several opportunities to write letters. While many of us, especially advanced writers and graduate students, feel we have already mastered the art of writing a quality letter in a professional setting, we can probably all find some helpful hints or suggestions in this section.

E-mails

E-mails are a good place to start a lesson on letter writing, as writing e-mails is something most current college and many graduate students grew up doing. For most of us, the format of an e-mail has become second nature. However, others have lost, or never learned, the appropriate way to compose an e-mail message. Therefore, it is an extremely misunderstood form of writing.

Since e-mails are generally used for casual conversations, too many people forget that is not all they are used for. Most students understand the respect due to a professor, professional, or other superior in a face-to-face interaction, yet those same people lose that understanding when they are safely behind their computer screens. You should also remember that, while your letter is addressed to a particular person, it is stored on a server and even deleting it

Figure 2.2

> To: Professor1@school.edu
>
> From: hotlips63@isp.com
>
> Subject: HEY Prof!
>
> HEY Prof!
>
> I need to get the homework from today. Can you email it to me ASAP?
>
> Thanks!
> Patricia

does not necessarily erase it. They can be copied, forwarded, and saved. They are very much public. This is a lesson that cannot be taught enough times, regardless of your level as a writer.

For someone who has never had to write and mail a professional letter, saying that writing a proper e-mail should be just like writing a formal letter is pointless. Instead, looking at an improperly written e-mail can allow us to understand the dos and don'ts of e-mail writing in a formal setting. Here, we will focus on writing a professional e-mail to a course professor. However, the same rules apply whether the e-mail is to a professor or to any other professional or person with whom you have a working relationship.

Header

While this is not exactly an issue of proper writing, it's something to think about if you want to become a professional in any field. When sending an e-mail, make sure to use an e-mail address appropriate for a professional setting. While the e-mail name you have always used may be hotlips63, it could just as easily be PatriciaJoy12 or PJ.Walker12. Most institutions provide their students with school e-mail addresses (.edu), which would likely make that process easier, but we understand that students do not always keep up with their school-issued e-mail addresses. It is not difficult to create a personal address to use with your professors or any other professional contacts you might have. Most e-mail clients will allow you not only to forward PatriciaJoy12's e-mail to hotlips63 but also to send e-mail from hotlips63's account as PatriciaJoy12, if you so choose. You can always delete the e-mail account once the course is over, but many people have a main account from which they collect and send e-mails from a variety of other e-mail addresses. Using an e-mail address with your name is ideal. If that is not possible, non-offensive words or a collection of letters and numbers (such as initials and parts of a date or address) are also acceptable.

Subject

The purpose of a subject line is to inform the receiver of your intent before she opens the e-mail. While not used as often, letters sent through the U.S. Postal Service can also have a "subject line." Sometimes the writer of a letter might write "Re: Your bill" on the outside of an envelope or on a message pad so the recipient knows that the enclosed is "regarding your bill." The same care should be used in an e-mail to a professor or other professional. What is the letter "regarding" or "in reference to"? A basic subject line could simply say, "The homework from May 14th." A more detailed subject line could read, "Request from P. Walker for the homework from May 14th." But be careful of length; your subject line should not require any scrolling.

Greeting

Another problem with the e-mail in the example is the "HEY!" in the subject line. This problem is similarly evident in the greeting. First, you do not want to start a professional letter by writing "hey." You should address a professional letter, specifically one to a professor, with "to," "dear," or even simply the professor's name and title (see the table below for a selection of titles). Unless you already know how the professor would like to be addressed, you should begin with Dear Professor (or Dr.) Monte. You can leave off the last name (i.e., "Dear Professor"), but its use tells the professor that you know who she is, as well as allowing you to be sure your message is going to the right person. Once you have written your first message, you can follow the recipient's lead in greetings and titles. Do not let a professor's use of your name be an example (although you can look at the type of greeting she used). Instead, make a note of how she has signed her letter. If she used her first name, unless she has already told you not to, you can probably use it when you address her in your next e-mail. If she uses her full name, you should address her as you have in previous letters. You should respond similarly if she has not used any name or used just her automatic signature.

Dear:	Should begin almost all letters; can be followed by names (Gwen), titles (Dean) or categories (Hiring Committee)
To whom it may concern:	Should be used only if you cannot uncover the name of the person
Hi, Hello, Hey	Should be used only for informal letters to people you are close to

If you are on a level playing field with the person you are corresponding with, rather than a subordinate to him, you can follow his example in terms of what he calls you and how he signs his name. If he addresses you as Emily and signs his name Mike, you can probably address him as Mike. Similarly, if you would like someone to whom you are not subordinate to call you by your first name, you can either tell him so or sign your letter with the name. If you have not been given any particular instruction in how to refer to someone, you should use a title.

Ms.: For an unmarried woman or if marriage status cannot be determined. Ms. is considered more politically correct than Mrs.

Mrs.: For a married woman using her married name. It should be used only if you have been told to use it.

Mr.: For a man with no other title

Dr.: For someone with a PhD, MD, DDS, or other professional degree

Professor: For someone who teaches at a college or university

Dean: The dean of an office

Director: The director of an office or institute

President: The head of an institution or office

If you need to address two people, you should use both of their names and titles with an *and* in between them. For three or more names, you may use "ladies" or "gentlemen," "colleagues," or "students," depending on who will be receiving the letter.

Finishing this section on the greeting, you should never use an exclamation point in a greeting to a professor. In fact, you should try to avoid them anywhere in your e-mail. In the words of F. Scott Fitzgerald, "Cut out all those exclamation points. An exclamation point is like laughing at your own jokes."[2] If you want to emphasize something in an e-mail, use a modifier—usually an adverb or adjective (or a word that acts as one) that adds description to the sentence—and explain your emphasis, rather than trying to elicit the emotion with a punctuation mark.

Body

Unarguably, the body is the most important part of your e-mail. This is why you are writing. This is where you explain yourself, make your argument, or ask your question. Yet even students who know exactly what they need often express themselves poorly in the bodies of their more professional e-mails. There are several important guidelines to remember. While these specifically center on writing professional e-mails, they can also be useful in writing an e-mail to anyone.

Recognize the Reader's Head. This means that, regardless of your intention, the reader will almost always take her mood, attitude, or feelings and breathe that life into the e-mail. If she is angry and there is anything at all ambiguous in your e-mail, she will hear it as angry. People often forget this attribute of letters and can both read emotional states in someone's e-mail that were not present and unwittingly send an angry e-mail to a friend. For this and many other reasons, it is important to read your e-mail before you send it out. Try reading it out loud with a different emotion in your voice. Can your receiver read something completely different in your letter than what you intended? If so, go back and try to change your words into something more neutral.

Additionally, intended emotions can also often be misread or missed all together. Sarcasm should never be in an e-mail to a professor, but if you are sending an e-mail to someone else, make sure you exaggerate the sarcasm. Without the inflection in your "voice," subtle sarcasm can easily be missed.

Don't Yell. Avoiding exclamation points was previously mentioned, but that is only one way your e-mail can seem demanding. You must keep in mind that you are likely sending this e-mail because you need something, yet your professor may not be able to assist you immediately. Avoid demanding terms such as *want* and *need*, and, at all costs, do not use phrases that signify that the receiver should stop what he is doing right away to help you—words such as *immediately*, *today* (except in a descriptive manner), *now*, and *ASAP*. Instead, remember you are asking the recipient to do something for you that may fall outside of his responsibility or course guidelines.

Write Properly. An e-mail to a professor is closer to a class paper than it is to a text message or a chat with a friend. You should follow the same conventions you would when writing anything for your professor. Write in full sentences with proper punctuation, grammar, and spelling. This includes not interrupting a sentence with an exclamation, words, or phrases the professor may or may not understand. Your professor doesn't want to hear that you are "LOL" or if something is "gr8." There should be no "text speak" in your e-mail. Similar to the Fitzgerald quote above, you don't need to LOL at your own jokes. If they are funny, they will be perceived as such. If they are not, no one will know they are jokes.

Follow Instructions. This is less about the actual writing and more about the considerations before you write. For example, in writing to a course professor, be sure to pay attention to what is listed in the syllabus or what your professor has said about e-mailing. If Professor Jones has told you that she will not accept late homework by e-mail, do not try to send it. If she has not given you an alternative, you may e-mail and ask if there is another way to drop off your work.

The structure of the body portion of your letter should mirror an essay in other ways as well. As in a basic essay, the main part of your e-mail should have an introduction, a body, and a conclusion.

The introduction can do many things. Depending on the purpose of the e-mail and how many e-mails you have already shared, you may need to introduce yourself:

My name is Colby Kent, and I am in your Sociology 101 class.

Or you may want to inquire as to how the recipient is doing:

I hope you are doing well.

However you begin, your letter can start with a casual tone but still fit within a formal structure. The body of your e-mail should explain your question, comment, or issue. You should keep it short and get to the point.

Closing

You should conclude your letter with an appropriate closing or a closing salutation. You can end by wishing your professor well or letting him know that you will be in class for the following session. You can also include something like "best," "best regards," or "sincerely." You should not, however, include salutations such as "love," "yours," and "truly." You should follow the closing salutation with your name, especially important if you have not introduced yourself or e-mailed before, or if your name is not part of your e-mail address.

Appropriate salutations for formal letters include the following:

- Sincerely
- Yours sincerely
- Respectfully yours
- Kind regards
- Best regards
- Warmest regards
- Many thanks
- Take care
- With appreciation

Finally, remember that a response may not be immediate, but you shouldn't push it. If the next class session and the office hours have passed and you have not heard anything, you can bring up the e-mail questions in person, but, unless it is an emergency, more than a week should go by before you send another e-mail, if you do at all. E-mails provide a quick way to communicate, but not everyone thinks of e-mails as needing an immediate response. The convenience of e-mails tends to overshadow the problems with them. If you can follow the guidelines in this section, you can be sure that you are able to address those problems.

Formal Letters

As a student, you may on several occasions need to write a business or professional letter. If you apply for a job, for example, your prospective employer may require you to write a cover letter. Some graduate or professional schools may require a cover letter with an application. Additionally, you may have a situation, separate from school, where you need to write a formal letter. Even if your letter is sent by e-mail, it is still important that it is in the correct format.

Writing a business letter was once something all students were required to do to graduate from high school. Now, in this age of e-mailing and texting, students are taught "snail mail" letter writing much later in their educations or never at all. Sometimes, like so much other writing, it is not until they have written a poorly structured letter that they are taught how to do it properly. Yet a well-written letter can assert authority, confidence, and competence.

Similar to e-mails, formal letters can be divided into different sections: header, introduction, body, conclusion, and footer. While the header and footer in an e-mail are often included in the e-mail client's programming, in a formal letter, you will write the header yourself and what is contained within it will vary depending on the type of letter.

The header of a letter usually includes the addresses of both the letter writer and the letter recipient. If you work at a school, have a professional job, or are a graduate student, you should use the letterhead of the institution where you work or go to school in sending a formal letter. Some schools have restrictions on students' use of letterhead, so you should check with your department. If you use a letterhead with an address, you do not need to include your address in the header. If there is no address, you should include one on the right-hand side of the header. The street address should be in the first row and the state, city, and ZIP code in the second row in the normal format for addresses. On the next line, the date should be inserted in the form "month, day, year" (although, if you are writing to an organization or company outside of the United States, "day, month, year" might be more appropriate). You may also include the day of the week preceding the rest of the date.

The receiver's information should be on the left on the following line in the same format, but it should also include the receiver's name in the first row. Alternatively, the sender's address and the date can be on the same side as the receiver's address (the left side) with an extra line break between each element. Finally, after another line break, you should write a salutation and the individual's title and name. In most cases, that salutation is "dear," and the title will depend on the individual.

As mentioned above, you should do your best to use the proper title of the person to whom the letter is addressed. If you cannot uncover the recipient's gender, you should use that person's full name. If you cannot find a name, you may use "To Whom It May Concern" (this can be written with each word capitalized or with only *to* capitalized); however, this should be used only as a last resort. Either greeting-plus-name combination can be followed by a colon; the combination that includes "dear" may also be followed by a comma. See above for additional examples of greetings and titles.

Figure 2.3

123 Electric Street
New York, NY 10023
September 18, 2012

Professor B. Johnson
Green Men Consulting
New Haven, CT 06511

Dear Professor Johnson,

Figure 2.4

123 Electric Street
New York, NY 10023
September 18, 2012

Professor B. Johnson
Green Men Consulting
New Haven, CT 06511

Dear Professor Johnson:

The body of your letter should begin after a line break and, like other types of writing in this book, should be divided into several pieces. The details within each section in the body will vary depending on the type of letter being written, but each will begin with an introduction within which you explain to the receiver your purpose for writing and give a little information about who you are. If you were directed to write the letter by someone or have a contact at the school or organization, that should also be mentioned in the introduction. In a longer letter, this could be a full paragraph. In a shorter letter, the introduction could be just one or two sentences. However, the meat of the body is where different letter types vary.

Job Letters

The introduction of a job cover letter should explain why you are writing the letter, such as "I am writing to apply for the position of statistical consultant at Green Men Consulting." Additionally, it should give a quick overview of your story and your qualifications: "My experiences in statistical analysis and software packages qualify me to fill your position."

The body of the letter is where you share the details of your qualifications. You should sound confident and competent. If it is a teaching job, you want to make sure to discuss your research, your teaching, and your service. If it is another type of position, check the qualifications required for the job and emphasize the experiences you have had that most closely fit the position.

Think about each of your former jobs, research you have conducted, organizations you have been a member of, or experiences you have had as a series of skills gained, responsibilities held, or activities completed. For example, if you worked as a college counselor, you probably had a lot of different types of responsibilities. You may have had to do administrative work, such as filing, data processing, and written communication. The job probably included advising, research, and/or other knowledge of the school or other schools. It may have also required registration, meeting with other faculty members, or organizing panels or meetings. These all become skills you can highlight in a cover letter. Remember that your résumé or curriculum vitae (see Chapter 11) will provide an overview of your jobs, skills, and service/volunteer work, so your cover letter should highlight particular experiences and draw the reader's attention to the ways you fit that particular position. In writing up your skills in a cover letter, make sure to emphasize what you actually did rather than what your title or official responsibilities were.

Organize your letter by skill, and, as usual, make each paragraph its own miniature paper. Introduce the skill, either with an introductory sentence or an example of the skill from your own experience. You then want to support your claim that you have that skill or can complete that task. You should try to avoid using more than three examples. Remember, they will have access to your résumé/curriculum vitae and can get further information from there. Follow up your skill paragraphs with a closing or transition sentence.

As you want the receiver of your letter to be excited about you, you should use active words that exhibit your achievements and bring them to life. Rather than saying that you "wrote a few summaries," tell them you "created reports to promote changes in your program" (see the Appendix for more examples of active words).

While much of your letter will be the same from position to position, make sure that you personalize each letter with the name of the school/organization/company and by addressing their particular needs and how your qualifications fit those needs. Also, the different jobs you apply for may have different emphases, so you should consider changing the order of the items in your letter. If you are applying for a position at a research-focused university, you should make sure your research experience is the first thing the receiver reads. If it is a teaching-focused university, your experiences with teaching should be addressed early in your letter. If the employer is interested in someone with nonprofit experience, any service work you have done should be mentioned as early as possible. This not only will ensure that the receiving parties recognize you as someone who fits their interests but also will give the impression that the letter was written specifically for them and their positions. While most will know that much of the letter is repeated for others, the effort is often appreciated (see the Appendix for a sample job letter).

Submission Letters

Generally, a letter of submission is included with a manuscript or book when it is sent to a scholarly journal or publisher. A journal or publisher may specifically request a cover or submission letter but can also omit that detail from the submission guidelines. Unless specifically asked not to (or if the method of submission does not allow for it), you should include a submission letter with anything you submit for publication.

The first paragraph of a submission letter is fairly straightforward. You should let the receiver know the purpose of your letter. This is usually as simple as saying, "I have enclosed for submission to [the journal] my paper titled [your paper title]." The second paragraph should describe your paper in much the same way as an abstract (see Chapter 8) would. To emphasize the importance of publishing your paper, you might want to include a third paragraph that adds some detail about the impact your manuscript could have on the field. Finally, you can end with a description of who you are and your reason for and interest in publishing in that particular journal (you can find a sample submission letter in the Appendix).

Letters to the Journal Editor

In your manuscript submission process, you may reach the revise and resubmit stage (see Chapter 8). Once you receive comments back from the reviewers of your manuscript, you will need to submit a letter to the editor detailing how you have addressed the comments you received. The letter can begin with a couple of sentences thanking the editor for accepting your work and letting her know that you have taken the revision process seriously.

If you have been given line-by-line edits, you should reply to the editor with a line-by-line response. For every line where a reviewer has provided a comment, you should include what you did to change it or why you chose not to. If you are working with a more general review, you can respond with something more general.

Request/Inquiry Letters

In a request letter, your tone is very important. As a sociology student, the request letters you write will most likely be requests for an update, recommendation letters, information, an interview or survey, or help. It is essential that the body of your letter present your request, cushioned by an understanding of the receiver's schedule and the commitment your request might require. This may include apologizing for taking up the receiver's time (unless your request is within the boundaries of his everyday duties). You will then want to present your situation and your request.

You should also be sure that you have done all you can on your own and have included or attached any information he might need to comply with your request. For example, if you are requesting letters of recommendation, a professor will require information on who he is writing to, who you are, and your experiences. Therefore, you should attach a copy of your résumé or curriculum vitae and a highlight sheet (see Chapter 11) that describes your qualifications to your recommenders. Also, a copy of your cover letter may be helpful. Some of the other letters might include an attached survey, interview, or web link. (A sample request letter is provided in the Appendix.)

Thank-You Letters

Thank-you letters, in any form, are a lost tradition. If someone sends you something, meets with you, or writes a letter on your behalf, it is always good to thank that person for her help and time. While you may believe the verbal thank you that you provided immediately after you received what you requested was adequate, it does not hurt to provide something in writing in addition. A thank-you note shows not only appreciation but also manners and, for many people, will add to their impression of you.

If you have primarily corresponded digitally, that is a perfectly acceptable method of sending your thanks. This may be done as either an e-mail letter or an e-card. However, if you have access to an address, sending a physical card or letter is still a good idea. A thank-you letter can be very brief. You should simply remind the receiver of the situation for which you are thanking her and then thank her for whatever action was helpful to you. Because of the short length of a thank-you note or letter, a card can work very well. Sending a thank-you letter shows common courtesy, but if the thanks is for something like a job interview, such a letter can also remind the interviewers who you are and ensure that your interactions with them remain in their minds. Generally, you want to send this letter within a few days of the action, but within a week is probably still okay. (You can see a sample of a thank-you letter in the Appendix.)

Whatever the type, your letters should conclude by briefly reemphasizing the purpose for the letter and thanking the receiver for reading it. If additional items are enclosed or will be forthcoming, that should also be noted. The conclusion should include your final personalization of the school, organization, company, or person and an invitation for further correspondence. Again, end with an appropriate closing salutation and your full name and title, if appropriate.

While much of our correspondence with each other has become fast moving and littered with grammar and spelling faux pas, the space still exists for communication in an intelligent and well-written format. This chapter represents the first step on your journey to becoming a better writer.

SUMMARY

This chapter provides an overview of the foundations of writing. We emphasized the following writing issues:

- How to organize the elements of a paper
- The concept of voice
- The writing of e-mails and formal letters

In our first "Writing in Practice," Dr. Katz Rothman describes the process of writing and what it means to her as a scholar and a person. She uses a trip to Germany to frame a discussion of the importance of books, writing, and sharing what is written.

WRITING IN PRACTICE

by Barbara Katz Rothman

Wie schrjft, die blijft.
Who writes, lives.

I really believe that Dutch proverb—writing is a way of living beyond our own space and time. My sociological research consists mostly of book-length projects. One was translated into German and has brought me to Berlin pretty regularly. Berlin is a city so filled with its own history that one cannot make it down a street without stumbling across memorials—literally, there are "stumble stones" embedded in the sidewalks with the names of people who were taken off to die in concentration camps. A quick trip to pick up a bike map ends up leading to a sign telling you that Eichman's office was located on this spot. I became used to it, sighed, nodded, and walked on.

But the memorial that brought tears to my eyes, the one that truly made me stumble, was the book-burning memorial. In front of Humboldt University, at the law school no less, there is a memorial marking the spot where the Nazis burned piles of the books they found offensive. You stand on a square of thick glass in the plaza and look down into a small white room lined with empty white bookshelves. I stood there and cried—the books! It wasn't enough they killed all those people; they had to kill their thoughts and their legacy. Of course they couldn't actually kill the books. Bodies go up in flames once and for all, never to return—but books, books hide in all kinds of places around the world. I could order any one of those burnt books and have a copy in my mailbox next week. I'm tempted to go find the list of books burnt that day and do just that right now.

So for me, writing is central—the way we leave parts of ourselves behind and send parts of ourselves forth, the way we enter the larger ongoing human conversation. And writing isn't just something I do—it's something I teach. I work mostly with graduate students, people doing their first major original piece of writing, making their own first contributions to the conversations they have been studying. Helping those people find their own voices fills me with as much joy as anything life has to offer.

This book is teaching you the early steps of finding your own voice. Do think of your writing as your voice, the way that ideas flow through you to others. Think about your "tone" as you write. People pick up "tone" and "accent" from others—ever notice yourself struggling in a conversation not to copy a strong accent? Or try this fun exercise—read Dr. Seuss aloud to some willing kid for a while, and then pick up a novel or textbook and read it to yourself. You'll probably find the singsong Seussian inflection bubbling inappropriately through. One lesson from that: Immerse yourself in the tone in which you want to write. To write academic papers, read a bunch. To write research reports, read them.

The other lesson to be had from thinking of writing as a voice in a conversation is to remember that writing is read as a voice is heard, that it exists in a meaningful way only when it is read. Share your writing—it improves with reading. Give a rough draft of a paper to a few friends, and listen to their comments. Before you record that voice for posterity, before you submit it to an editor or to a grader, get it read by people who will let you know what they are hearing in it. We all sometimes say things we don't quite mean, express ourselves awkwardly or badly—and others can help us see that. I don't—even now, having written a respectable small shelf full of books—submit a piece of writing without having a few sets of friendly eyes go over it for me first.

Write. Live. Read and share. Join the conversation.

—Barbara Katz Rothman, PhD, is a professor of sociology at the City University of New York.

NOTES

1. Tyner-Mullings, Alia R. 2012. "Redefining Success: How CPESS Students Reached the Goals That Mattered." Pp. 137–65 in *Critical Small Schools: Beyond Privatization in New York City Educational Reform,* edited by Maria Hantzopoulos and Alia R. Tyner-Mullings. Charlotte, NC: Information Age.

2. Graham, Sheilah and Gerold Frank. 1958 [1974]. *Beloved Infidel: The Education of a Woman.* New York: Bantam Books.

CHAPTER 3

WRITING AND THE SEARCH FOR LITERATURE

Proposals, Library Research, and the Preparation of Literature

This chapter will address the different types of writing involved in the beginning stages of a research project. While writing is not necessarily associated with the early stages of research, properly phrasing your search terms, research topics, and study interests will greatly aid you in the literature search process. This chapter will include developing a research topic and conducting library research, as well as the use of keywords and other strategies used for research both online and in the library. We will provide helpful hints and information on gathering references, reading, evaluating research, and using software to assist in the research and writing process. We also explain how to write from sources and how to properly attribute and include the work of other researchers in your own writing. In this chapter, we also review how to write outlines, summaries, and annotated bibliographies. These writing tools will help you stay organized and focused in preparing for a more formalized writing project. This chapter concludes with a discussion on organizing the literature, such as articles, books, and dissertations that you find to support your research. We begin with how to select and focus your research topic.

SELECTING A RESEARCH TOPIC

From start to finish, writing is an integral part of the research process. Most of us write down our thoughts and ideas, or brainstorm, to help us formulate our research projects and writing. Before you can begin a project, you first need to select a research topic. Your topic will generally be determined by why you are undertaking the project. If, for example, you are writing a course paper, it is likely that your topic will be based on the area addressed by the course—for instance, writing a research paper on racism for a course titled "Race and Ethnic Relations." However, if you are not writing a course paper and do not have an assigned topic, developing one on your own can seem challenging.

In selecting a topic, think back to your "Introduction to Sociology" class. A topic or area within sociology likely jumped out at you. It might have been a theory or a particular study that caught your interest. For example, do you find yourself taking classes and writing your papers on issues pertaining to gender, deviance, or education? Most sociologists have at least three areas of focus or interest within sociology that we concentrate on and examine. If you look through your professor's curriculum vitae, or academic résumé, you will probably see that you can group your professor's publications and presentations into several similar topics within sociology. She may study one type of population, utilize the same methodology in most of her research, or focus on the same theories.

There are a few steps you can take in selecting and developing your topic. The first step is to brainstorm and come up with the areas of interest to you in the field of sociology. You may also be able to combine your research interests into a topic and refine that topic so you can use it as the basis of your writing. Each step is examined below.

Brainstorming

The first major challenge new sociologists must face is figuring out what to study. This is a lot easier if you are writing a course paper or you have been assigned a topic. If you are selecting your own topic, the task can seem quite daunting and may feel overwhelming for a new researcher, as the field of sociology is quite broad. This is also one of the great things about sociology—we can study a variety of different aspects of society, from a variety of different theoretical and methodological perspectives. We study everything from crime to the economy, from sexuality to deviance. We apply Marxist theories and functionalist theories to our analysis of urban education. We conduct interviews, ethnographies, and distribute surveys to examine one's level of religiosity. However, sociologists, no matter how well informed on a variety of subjects both in and out of sociology, neither know everything nor are interested in all areas within sociology. Thus, the majority of our research tends to fall within a few very specific areas of study. We have areas of focus. While we may select these areas of focus early in our careers, they may change as our research interests and tastes change. Often this is a good place to begin when trying to develop ideas for research. Below, we present four suggestions to help you select your areas of focus.

American Sociological Association

One way to help you choose your areas of interest within sociology is to go to the American Sociological Association's website (www.asanet.org). The American Sociological Association (ASA) is an organization made up of more than 14,000 academics, researchers, and professionals who work to advance sociology as a discipline and who teach in academia or work for nonprofit and for-profit organizations and agencies. ASA publishes journals and newsletters, and it organizes the largest annual sociology conference in the nation. Many of your professors are likely members of ASA. ASA also welcomes student members (we will discuss that in a little more detail in Chapter 11). On the ASA website, the link labeled "Sections" will take you to the current list of sociology sections—smaller committees focused on specific areas or fields of study within sociology that are tasked with promoting research and interest in those areas. As of 2012, the ASA has 52 sections.[1]

Figure 3.1

Aging and the Life Course	Body and Embodiment
Alcohol, Drugs, and Tobacco	Children and Youth
Altruism, Mortality, and Social Solidarity	Collective Behavior and Social Movements
Animals and Society	Communication and Information Technologies
Asia and Asian America	Community and Urban Sociology

(Continued)

Figure 3.1   (Continued)

Comparative and Historical Sociology Consumers and Consumption	Medical Sociology
Crime, Law, and Deviance	Mental Health
Culture Development	Methodology
Disability and Society	Organizations, Occupations, and Work
Economic Sociology	Peace, War, and Social Conflict
Education	Political Economy of the World-System
Emotions	Political Sociology
Environment and Technology	Population
Ethnomethodology and Conversation Analysis	Race, Gender, and Class
Evolution, Biology, and Society	Racial and Ethnic Minorities
Family	Rationality and Society
Global and Transnational Sociology	Religion
History of Sociology	Science, Knowledge, and Technology
Human Rights	Sex and Gender
International Migration Inequality, Poverty, and Mobility	Sexualities
Labor and Labor Movements	Social Psychology
Latino/a Sociology	Sociological Practice and Public Sociology
Law	Teaching and Learning
Marxist Sociology	Theory
Mathematical Sociology	

Source: American Sociological Association. 2012. "Current Sections." Washington, DC: American Sociological Association. Retrieved March 22, 2012, http://www.asanet.org/sections/list.cfm.

There are more areas of sociology that people may be interested in that are not listed above, but for most of us, our interests fall within one or several of the categories listed. Go through the list and see which topics interest you or what you may want to research further. Try to select at least three sections that contain your topics of interest.

News and Current Events

As an emerging sociologist, it is imperative that you keep up on current events. News stories can change every day, and we are constantly learning about aspects of society. As a sociologist, you should be engaged in the world. Get a newspaper subscription. Read CNN.com, *The New York Times*, *The Boston Globe,* and/or *The Washington Post.* Since you can now read newspapers online (typically for free), there really isn't any reason why you shouldn't be well versed in current events. What issues are timely or of interest to you? For example, obesity has become a major cause for concern in the country, and news outlets have focused on this epidemic. Are you interested in obesity or other health issues? If so, you will want to look into the ASA section on "Medical Sociology" or "Body and Embodiment."

Studying Yourself

As strange as this may sound, it is something that many sociologists do quite often. We are inherently interested in the social world, which is why we want to study it, but there are also many, often contested, aspects of our own lives or identities that fascinate us. Maybe you are a person of color and issues of race interest you. Maybe you are male and men's issues are of concern to you. Think about the issues that fascinate you. Think about the aspects of your life or identity that you want to learn more about. What are the larger topics—such as an ASA section—that these issues fall under? For example, if your upbringing by a single mother interests you, then maybe one of your areas of interest could be sociology of the family.

Active Reading

Active reading is the process of reading to enhance your understanding of a topic or concept. However, active reading is useful not only for conducting research; it can also be useful in thinking about a topic. While you read the research others have done, keep note of what interests you. What do you think the authors did well? What could have been done better? Is there another perspective you think is missing? If you are reading an article on math education in urban schools and you think the article is missing the perspective of women, maybe that is an area of interest for you and you may want to think about studying gender. (Active reading as part of the writing process is discussed in more detail in the following chapter.)

Now that you have selected your areas of interest, you may want to come up with ways to combine them into one research topic. While you might keep some areas separate for future research, you may find that combining your areas of interest leads to a more developed research topic. For example, what kind of project could combine research interests within the areas of "Sex and Gender" and "Body and Embodiment" (as taken from the ASA sections list) into one research topic? One potential research topic could involve assessing gender differences in perceptions of the body.

Focusing Your Topic

Once you have a general topic based on your areas of interest, you will need to focus it. Sociologists tend to organize their research around larger demographic questions (e.g., race, class, gender, sexuality, religion, nationality). Will your topic pertain to race issues? Gender issues? And, if so, which issues in particular do you want to examine? Which gender, specifically, will you study? In what geographic area will you assess this issue? Will you focus your work on the United States, or will you study some issue pertaining to gender in another country? Does a particular age group interest you?

The topic of gender differences and perceptions of the body, for instance, is much too broad. You will need to focus this topic to research and write about it effectively. What aspect of society influences or can be influenced by perceptions of the body? One aspect might be the media and their influence on perceptions of the body. Is that a lens you could use to examine your topic? Will you want to focus on women or on men, or compare the two? Will you be looking at a particular age group or the differences between multiple age groups? What aspect of the media will you focus on? The more defined your topic is, the easier it will be for you to conduct your research.

To help focus your topic, you may want to take a look at some review articles. These are articles written to provide academics with an overview of a particular field. Unlike a focused piece, a review article tries to incorporate all the main issues within that larger topic. A review article on the sociology of sports would include sections on the historical and current research on sports and sociology. This may cover issues of race, gender, sexuality, education, funding, deviance, and nationality. A review article can help focus your topic because it can give you the important issues within that topic. The journal *American Sociological Review* is one place to find such articles.

Once you have selected a topic and focused it, you should ask for advice from a colleague, professor, mentor, or advisor. If you are new to research, you should never select a topic to research and study without first seeking advice. Your professor likely knows more about the topic you chose than you do. She may have suggestions on how to focus your project or may already be aware of literature on this topic. This informed perspective could save you a lot of time and frustration.

SEARCHING FOR LITERATURE

Now that you have your research topic, it is time to begin researching the literature previously published on your topic. Your review of the literature will show you the existing literature on your topic, where it is lacking, and where it can be improved. The first place most academics go to begin this process is the library.

Your college or university library is the best place to start your search for literature. As we are sure you have noticed, there are several differences between your college's library and your local neighborhood public library. Although public libraries are great resources for high school students, they rarely provide access to databases that search through scholarly journal articles and other academic texts. Some cities, such as New York City, have what are known as research libraries. These libraries subscribe to social science and other scientific journals, as well as books based on research reports and projects. However, chances are you will conduct most of your research at a campus library. Your college or university library has many resources that will help you conduct your research and write up your research report. These resources include databases, research librarians, interlibrary loan, and bibliographic software. Each will be described in more detail below.

School Library Databases

Hundreds of databases exist to help you search through books, articles, newspapers, research reports, dissertations, and theses. The databases you will have access to will vary depending on your institution's subscription plan. As sociologists, we have a number of databases that help us find sources on our topics. Some of the most popular databases include the following:

- Academic Search Premier
- Anthropology Plus
- Black Studies Center
- Contemporary Women's Issues
- Criminal Justice Abstracts
- ERIC (via EBSCOhost)
- JSTOR
- LGBT Life with Full Text
- PAIS International
- POPLINE
- ProQuest Dissertations & Theses
- PsychINFO
- Psychology and Behavioral Sciences Collection
- SAGE Journals Online
- Social Sciences Citation Index
- Social Sciences in ProQuest
- Social Services Abstract
- Social Work Reference Library
- Sociological Abstracts
- Substance Abuse and Mental Health Data Archive
- Web of Science
- Women's Studies International

The nature of your project will also determine which database you examine. For example, if your project explores issues relating to education, you may want to focus your literature search on databases that specialize in research pertaining to education, such as ERIC.

Most databases allow you to search for journal articles, books, book reviews, and even newspaper articles by focusing on a number of fields. Databases also usually allow advanced searches that give you the option of three to five search fields. These fields often are separated by boxes that contain the Boolean search terms *and*, *or*, and *not*. These will help you refine your search if you are using more than one search term. For example, if you were conducting research on HIV/AIDS among heterosexual Latino men using the Sociological Abstracts database from ProQuest, you would focus on the terms *Latino, heterosexual,* and *HIV/AIDS*. You could separate the words by the terms *and*, *or*, and *not*. For example, you could search "*Latino* and *HIV* or *AIDS*"—which would include resources mentioning *Latino* and *HIV* or *Latino* and *AIDS*—and "*heterosexual* not *homosexual*"—which would add a focus only on the resources that include the term *heterosexual* and not *homosexual*. Some of the databases have implied Boolean searches, where entering any two terms implies an *and*.

Figure 3.2

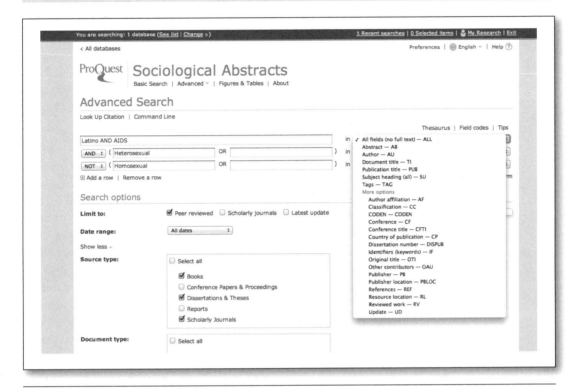

Source: www.Proquest.com.

In your search, you can often include the following fields:

Title—Insert the title of the article or book.

Name—Insert the author's last name (e.g., "Smith" or "Smith, John"). Some databases will allow you to search by author's first name or include the first name in the search. Others allow you to search only by last name.

Keywords—These are search terms or phrases that databases look for or filter out to find the appropriate resources for your project. The more appropriate or focused your keyword, the more likely you will find sources on your topic. Keywords are often the nouns and/or adjectives in your thesis statement/question or overall topic. For example, if you were conducting research on infant mortality among Indian women, you would search keywords *India*, *women*, and *infant mortality*.

Affiliation—This will allow you to search by the author's affiliation. For instance, if you knew that you wanted to seek out a researcher who worked at a particular think tank or research institute, you could instruct the database to filter for the author's affiliation (e.g., Ithaca College).

Journal name—If you want to limit your search to a particular journal, you can search through the databases by journal name. If the journal is *American Journal of Sociology,* you can simply type that name into the search, along with any other search terms, and the database will search for key terms and phrases within that particular journal.

Time—You are also able to narrow your search by focusing your work within a particular time frame. The nature of your project will often determine the time frame you will need to focus on in your search. It is usually ideal to stick with research published within the past 10 years, as the data and the research are more recent and, thus, more likely to still be applicable to your project. An article exploring gender roles within the home that is published in 2007 will likely yield very different findings than will an article on the same topic published in 1964 or even 1984. As sociologists, we study society, and since society is constantly changing and evolving, our research and theories also evolve. As such, if your topic allows, searching for more recent articles will likely be more reliable. However, if your interest involves a historical perspective or changes over time, older documents are acceptable.

Scholarly/peer-reviewed articles—This will allow you to narrow your search to only articles that are peer reviewed. Peer-reviewed articles and scholarly papers are reviewed by scholars in the field before being published, thus giving the work more credibility within academic circles. As will be explained further below, including newspaper or magazine articles in your research is often ill advised because they are not peer reviewed.

After you input your search words or phrases into the database's search engine, you will receive a number of results. If your search produces a book, you will be provided with the book's title, author's/editor's name, year of publication, place of publication, and the name of the publishing house. If your search produces a journal article or newspaper/magazine article, results will include the article's citation, including author's name, title and journal/magazine/newspaper name, date of publication, and issue and volume number so you can find the article, as well as the article's abstract or summary. Depending on the database and what journals your university subscribes to, you may also get a link that will bring you to the actual article online or will provide a PDF or the

HTML link to the article. This will allow you to get your article easily without physically going to the library, searching through the stacks for the journal and specific issue number, and photocopying it.

The number of search results you receive depends on how specific you are. Depending on your search terms, you can receive no results or thousands. If you find more than 50 articles on your topic, your search terms are too broad and should be better focused. As described above, this could include narrowing to a particular time frame, journal, or even gender of the group being researched. If you find you have too few articles/books, you should include a variety of search terms and phrases to increase the number of results. For example, if you are researching African American boys and school playgrounds in urban areas, you should consider that researchers may have used different words to categorize their research. You may want to search for the broader term *Black*, in addition to *African American*. You could also add *yards* to your search for *playgrounds* and *children* or *male* to your search for *boys*. Keep track of the different search terms used in the search fields so you don't keep producing the same books, articles, and other literature in your search.

Additionally, you should also keep in mind that search terms can change over time. The word *Negro*, for example, was used before the 1980s to describe the group of people now often referred to as "African American" or "Black." Some people who were born before that time may still refer to themselves in that way, and research conducted in the 1950s and 1960s may use this terminology. If you are looking for information on African Americans in previous time periods, considering the change in terms is important. Other terms that have changed over time include *special education*, *developmentally disabled*, *bilingual education*, and *adolescent*. Broadening a search may include being aware of or researching the terms themselves.

Resource/Research Librarian

These librarians work within college and university libraries, often in a research capacity, to aid faculty, students, and staff with library research and literature collection. Many research librarians specialize in particular areas of study, such as education, medicine, and the social sciences. These librarians serve as excellent resources, as they can help search for books and articles, as well as Internet sources. They can also help you come up with search terms and look for databases. Remember that these individuals have been trained and are paid to help you with your research. You should take advantage of their presence. You can typically make an appointment to meet with these librarians in person, and at some universities you can also chat with research librarians via telephone or online.

Interlibrary Loan

If you discover that your college's library does not have a particular book or article, before beginning the arduous task of searching for these sources on your own, find out if your school library participates in an interlibrary loan (ILL) consortium. Participation in the ILL will allow you access to sources such as books, journals, theses, and dissertations located at other libraries that participate in the consortium. The ILL consists of a consortium of libraries, typically university libraries, across the country. Not all university libraries are part of a consortium; however, most large universities and colleges provide this service to students, faculty, and staff. With most ILLs, you will need to complete a form with your name and contact information to order the text. Depending on how rare the book or article is, for example, you can receive the source any time from a few days to a few weeks. In the case of articles, many times they can simply be e-mailed to you as a PDF attachment or link.

Bibliographic Managing Software

Bibliographic Managing Software helps you keep track of and store your references. The two main bibliographic software packages are RefWorks and EndNote. These packages allow you to store an unlimited number of references, as well as a limited number of abstracts and notes in a file, often relating to the topic, for easier retrieval and reference. In fact, both software packages even create bibliographies for you in the correct citation style (e.g., ASA style, American Psychological Association style, or Chicago style) for inclusion in the reference section of your paper. These software packages are quite similar, but the main difference between the two is that EndNote requires a software program on a Mac or PC. This means that you must save the program to your computer to access your references. RefWorks is a web-based program, so you can access your references anywhere you have an Internet connection. These software packages also allow you to export your records so you can share references with other users of the software package, which aids in collaborating on research projects.

SELECTING APPROPRIATE LITERATURE

Not all literature is created equal. You want to be certain that the literature you use as resources on your topic is high quality and, importantly, reliable. Although scholars sometimes cite newspapers and magazines—usually because of their relevancy and timeliness—or theses or dissertations (these will be discussed in much more detail in Chapter 11) for more obscure topics, most scholars rely on articles published in scholarly journals and books as resources for their work.

Scholarly Journals

One of the most common and well-respected forms of sociological and academic writing consists of research reports or writings published in scholarly journals. Scholarly journals contain research reports or empirical studies based on original research, theoretical papers, and reviews of the literature, as well as review essays and book reviews. The purpose of these journals is to disseminate new knowledge about a particular area of study to other researchers interested in the topic who subscribe to these journals. A manuscript submitted for peer review is first reviewed by the editor to make sure it is appropriate for the journal. Once the submission goes through this initial review, it is then sent out to other scholars in the field so they can review the paper for reliability. If they deem the paper an important contribution to the field, the paper is published.

Scholarly journals are small booklets of varying length; some are quite slim, 100 pages or so, while others can be a few hundred pages or more. Each journal issue or volume contains varying numbers of articles or reviews. Some journals publish several volumes a year, while others publish only one. There are also journals that focus on specialized topics and others that are more general.

Larger publishing companies, such as SAGE, or organizations and associations such as the ASA publish research journals. Departments within universities and colleges also sometimes publish journals. Some journals are published in print, and, increasingly, others are being published solely online. If you are ever unsure of whether or not a source is peer reviewed or comes from a scholarly journal, you can always search for the name of the publishing source in a search engine.

Books

As social scientists, we want to make sure we select the proper books as resources. Most important, we must make sure the work is reliable. It is a little harder to verify the reliability of a book than of an article. Since most articles in scholarly journals are peer reviewed, you can be a little more certain that the article is reliable and a contribution to the field. However, this is not necessarily the case with books. Some books make excellent resources, but literally anyone can publish a book.

The type of research you conduct will likely determine the books you will need. Academic presses tend to publish the most reliable book information. There are a variety of academic presses; some are university presses, such as Harvard University Press and the University of Chicago Press. There are also academic presses that are not affiliated with a university, such as SAGE. Additionally, there are popular presses that publish academic books, such as McGraw-Hill. It is always important to note the publisher of the text and to use scholarly sources as your references.

Some books, known as edited volumes or anthologies, consist of a number of essays written by multiple authors that are compiled and edited by one or multiple editors. Anthologies provide excellent resources, as they often focus on more specialized topics and provide a variety of perspectives on your topic.

Although books are quite helpful as they provide a more thorough analysis of a particular subject, they are also quite time-consuming to read and analyze. You can read a dozen articles with dozens of methodologies, theories, and findings in the same time it would take to read one book. Books also take longer to publish, and, therefore, the information within them is probably older than what you find in articles.

Reference Sections

The reference section or bibliography of a book or article lists the materials and literature referenced in the text. These reference sections potentially serve as great starting points for a literature search, as they already provide a list of materials on the research topic. The reference pages of dissertations and theses are also especially helpful. Go through the references the authors cited in their text and you can see if there are any titles or works you may want to examine. This is particularly helpful if you have an obscure topic or are having difficulty finding sources. You might also consider reverse-citation searches, which Google Scholar and JSTOR provide. These will allow you to find other sources that have cited the article you are reading. While examining an article's reference section exposes you to older articles, reverse-citation searches open up the field to newer articles. Looking through the references of the various essays included in an anthology can also be particularly helpful because, with all the articles contained in the collection, you may have access to hundreds of potential references on your topic. You don't have to reinvent the wheel while collecting references.

Encyclopedias

These provide great resources if you need an overview of an issue or the background story on a topic (we review encyclopedia articles and how they are written more extensively in Chapter 4). As social scientists, we typically conduct research that is much more focused than what you would find in your typical encyclopedia entry. As useful as a traditional encyclopedia can be, it is not as helpful if you are interested in doing research, for example, on the impact of stigma on the lives of those with AIDS. There are a number of more focused encyclopedias that we use in the social sciences, such as the *Cultural Encyclopedia of the Body* and the *Encyclopedia of AIDS*. Encyclopedia entries often provide a list of the works referenced in the entry or further suggested readings on the topic.

Webpages

Many websites contain valuable and reliable information, but many more do not. Websites often contain false or biased information and, as such, do not always make suitable sources. There was once a time when professors would caution their students against or even forbid them from using online sources as references in their research papers and projects. As the nature of the Internet has changed, professors have come to realize that some websites can be valuable resources.

But not all websites are created equal. That is, not all webpages are reliable and appropriate for referencing in a course paper or professional report, so you should always cite webpages with caution. As anyone can create a ".com" webpage, we typically advise that such websites be fully researched before citation. With ".com" sites, it is important to check when the website was created and who or what organization or individual created it. You should consider whether this information adds or takes away from the webpage's reliability. American websites ending in ".gov," ".edu," or ".org" are usually more reliable—especially those ending in ".gov," as they are government websites and contain findings from government reports and documents. Websites ending in ".edu" belong to educational institutions and are typically more reliable sources, as are ".org" websites, which are often run by nonprofit organizations. However, ".org" is an open domain that anyone can use, so it should also be fully vetted. A number of scholarly journals are published only online, and those may be suitable sources because many of them are peer reviewed. Keep in mind that some websites are more accurate than others, and you should always be careful when using online sources. Below, we present several questions you should ask yourself to help evaluate the potential reliability of a website's information.

- What is the webpage's focus?
- What is the webpage's content?
- Is the webpage well written or does it contain many grammatical/spelling errors?
- Who created the webpage?
- Is the author an expert on the issues addressed on the webpage?
- What are the author's qualifications?
- When was the website first created?
- When was it last updated?
- What sources and information does the webpage cite or reference?
- Can you verify the information?
- Can you contact the author?

To verify the webpage's author, you can always search her name using a search engine such as Google.com. You can also look up her institutional affiliations. Additionally, to verify the content, you can search for the references cited on the webpage in library or online databases such as JSTOR or Google Scholar. In the end, you (and your professor) will have to use your best judgment to determine if a webpage is suitable for use and if it will help enhance your research.

WRITING FROM SOURCES

Once you have selected the relevant literature for your project, the process of incorporating these sources into your own work to help inform your research begins. You can incorporate the work of another author or a particular source through the use of summaries, paraphrasing, and direct quotes, but all this must be properly cited. Each discipline has an appropriate way of citing sources, and we will examine how this is done within sociology using the two most frequently used styles, ASA and American

Psychological Association (APA). First, however, we will briefly discuss (and caution against) plagiarism.

Plagiarism

To plagiarize is "to steal and pass off (the ideas and words of another) as one's own" or "to use (another's production) without crediting the source."[2] This means if a writer uses the words, ideas, or language of another and is not authorized to do so (either under fair usage, which must be cited properly, or by permission), he is committing plagiarism. However, most plagiarism is not intentional but, rather, the result of sloppiness or disorganization. As we will show in several of our chapters, the writer may find that much of the information in the first few sections of his document will be cited information, as the early sections of a paper are where the research gathered has not yet come together to create the writer's own perspective. When something isn't cited, it is usually a known fact or the researcher's own contribution. If there is a question as to whether something should be cited, citing the work is always best. The writer must remember this one rule about citations: Every piece of information that is not the writer's must be credited.

Plagiarizing is highly frowned on in academia, as colleges and universities are in the business of producing knowledge. As a result, the consequences of plagiarism can range from a failing grade to expulsion from one's school or place of employment. Every institution has its own rules, definitions, and guidelines concerning citations and plagiarism. Rules regarding plagiarism can typically be found in the student handbook, the school guidebook, or several other locations on a school's website.

Summary and Paraphrasing

There are several ways to organize and use the information the writer has extracted from academic sources. The first is through summarization. A summary overview is not a common assignment within sociology, but the most common place where a summary is used is in writing an abstract. Most other summary-type writing will focus on a particular theme or question and will not be a simple summary of the whole piece. Even in completing a book review, as will be elaborated on in the next chapter, there will be a focus on a few areas of importance rather than describing the entire piece as a whole.

The more common use of a summary is found in paraphrasing or indirect quotes. Paraphrasing someone else's work is a way to synthesize various pieces of information. Here, the writer has the opportunity to summarize a particular idea or several ideas from one or multiple authors. As these are not the writer's original thoughts, even if the ideas have been put together in unique ways, they must be cited.

Initial quote:

"According to domestic and transnational polls on religious beliefs and commitment, 'American Blacks are, by some measures, the most religious people in the world.'"[3]

Possible paraphrasing:

Research indicates that African Americans are among the most religious racial/ethnic groups in the world (Pattillo-McCoy 1998).

Direct Quotes

Direct quotations are, as the name suggests, directly borrowed from the book or article and included in the writer's piece. The initial quote above is an example of a direct quote. The quote either will be no more than a few sentences—in which case, it can be set in line with the rest of the paragraph—or will be longer and set as a block quotation—that is, set off from the rest of the text in a manner that varies by discipline. In sociology (ASA format), four or more lines of text should be structured as block quotations, which are indented on both sides and single spaced. Short quotations always include quotation marks at the beginning and end as well as a citation, which in sociology is the author's last name, followed by the date, a colon, and the page number. Longer quotes also include citations but not quotation marks. Unlike paraphrasing, the citations for direct quotes must include page numbers.

The exact wording from the original writing should also be used in a direct quote. When it is necessary to edit, the writer must note that changes have been made through the use of ellipses (. . .)—which indicate missing words—or brackets ([ ])—which indicate changed words, when, for example, a personal pronoun must be changed or a word needs further explanation or translation.

Initial quote:

"The school was difficult for me. I really wanted a lot more than I was able to receive there. I felt I put my all into my work and didn't see the rewards" (Jenkins 2008:53).

Possible revision:

According to Jenkins, Jade's "school was difficult for [her]. . . . [She] felt [she] put [her] all into [her] work and didn't see the rewards" (2008:53).

Below, we provide a passage and show how a direct quote, summary, and paraphrase can be written based on the passage.

"Yet in spite of this gender development, attitudes to female football supporters remain strikingly sexist. One man who witnessed women throwing bottles and punches at Fulham Broadway said female fans only wanted 'to watch Beckham's legs and marry Wayne Rooney.' A policeman regularly deployed at football grounds, who conceded that women were increasingly engaging in disorderly [behavior], rejected the idea that rowdy female fans could be serious about the sport. 'The girls are just trying to impress the boys, aren't they?' he said. 'They've had one too many Smirnoff Ices.'"[4]

Direct Quote	Summary	Paraphrase
According to Wake, many football fans believe that women are interested in the sport only to "watch Beckham's legs and marry Wayne Rooney" (Wake 2008:20).	The article describes the ways female fans of football (nee soccer) are still referred to in sexist ways. According to Katie Wake, women who are fans of football are interested in it only because they connect with the players in a sexual way, believing that they have attractive bodies or are husband potential. Women may also find that interest in the sport attracts the attention of men. Overall, many men tend to look at female fandom with skepticism and, even when faced with female hooliganism, still see it as based on women's relationship with men and not their own interests (Wake 2008).	Researchers have found a lack of understanding of female fandom, such that men often believe women get involved because of their attraction to the players or to get attention from men (Wake 2008).

As illustrated in the above example, remember that when you refer to an author of an article or a book, you do not need to use the name of the article but simply the author's last name. Also, you do not need to keep saying, "he said"; let the audience know who "he" is by referring to the author's first and last name the first time you mention the article and the last name alone for each subsequent mention.

In-Text Citations and References

The ASA and APA citation styles are the most commonly used reference styles within sociology journals and papers. American Anthropological

Association (AAA) is the style cited by anthropologists. Chicago style may also be used in courses that don't emphasize a particular social science format. Since ASA and APA are the styles most frequently used by sociologists, we will focus on those two styles in this chapter. We discuss AAA and Chicago styles in the Appendix of this text. However, it is always good to have a style guide on hand for more details and to keep abreast of changes in the citation styles when they occur. Each professional organization should have a hard copy of the style guide available for purchase on its website. Some of the organizations also provide access to free digital versions.

American Sociological Association Style

When you use direct quotes in ASA style, you incorporate short in-text quotations into the text of your paper and enclose them in double quotation marks. The accompanying citations are written in this format: ([author's last name] [year]:[page number]). If the quote is indirect or you are referring to the entire book, you do not need to include the page number. There is a space between the author's last name and the year but not between the year and the page number. If you include the author's name in explaining your quotation, you do not need to repeat the name in the parenthetical citation; likewise, if you include the year of publication with the author's name, you need not include it in the parentheses at the end of the quotation. In-text citations in these instances should precede the ending punctuation.

Finally, if one volume has more than two authors, you should include each author's last name (up to three names) with commas between them and an *and* before the last author name. For all subsequent citations for these authors, write only the first author's name and use *et al.* for the remaining authors. If a work has more than three authors, include only the first author's name and use *et al.* for the other authors in the first citation as well as in all subsequent citations. If you are citing multiple works within one set of parentheses, they can be ordered either alphabetically by the authors' last names or chronologically and should be separated by semicolons. However you decide, be sure that all your citations follow the same format.

Block quotations, those of more than 40 words or 4 lines, should be indented with a space before and after the quote. They are often single spaced. You should introduce the quotation with either a comma or a colon. In a block quotation, the in-text citation should follow the ending punctuation. If the author's name and the date are included in the quotation, in the parentheses, add a capital *P* for page, followed by a period and then the page number.

Figure 3.3

Citing the entire book:

- Garcia (2003) strongly agrees.

Citing one author—name not in text:

- "the issue with public health" (Garcia 2003:29)

Citing one author—name in text:

- As Julio Garcia suggests **[first and last name used on first mention; only LAST name used afterward],** "the issue with public health is that time and again funding is often denied to the groups and organizations most in need" (2003:29).

Citing two authors—name not in text:

- (Lopez and Best 2010)

Citing three authors—names not in text:

- (Leon, Pace, and Chang 1999)
- After first citation: (Leon et al. 1999)

Citing four or more authors—names not in text:

- (Leblanc et al. 2010)

Citing multiple works by the same author—different years:

- (Pugh 2008; 2009)

Citing multiple works by the same author—same year:

- (McGruder 2009a; 2009b)

Citing multiple works—alphabetical order:

- (Bartley 1982; Carrillo 2000; Torres 1999)

Citing multiple works—chronological order:

- (Carrillo 2000; Torres 1999; Bartley 1982)

Citing a work with an unknown author:

Use the least amount of information needed to identify the reference in the reference list.

Citing a work with multiple editions:

If you are using a later edition of a volume than its original, place its earliest date in brackets first and then follow it with the date of the volume you used.

Citing a work with an unknown date:

Tyner (n.d.)

The heading for the reference section is generally a first-level heading. Each item should be double spaced and formatted as a hanging indent (first line is left justified; all subsequent lines are indented below it) and in title case. References should list all the articles, in alphabetical order, by author's last name. All authors' full first and last names should be included in the reference section (no *et al.* or initials, unless that is how they have referred to themselves in their document). For multiple works by the same author, list them in chronological order from oldest to newest. If an author has completed both solo work and multiauthored work that you have cited, include the solo work first, followed by the multiauthored work. Be sure that the letters following the dates of works by the same author published in the same year match up with those used in the in-text citations.

Figure 3.4

Books, one author:

- Anyon, Jean. 1997. *Ghetto Schooling: A Political Economy of Urban Educational Reform.* New York: Teacher's College Press.

Books, multiple authors:

- Attewell, Paul and David E. Lavin. 2007. *Passing the Torch: Does Higher Education for the Disadvantaged Pay Off Across the Generations?* New York: Russell Sage Foundation.
- Bryk, Anthony S., Valerie E. Lee, and Peter B. Holland. 1993. *Catholic Schools and the Common Good.* Cambridge, Massachusetts: Harvard University Press.

Edited volumes (entire):

If there is a volume or edition, it should be after the title and not italicized.

- Arum, Richard, Irenee Beattie, and Karly Ford. eds. 2011. *The Structure of Schooling.* 2d ed. Thousand Oaks, CA: Pine Forge Press.

Edited volume (chapter):

- Coleman, James, Ernest Campbell, Carol Hobson, James McPartland, Alexander Mood, Frederick Weinfeld, and Robert York. 2011. "Equality of Educational Opportunity: The Coleman Report." Pp. 120–36 in *The Structure of Schooling,* 2d ed., edited by R. Arum, I. Beattie, and K. Ford. Thousand Oaks, CA: Pine Forge Press.

Journal articles:

- Battle, Juan. 1997. "The Relative Effects of Married Versus Divorced Family Configuration and Socioeconomic Status on the Educational Achievement of

African American Middle-Grade Students." *The Journal of Negro Education* 66(1):29–42.

- Aguirre, B. E., Dennis Wenger, and Gabriela Vigo. 1998. "A Test of the Emergent Norm Theory of Collective Behavior." *Sociological Forum* 13(2):301–20.

Articles from magazines or newspapers:

- Neergaard, Lauran. 2012. "Use of Condoms Stalls: CDC Issues Report on Teens' Sexual Behavior." *Milwaukee Journal Sentinel,* July 25, p. 3A.

Information posted on a website:

- Botsch, Carol Sears. 2000. "Septima Poinsette Clark." *USC Aiken.* Retrieved July 15, 2012 (http://www.usca.edu/aasc/clark.htm).

Blog posts:

- Lewis-McCoy, R. L'Heureux. 2012. "58 Years After Brown: More Separate, Less Equal." Uptown Notes Blog. Retrieved May 25, 2012 (http://www.uptownnotes .com/58-years-after-brown-more-separate-less-equal//).

American Psychological Association Style

APA format is used for publications associated with the APA but also may be found in other disciplines and journals that sociologists might encounter, such as in the field of education. Some professors and sociological journals still accept or even prefer articles in APA format. For these reasons, we thought it was important to include a discussion of APA style in this volume.

When incorporated into the text of your paper, short in-text quotations in APA should be enclosed in double quotation marks. In-text citations of direct quotes in APA format are written in this format: ([author's last name], [year], p. [page number]). If the quote is indirect or you are referring to the entire book, you do not need to include the page number, but APA recommends it. There is a space between the comma after the author's last name and the year and before and after "p." Similar to ASA style, if the author's name is included in your explanation of the quotation, you do not need to repeat the name in the parenthetical citation, and if you include the year of publication with the author's name, it does not have to be included in the parentheses at the end of the quotation. Finally, if there is more than one author for one volume, you include each person's last name (up to five authors) with commas between them and an "&" before the last author. For all subsequent references to these authors, write only the first author's name and use *et al.* for the remaining authors. If a work has more than five authors, include only the first author's name and use *et al.* for the other authors in the first as well as subsequent references. If you are citing multiple works within one set of parentheses, they should be written in the same order they are listed in the references (i.e., alphabetical) and separated by a semicolon.

Block quotations, those of more than 40 words, should be indented half an inch. Most journals will also allow them to be single spaced. You should introduce the quotation with either a comma or a colon. The in-text citation should follow the ending punctuation.

Figure 3.5

Citing the entire book:

- Garcia (2003) strongly agrees.

Citing one author—name not in text:

- "the issue with public health" (Garcia, 2003, p. 29)

Citing one author—name in text:

- As Julio Garcia (2003) **[first and last name on first mention of the author; only LAST name afterward]** suggests, "The issue with public health is that time and again funding is often denied to the groups and organizations most in need" (p. 29).

Citing two authors—name not in text:

- (Lopez & Best, 2010)

Citing three to five authors—names not in text:

- (Leon, Pace, & Chang, 1999).
- After first reference: (Leon et al., 1999)

Citing six or more authors—names not in text:

- (Muhammad et al., 2009)

Citing multiple works by the same author—different years:

- (Pugh, 2008, 2009)

Citing multiple works by the same author—same year:

- (McGruder, 2009a, 2009b)

Citing multiple works by different authors—alphabetical order:

- (Bartley, 1982; Carrillo, 2000; Torres, 1999)

Citing a work by an unknown author:

You should use the title of the work in the body of the text or the first couple of words of the title in the parenthetical citation. Use the abbreviation *n.d.* if the date is unknown.

Citing a work with multiple editions:

If you are using a later edition of a volume than its original, place the original publication date first and then the date of the newer volume you used; separate the two dates with a backslash (e.g., 1970/1988).

Citing a work with an unknown date:

- Tyner (n.d.)

The reference heading should be centered at the top of a new page. Each item should be double spaced and formatted as a hanging indent. All major words in paper and journal titles should be capitalized, but titles of chapters, articles, books, and websites should be set in sentence case. References should be in alphabetical order by author's last name. You should use the authors' last names and first initials for all authors up to six. If there are seven or more authors, follow the sixth name with *et al.* If you have multiple works by the same author, list them in chronological order from oldest to newest. If an author has completed both multiauthored and solo works, include the solo works first, followed by the multiauthored works. Be sure the letters that follow the dates of works by the same author that were published in the same year match up with those used in the in-text citations. Books and journal titles should be italicized.

For online information, cite exactly as you would for the print version of the work. If the work is available only online, also include the URL. If there are no page numbers, use the abbreviation "para." and include the paragraph number.

PREPARING TO WRITE

Now that you have your topic and a pile of scholarly journal articles and books that you think will be helpful and inform your research topic, you are ready to begin organizing the literature so you can prepare yourself to write. The three forms of writing that will help you prepare your research are annotated bibliographies, proposals, and outlines.

Figure 3.6

Books, one author:

If there is a volume or edition, it should be placed in parentheses after the title and not italicized.

Goffman, E. (1990). *The presentation of self in everyday life* (15th ed.). New York: Penguin Books. (Original work published in 1959)

Books, multiple authors:

Attewell, P., & Lavin, D. E. (2007). *Passing the torch: Does higher education for the disadvantaged pay off across the generations?* New York: Russell Sage Foundation.

Bryk, A. S., Lee, V. E., & Holland, P. B. (1993). *Catholic schools and the common good.* Cambridge, Massachusetts: Harvard University Press.

Edited volumes (entire):

Arum, R., Beattie, I., & Ford, K. (Eds.). (2011). *The structure of schooling* (2nd ed.). Thousand Oaks, CA: Pine Forge Press.

Edited volume (chapter):

Coleman, J., Campbell, E., Hobson, C., McPartland, J., Mood, A., Weinfeld, F., et al. (2011). Equality of educational opportunity: The Coleman Report. In R. Arum, I. Beattie, & K. Ford (Eds.), *The structure of schooling* (2nd ed., pp. 120–136). Thousand Oaks, CA: Pine Forge Press.

Journal articles:

Battle, J. (1997). The relative effects of married versus divorced family configuration and socioeconomic status on the educational achievement of African American middle-grade students. *Journal of Negro Education, 66*(1), 29–42.

Aguirre, B. E., Wenger, D., & Vigo, G. (1998). A test of the emergent norm theory of collective behavior. *Sociological Forum, 13*(2), 301–320.

Articles from magazines or newspapers:

Neergaard, L. (2012, July 25). Use of condoms stalls: CDC issues report on teens' sexual behavior. *Milwaukee Journal Sentinel*, p. 3A.

Information posted on a website:

Botsch, C. S. (2000). Septima Poinsette Clark. *USC Aiken.* Retrieved from http://www.usca.edu/aasc/clark.htm

Annotated Bibliographies

There are two different types of annotated bibliographies. In addition to what we will talk about in this chapter, there are also the annotated bibliographies written and published in research reports and journals to help other scholars ascertain the work in a particular field or area of study. These will be discussed further in Chapter 4. This chapter will discuss those written by researchers in the beginning of the research process, as they help organize the literature on a specific topic.

An annotated bibliography is a list of articles, books, or other research that pertains to your topic, along with the bibliographic citation (generally written in ASA or APA format), a short description, and an evaluation/ analysis. The analysis part is very important because it will help you construct your literature review when you write up your research report. Citations in annotated bibliographies are commonly listed in alphabetical order by the first author's last name and are analyzed one by one. However, instead of arranging this annotated bibliography in alphabetical order by author's last name, we would suggest arranging it by theme/concept. This can help you see where your deficiencies may lie and will help you organize your research topics.

Annotated bibliographies save a tremendous amount of time in the writing process, as they help you keep track of the literature you have and, therefore, you won't have to reread all the literature to remember how it relates to your research when you sit down to write it up. Also, if you plan on writing a literature review (see Chapters 4, 6, and 8), arranging the annotated bibliography entries by theme will help you begin to organize your literature review.

The structure of the annotated bibliography typically consists of the following: an introductory paragraph; a series of annotations, including the citation of the source; and a concluding paragraph.

Introductory Paragraph

Many annotated bibliographies begin with an introductory paragraph that is about 150 to 250 words long, introducing the annotated bibliography as well as the literature. This paragraph should contain background information on your topic as well as the questions that interest you about the topic and an overview of what you learned from this particular body of literature. Why did you choose to include this literature in the annotated bibliography? Explain the overall themes you found in all the literature presented in the annotated bibliography.

Annotations

Each annotation should start with a full citation of the source, preferably in ASA or APA format. Annotations are generally concise. Each description should range from 150 to 250 words; excess words and phrases should be omitted. Remember, each annotation should be succinct and to the point.

Actual annotation styles can vary, but they generally begin with a brief summary of the article or book. Articles and books already contain summaries either at the beginning or the end of the piece. Your summary, however, should not focus on the whole piece but should pay particular attention to how the book or article relates to your research and your topic. It is important that your annotation is critical and explains the author's argument. Briefly explain how this research relates to, contributes to, or refutes what other scholars have found. This part is particularly important, as it will aid in the construction of your literature review. At the end of the annotation, you should include a few short sentences that explain how this particular work will contribute to your potential project or overall topic. The purpose of the annotation is not just to help you begin to think about the literature but, more important, to help you discover how it relates to your larger research topic.

Concluding Paragraph

After you have listed all your annotations, you should include a concluding paragraph that assesses what you have learned as a result of your literature search, as well as how you will use these resources. This, too, is typically 150 to 250 words long. Importantly, you should include a thesis statement, or what you propose to argue or research as a result of the literature you examined. Explain what research questions you now have and how this literature will aid you in your project. The concluding paragraph should help you form your research question based on your search topics. What has the literature, overall, said about your research topic, and what resulting research question do you now have? This question forms the basis for your project.

For example, if you are interested in exploring the influence of the media on the perceptions of body image for men, you will probably find a variety of sources. Based on your research, how can you focus your topic into a concise research question? What aspects of the media do you want to focus on? Television? Magazines? Additionally, you may want to focus your sample of men by age. One resulting research question could be, "How do teenage boys react to the depictions of the male body on exercise and weightlifting magazine covers?"

Research Proposal

Now that you have your annotated bibliography, or list of readings, and your research question, it is time to develop a research proposal and begin thinking about your thesis statement and/or hypothesis. As discussed in the previous chapter, a hypothesis is an early answer to the research question(s) you developed as a result of your literature search, and a thesis is developed after more extensive research has been conducted. As you focus your topic, think about how a sociologist might examine this issue. As sociology is the scientific study of society, you want to be certain that you examine your issue from a sociological perspective. You should begin this process by pre-liminarily answering your research question. For example, if your research question is,

"How do teenage boys react to the depictions of the male body on exercise and weightlifting magazine covers?"

a statement that answers this question could be,

"Depictions of the 'idealized' male body on weightlifting and exercise magazine covers have a negative influence on the body image of teen boys."

This statement could serve as the hypothesis, or the answer to the research question. To develop the hypothesis, you should first think about the purpose of your project and what you hope to accomplish as a result of your study. Based on your review of the literature, what do you expect to find? Although there could be a number of possible reactions to these depictions, you will need to work to focus your hypothesis so it is neither too broad nor too general. This will help guide you through the rest of the research process.

Writing a research proposal will help you think about the process of developing and proving your thesis statement. Research proposals explain the proposed research and what it will entail. Proposals can be written for yourself as a reminder of what you plan on doing for your project, but they can also be written for professors and different agencies and organizations. Research proposals can vary in length depending on the size and nature of the intended project. Some could be as long as 20 pages, while others could be only 500 words. These proposals help prepare you for your project and keep you on track. Importantly, these proposals are handy in helping you articulate your project to a professor or colleague. Although the structure of research proposals may vary, they contain the following basic parts: an introduction to the problem/issue, background for the problem/issue, a description of the proposed research, and a list of references.

Introduction to the Problem or Issue

The issue is the problem you find, or expect to find, based on a particular research topic. If the topic is the economy, the issue may be the high unemployment rates found within minority communities. This introduction should introduce the reader to the issue. This may seem a bit confusing if you are writing a research proposal for yourself, but you may want to have your professors or colleagues read your proposal for their insight and feedback. An introduction that adequately and briefly introduces the issue should provide the necessary background information for readers. Explain what this problem or issue is and why you are interested in examining it.

Background to the Problem or Issue

Provide a background to the overall issue. Here, you will briefly explain how this issue became a problem. At the end of the description, state your thesis statement and explain how you came upon it. This may include explaining your research question(s) and the resulting hypothesis as well.

Description of Proposed Research

Explain how you plan on proving your thesis. You should have an idea in mind of what kind of data you plan on collecting and how you plan on gathering this data. Describe the methodology you propose to utilize to explore your thesis statement. Given your time and resources, think about what methodology will be feasible so you can explore your thesis. You don't want to propose a methodology that is too costly or too difficult for you to conduct on your own. Also, think about what has been done before and how. When you look back at those other articles, or the annotated bibliographies you created from them, think about the methods they used. What did you think worked and did not work? Are there ways you could expand on or change their methodology? You will already have an idea of the different work on your topic, as you have conducted a review of the literature and have written about your overall findings within the literature in your annotated bibliography.

References

Provide a list of the key references that helped inform your research hypothesis and that you plan to cite in your research. You do not have to include all the references you plan to use in your project, but you should list the important ones in the area of study. Again, this will be helpful to your professors or colleagues, as they can see which research you have or have not cited. This way, they can provide some suggestions on intended literature.

Outline

Although not necessarily part of the research process, writing an outline is certainly part of the writing process. We are including a discussion of outlines in this chapter because, while outlining does not necessarily help you prepare your research, it does help you prepare to write, and lay out, your paper. Whether you are writing a research paper or literature review, an empirical research report, or even a book review, an outline should always be part of the writing process. Like the proposal, an outline can help you organize your thoughts and ideas. Ideally, the outline should be written once all research is conducted, or once you are ready to write up your paper. However, some people write outlines as part of their process of thinking through the topic (for more information on writing an outline at this stage, see Chapter 9). In creating an outline, you will want to think about how you plan on breaking up your paper and what you plan to include in it. It will be easier if, before writing the outline, you already have an idea of the overall purpose of your paper and already know its structure as well as your intended format. Since there are a number of different types of papers and formats, this section will focus on a standard empirical paper (with the following sections: introduction, literature review, methods, results, discussion, conclusion) as an example. Chapter 8 includes some other examples of paper formats.

Outlines follow the logical progression of a paper, as they contain some kind of summary of the introduction, the body of the paper, and the conclusion. They concisely state what will be included in each section of your paper and use numbers, letters, and/or Roman numerals to identify how the proposed project is broken up and its subheadings.

You can begin writing an outline in a number of ways. We suggest beginning by listing the sections you know you will include in your paper, organized in a logical order. These sections could also translate into subheadings in your final paper. This will serve as the basic skeleton of your outline. If you were to write an empirical paper, you would include the following sections:

I. Introduction

II. Literature Review

III. Methodology

IV. Results

V. Discussion

VI. Conclusion

Once you have the major headings, you can begin to flesh out the skeleton by listing what you plan to include within each section. Again, this keeps you organized and helps your paper follow a logical progression. Your outline should begin with an introduction to the essay or paper and your topic. Depending on the level of detail you want to include in your outline, you can also explain what specific topics you will address.

I. Introduction

   a. Introduction to topic
   b. Introduction to paper
   c. What you will discuss in your paper

      i. Issue 1 you will discuss

      ii. Issue 2 you will discuss

You can see that here the general structure is indicated by uppercase Roman numerals, while the details of the introduction use lowercase letters. If you further break down those details, you might use lowercase Roman numerals, capital letters, numbers, or bullet points.

As you further develop the section on literature reviews, for example, you could list all the citations you plan to include in your paper.

II. Literature Review

    a. Introduction to literature review

        i. Collins (2001); Smith and Rodriguez (1989)

    b. Literature on topic

        i. Chu (2011); Goodhand (2010); McGuire (1999)

The various sections of your outline can serve as subheadings as you transition from one topic to the next. Remember, outlines help keep you focused so you know what you will include in your paper and where you will include it. It is also helpful to show your developed outlines to a professor or colleague and ask her for feedback on what you should or should not include in your paper before you actually begin to write it.

After you have completed your library research, review of the literature, annotated bibliography, research proposal, and outline, and you have an understanding of how to cite the literature on your topic, you should have a clear picture of the paper you are about to create. You are then ready to begin the work on that construction. The next chapters in this text explore the various types of writing you are likely to encounter as a sociology student and scholar.

SUMMARY

This chapter examines the common writing styles often used in conducting library research and in the beginning stages of the writing process. We explored the following areas:

- Ways of developing research topics, such as brainstorming for topic ideas, combining areas of interest, and focusing research topics
- Conducting library research and the resources available in a typical university or research library
- How to select appropriate sources, such as books, refereed journals, encyclopedias, and websites
- How to avoid plagiarism and incorporate the proper citation styles into your text

- How to reference sources in ASA and APA formatting styles
- The different types of writing that help you develop a larger writing project, including annotated bibliographies, research proposals, and outlines

The following "Writing in Practice" piece was written by Cynthia W. Bruns. This essay explains her role as a reference librarian. It also provides advice on developing a research topic as well as conducting library research.

WRITING IN PRACTICE

by Cynthia W. Bruns

I am a reference and research librarian specializing in sociology. I have a master's degree in library and information science and a second master's in American studies. As a librarian, it is my job to select the sociology resources and the research databases that the library purchases and to instruct students in the process of effectively manipulating these databases. I work with sociology classes, the faculty, and with individual students to assist in the process of discovering the literature of sociology and locating materials on the topics under investigation.

I work daily with research databases, and it is easy to forget that our students do not automatically recognize the existence or effectiveness of these resources. I can recall that as a college freshman, I had my first experience with journal articles when I was given the assignment to read an article of my choice. The only parameter I was given was that the article could not come from a magazine. What a shocker! Even though I had attended an excellent high school, I had no idea that journals existed, or how to access one. I don't remember how I was able to locate that first journal article, but I must have, because I passed that class. I have focused on this snippet of a memory to remind me that students do not arrive at a university well versed in all aspects of research and often may not have any awareness of the breadth of quality research information available to them. This is where I can help.

I worked for a number of years as an instructional librarian after receiving my first master's. Assisting the students, I found that the most challenging aspect of researching a paper can be beginning the process. Narrowing and focusing a research question is a stumbling block for many students and yet is a critical portion of the research process. A poorly chosen topic or a subject that does not interest the student can turn the research process into pure drudgery. Students have told me that when they meet with faculty members, they are generally directed to research a narrower and more focused topic. This is actually very good advice and will make the paper much easier to research and write.

As an instructional librarian, I had watched students struggle with choosing a topic. When I went back to school and started my second master's, I had the same challenges. I knew I was especially interested in researching the changing American attitude toward our environment as reflected in our outdoor recreation choices. However, I needed to turn my interest into a manageable question. Instead, I found myself exploring and reading everything on outdoor recreation and even more on environmental attitudes. First, I started with books, then moved into the popular press, then on to journal articles, and, eventually, started looking at legislation. As a result, I ended up with a great mishmash of everything. The more I read, the more avenues of inquiry opened up for me. It can be a hazard of my profession, having easy access to all types of information. I found it all very interesting but also quite distracting, as I was thoroughly mired in my topic. It was a problem because I was not making progress in producing a thesis. I needed to step back and do what I had always recommended to students: concentrate my research on a concise topic and then stick to my established constraints.

The best way for me to start focusing was to meet with my faculty advisor to discuss my research. I took advantage of the advisor's expertise in the discipline and listened carefully to the suggestions. The questions presented to me challenged some of my ideas, clarified my thoughts, and established the boundaries for my paper. First, I needed to limit my research by time. Therefore, I chose to work with the decade surrounding the first Earth Day in 1970. I also needed to narrow it to one particular type of outdoor recreation. I chose backpacking in the wilderness.

Further, I needed to start taking my own advice. I had always suggested that students start the research process by reading the introductory and background information on the overall topic to develop a global understanding of the larger issues involved. This was really necessary with an issue such as environmental attitudes. After doing so, I knew the dates of significant events, names of people involved, important legislation of the period, had an idea of the theoretical framework, and had a plan of where I was going with my research. I began to see overall patterns, learned the names of some researchers in the area, and found that I was much less likely to spend my research time on tangential issues. Finally, the research began to take shape. The paper would take many more hours of researching and writing; however, after focusing my time on a succinct subject matter, I was able to make effective progress toward completing my thesis and, eventually, was very pleased with the resulting paper.

—Ms. Cynthia W. Bruns, MA, is reference coordinator at Pollak Library, California State University, Fullerton.

NOTES

1. American Sociological Association. 2012. "Current Sections." Washington, DC: American Sociological Association. Retrieved March 22, 2012 (http://www.asanet.org/sections/list.cfm).

2. *Merriam-Webster's Collegiate Dictionary.* 2012. 11th ed. Springfield, MA: Merriam-Webster.

3. Pattillo-McCoy, Mary. 1998. "Sweet Mothers and Gangbangers: Managing Crime in a Black Middle-Class Neighborhood." *Social Forces* 76:747–74.

4. Wake, Katie. 2008. "Uncivilising Influence." *New Statesman,* June 9, pp. 19–20.

CHAPTER 4

WRITING TEXTUAL ANALYSES

Literature Reviews, Book Reviews, Annotated Bibliographies, and Encyclopedia Entries

Sociologists do not just write articles and books; we also analyze and summarize text through our writing of literature reviews, book reviews, encyclopedia entries, and annotated bibliographies. Although we already discussed in the previous chapter annotated bibliographies and how they aid in the writing preparation process, this chapter will focus on how annotated bibliographies are written as a form of textual analysis. We will discuss how to write these critical evaluations and analyses of social science books and articles, as well as encyclopedia entries in social science volumes. We will also explain the application of active reading to help you evaluate these texts before you begin your analyses.

EVALUATING TEXTS

A textual analysis examines and interprets discourse, or ways of communication. It is both a way of analyzing data and a form of data collection. Additionally, textual analysis can help the researcher and writer learn more about a particular group of people or culture. Anything that can be used as a form of communication can be considered a text, such as language, a book, newspaper, magazine, painting, film, etc. As this is a writing book, we will focus on analyzing written text.

A writer performs a textual analysis when she seeks to understand and interpret what the author of the text is attempting to communicate to her audience.

Typically, the author of a textual analysis will attempt to answer the question, *What does the author hope to accomplish by creating this piece?* In a textual analysis, you will discuss not only how you see the text but also how you believe the audience will interpret the material.

It's important for you to remember that books and articles are written with a particular agenda in mind. When you are reading them, you should ask yourself what that agenda is. How does the author expect the work to be read? What issues can you deduce as important to the people reading this text? How do you make sense of this text? Other questions to contemplate include the following:

- Who is the writer?
- What is her position in the discipline of sociology?
- Why is she writing this piece?
- Who is the intended audience?
- How does the author expect the audience to interpret the text?
- What does the audience learn as a result of reading the text?
- Is this text beneficial for its intended audience?

While our focus in this book is on sociological writing, we would like to take a few pages to talk about active reading for the purposes of understanding and interpreting a text.

When we first began to read scholarly materials, most of us had a particular method of reading. We probably allowed the words to wash over us and picked out what we could use in class, papers, or exams. To be a writer in sociology, however, our methods of reading have to change from what they once were. We have to be able to engage with what we are reading—to remember it, analyze it, and understand it—and it is through engaging with reading that we expand our knowledge and gain a deeper understanding of how to write.

To actively read, you should begin with a preview. There are several places in academic writing that you could examine to understand where the piece is going. These places should also be kept in mind when writing, as the same elements could be read in your own writing as a preview for interested readers.

If you are reading a book, the table of contents is always a good place to start. The table of contents provides the path the writer takes through writing and can also provide information on her theories or the types of evidence used. Prologues, chapter summaries, and introductory chapters can similarly provide a reader with an explanation of the structure of the book as well as a preview or summary of what is in each chapter. Prologues and introductory chapters often also include some synthesis that may or may not be found in other places in the work.

With an article, the abstract provides much of the important preview information. If written correctly, the abstract can give the reader a basic outline of the entire document. A good abstract will include an introductory sentence (or two), a thesis sentence, and sentences on the methodologies and important findings, and can even include implications and suggestions for future research.

This abstract introduces the article with the thesis that Oscar Lewis's culture of poverty theory has been misinterpreted. It goes on to tell us that the article will correct this misperception through the "sociology of knowledge" theoretical perspective by exploring the historical origins of the theory and showing "how current poverty scholarship replicates this erroneous interpretation." The findings are that Lewis's work is "firmly grounded in a Marxist critique" and is a "celebration of the resilience and resourcefulness of the poor" (Harvey and Reed 1996:465).

Headings and subheadings are another useful way to preview an article, but if you are not already familiar with the topic, they can be difficult to follow. Often headings include terms or phrases explained within the body of the document and, therefore, may provide less information for someone who is not yet familiar with the terms. If the reader understands the headings, or if the writer has taken care to create clear and informative headings, these can be a useful road map.

While it is always important to read an article in its entirety, the introduction, discussion, and conclusion sections can provide much initial information on what the writer intends to do, how she has interpreted the data, and what the data mean to her larger questions. This can provide a solid framework for the reading that follows.

Figure 4.1

Abstract: For three decades, Oscar Lewis's subculture of poverty concept has been misinterpreted as a theory bent on blaming the victims of poverty for their poverty. This essay corrects this misunderstanding. Using a sociology of knowledge approach, it explores the historical origins of this misreading and shows how current poverty scholarship replicates this erroneous interpretation of Lewis's work. An attempt is made to remedy this situation by arguing that Lewis's subculture of poverty idea, far from being a poor-bashing, ideological ploy, is firmly grounded in a Marxist critique of capital and its productive contradictions. As such, Lewis's work is a celebration of the resilience and resourcefulness of the poor, not a denigration of the lower class and the cultural defenses they erect against poverty's everyday uncertainty.[a]

[a] Harvey, David L. and Michael H. Reed. 1996. "The Culture of Poverty: An Ideological Analysis." *Sociological Perspectives* 39(4):465–95.

Once a preview has been conducted, the rest of the piece should also be read closely. Breaking the work down into some of the structural elements discussed above and in Chapter 2 helps you fully understand what has been read. Remember that each section or paragraph is like its own small paper. It should include an introduction, a conclusion, and the body between them. The reader can also make a distinction between what is core material and what is elaboration. All the material should be read; however, the core material is usually most important and should receive the most attention.

An understanding of these types of information is also important in highlighting or taking notes. The information the reader is most likely to need to return to is the core material, rather than the elaboration; therefore, the core material is what should be saved. This type of information is likely less than 10 percent of the entire document, and your highlighting should represent that. The elaboration material can usually just be summarized.

Notes on the reading can also be kept in the margins of books (if it belongs to the reader) or on Post-Its or other sticky notes made especially for that purpose. Once notes are removed from the actual reference, however, the writer/reader must still ensure that all information is referenced back to its original source.

These reading and note-taking hints should help you read through and prepare to evaluate social science texts to create textual analyses. The main forms of textual analysis that social scientists write are book reviews, annotated bibliographies, and literature reviews. As encyclopedia entries include an overview of text on a particular topic, a discussion of them will also be included in this chapter.

BOOK REVIEWS

Book reviews are quite different from the book report you may have been asked to write at some point in your education. A book report is simply proof that you read and understand the assigned book. Book reports also provide basic information on the book, such as who the author is and a summation of the book. Book reviews, on the other hand, provide a deeper analysis of the text and evaluate the content and its potential influence. There are generally two different types of book reviews: book reviews for the general public and book reviews for the academy. Book reviews for the general public are those you read in newspapers and magazines such as *The New York Times* and *Reader's Digest*. These reviews tend to focus more on the readability of the text, not necessarily its contribution to a particular academic field of study.

Academic book reviews, on the other hand, are written by experts in the field of study for which the book was written. These expert reviewers describe the overall text and its content, provide a critical evaluation of the book's potential relevance and influence, and assess its contribution to the overall field of study. Reviews also explain where the book stands in relation to similar books in the field.

Academic book reviews are usually published in academic journals. Many journals will publish three or four book reviews in each issue. These books normally relate to the overall theme of the journal. For example, *Gender and Society*—a journal geared toward readers interested in gender and sex—included a book review[1] for *Intersex and Identity: The Contested Self*, written by Sharon E. Preves (2005).[2]

How Reviewers Are Selected

When authors have written a book they believe the readership of certain journals would appreciate, often the book's publishers will send copies of that text to those journals for contributors to review. In many cases, journal editors receive hundreds of books per year from publishers and authors hoping to receive favorable reviews. In many instances, editors receive more books than they have potential reviewers. As a result, editors are often eager to hear from potential reviewers. Most often, those selected to write book reviews are faculty, graduate students, and professionals within a particular field, such as public policy.

Most often, reviewers are selected in one of two ways to write a review of a book. In some instances, the editor of a journal or the book review editor (sometimes they are two different people) will contact a potential reviewer with a request to review a particular book because the editor is familiar with that reviewer's research. The second way is for the potential reviewer to select a journal that publishes reviews based on her areas of expertise or the journals she tends to cite most frequently in her research. She should then go online to check how book review submission requests are handled. Some journals require that the potential reviewer provide the journal's editor with a copy of her curriculum vitae, or CV (discussed in more detail in Chapter 11), and a brief introduction explaining her research interests. In this case, the editor may select a book she feels is appropriate based on the reviewer's interest and expertise. Other journal editors allow the potential reviewer to select her book of interest from a list of books. In this case, the editor will often list the books on the journal's website or in a sociology/social science newsletter. Once the potential reviewer selects the book she would like to review, she contacts the editor with her CV; a brief description of her research interests, including an explanation of why she is qualified to evaluate the book; and the title of the book she wants to review. If the editor thinks it is appropriate, and if the book is still available, she will assign the book to the reviewer. Either way, we would suggest that you look the book up online and pay attention to the book length and book synopsis; before agreeing to review the text, make certain you are familiar with the book and the area of study and estimate how long it may take you to read the book.

It is important to note that, as with scholarly journal manuscripts, most academics are not paid to write book reviews. A reviewer is paid in her intellectual contribution to the field of sociology as well as with another line on her CV; she also gets to keep the book.

Evaluating the Book

Once the editor sends you the book in the mail, you will want to pay attention to the following things, though not necessarily in this order.

Book Structure

The two most commonly reviewed types of books are traditional books and anthologies. Traditional books are written by one or multiple authors on a given topic. The majority of the books you read are traditional books. *Nickel and Dimed: On (Not) Getting By in America*[3] by Barbara Ehrenreich (2001), *The Power Elite*[4] by C. Wright Mills (1956), *The Craft of Inquiry*[5] by Robert R. Alford (1998), and *Moby Dick*[6] by Herman Melville (1967) are all examples of traditional books.

Anthologies are essays or other forms of writing compiled into one text (or a series of texts) by an editor or multiple editors. These books often contain essays, speeches, poetry, or a combination of the three that focuses on a particular theme. For example, *Let Nobody Turn Us Around: Voices of Resistance, Reform, and Renewal*[7] by Manning Marable and Leith Mullings (2009) contains essays and speeches such as Henry Louis Gates Jr.'s "Black Anti-Semitism"[8] ([1992] 2009) and "Ain't I a Woman"[9] by Sojourner Truth ([1851] 2009).

Writing a book review for an anthology is a little bit different from writing one for a traditional book. Although the overall elements of the book review are similar, in anthologies, the reviewer does not usually have enough space to focus on each essay individually. Instead, when reviewing anthologies, the reviewer will need to focus on how well the different essays and pieces contribute to the overall goal of the anthology, as expressed by the anthology's editor. You will therefore want to pay particular attention to the preface, introduction, and/or conclusion to the book and each section of the anthology. Typically, the introduction explains what the editor hopes you will learn as a result of reading this selection of essays and provides the overall context of the essays. The conclusion of an anthology often reiterates the editor's goals.

Book Title

Read over the title of the book a few times and really think about what it means. Many academic books also have a subtitle. Ask yourself, what does the title suggest? Authors (and often publishers) put a lot of effort into the titles of their books. The best titles accurately describe the text and the material discussed in the text. Often, a book will have a formal title that describes the text and then a catchy subtitle, or vice versa. For example, *Black Picket Fences: Privilege and Peril Among the Black Middle Class* (Pattillo-McCoy 1999).[10] The main title is *Black Picket Fences*, a relatively catchy title playing on the phrase "white picket fences." What can you gather from such a title? The subtitle is *Privilege and Peril Among the Black Middle Class*. What information about the book do you gather from the subtitle?

Author

Almost all books currently published contain information about the author besides simply her name. Books will often say where the author is from, where she lives, and, in the case of academic books, where she works or has worked and what she teaches and researches. Anthologies tend to provide similar information concerning their editor(s). In the case of anthologies, editors usually also provide some descriptions of the volume's contributors.

Before you read the book, you will want to find out some information about the author/editor. You can always begin by looking the author up online. If she is an academic, she may have a webpage on her university's website or her CV may be posted online. Make sure to note the following:

- Are you familiar with this person's previous work?
- What is the author's area of research?
- What is the author's highest level of education?
- Is the author associated with a particular university, hospital, government institution, or think tank? If so, what type?
- Is the author an academic or a practitioner in a particular field, etc.?

This information is important to best understand the text and to see if the author has a particular agenda in writing the text. This also helps prepare you in case there is a level of bias in the author's work.

Publisher

Within the first few pages of the book, you will find copyright information and information about the publisher, as well as the date and location of the book's publication. This information is not only important to write a citation of the book for the journal but also because it provides you information on the publishing process of the book. You will want to pay particular attention to the publisher of the book. As we mentioned in the previous chapter, university presses, such as The University of Chicago Press, and non-university academic publishers, such as SAGE, publish academic books. In most instances, academic books go through a review process similar to that for scholarly journals, where other academics in the field may have reviewed the manuscript prior to publication. Pay particular attention to the following:

- The date of publication, as the book could have been written years ago. If so, how relevant is the book now?
- The publishing company. Are you familiar with it? What other books does it tend to publish?
- The publishing location. Where was the book published? Was it published in the United States? Abroad? Is there a connection between where the book was published and the topic?

Endorsers

Often, other well-known academics or researchers will endorse the book. These are people whom the author and/or publisher have identified as experts in the field in which the book was published. These endorsements are typically about a paragraph long and briefly describe and praise the book and the author. Pay particular attention to who these endorsers are. Where do they teach? What have they published themselves? How does their expertise compare to that of the authors?

Book Layout

Focus on the book's layout. Most academic books are around 200 pages long. Is the book shorter than that? Is it more than 400 pages? How many chapters are in the book? How did the author title each chapter? Do the titles describe what the chapters address? How is the book broken up? Are there different parts or book sections that consist of a particular grouping of chapter topics?

References

You always want to pay particular attention to the reference section of any book or article. This is especially important in writing a book review. The reference section provides a list of all the articles, books, and other resources referenced in the text. How many pages of references are there? The number and types of references will tell you whether or not the book was well researched. Is there an important book or article on this topic that the author did not reference? Is there an aspect of a book or article the author did reference that is missing from his argument?

Index

The index of the book lists the names, books, terms, etc. most frequently used in the book and on what pages they are located. What types of words, phrases, or field-specific jargon do you see in the index? How often do these words or phrases appear in the text? Is there anything that should be in the index (or in the text) that isn't?

Preface

The preface is an important part of the book that is often overlooked. The preface often provides background information on the book and/or study on which the research presented in the book was based. The preface can also include information on the author's approach to this work. Is the research presented in the book part of a larger project? Who does the author acknowledge? Who were the author's influences? Where did the author receive funding?

Appendix

The appendix typically contains additional information that clarifies a variety of aspects pertaining to the book and/or the research. For example, if the book is a qualitative study, the appendix will typically contain a list of interview questions or a description of respondents.

Writing the Review

Most academic book reviews in a scholarly journal have very specific guidelines—they will specify the word count, font size and style, margin width, and overall format of the review. Also, editors sometimes request that reviewers create titles for their book reviews. Make sure to note if your editor has any particular specifications for how the book review must be formatted and, importantly, if there is a page limit/word count for the book review, as that will determine what can and cannot be included in the review.

Focus of the Review

Before sitting down to write the book review, make sure you look at several examples of book reviews. If you plan on submitting your book review to a particular journal, you should read over reviews that have already been published in that journal and use them as samples. If you are writing a book review for a course, you should think about the overall topic of your book and of your class, and how the two relate. What subject areas does the book address? What course are you taking? Take the book *Magical Urbanism: Latinos Reinvent the U.S. City* by Mike Davis (2001)[11] as an example. This text explores issues of immigration, urban studies, and Latina/o studies. Reviews for this text can be found in the scholarly journals that address these issues, such as *Race and Class,*[12] *International Journal of Urban and Regional Research,*[13] and the *Harvard Journal of Hispanic Policy.*[14] Each review focuses on the research concerns of the journal's readership. If you are in an urban studies course, you may want to focus your review on how well Davis explores the impact Latinos have had on the urban landscape. Taking into account what you learned in class as well as what you have learned in other courses, and based on the author's expressed goals, what do you expect from the text?

Make sure to keep a notebook and pen handy as you read through the book (see the discussion on active reading toward the beginning of this chapter). You want to take notes frequently throughout the text. You want to focus your notes on both what stands out to you and what is hidden in the text. You should be as thorough as possible in your read of the text so as not to criticize or praise the author for something he may not have done. While reading the text, you want to remember to note what the author's claims are and whether or not he has supported these claims.

Structure of the Review

Book reviews are typically short (about 900–1,200 words) and usually contain three basic parts: the introduction, your evaluation of the book, and the conclusion. You want to present your argument and overall review of the book, and then you want to defend your opinion/evaluation—why you feel the way you do about the book—to the reader and, in some way, to the book's author. The two main purposes of a book review are to introduce the reader to the text and to evaluate the text based on the author's expressed goals and the text's potential contribution to the field of study. The introduction and evaluation also serve as the basic elements of your book review.

Introduction

Most of the people who will be reading your review have not yet read the book, so your review will serve as an introduction for them. In the introduction to your book review, you will describe the book and introduce your overall review to the reader. Here, you will clearly identify the title of the book, the author, the publisher, and the year of publication. You will also introduce the reader to the overall issues addressed in the book, as well as prepare the reader for your analysis of the text. The introduction describes whether or not the book is an anthology and identifies the book's intended audience. In the introduction, you want to grab the reader's attention. One way to do this is to start by referring to a current event that relates to the issues addressed in the book.

In your introduction, make sure to inform the reader of your overall evaluation of the text and provide a brief reasoning for your evaluation. This will prepare the reader for the position you take in your evaluation of the text. You want to clearly spell out how you see the author's stated goals.

Evaluation

The most important part of your book review is your evaluation—the actual review. Based on the author's expressed goals, how would you evaluate the book? Does the author meet her objectives? Does the book accomplish the author's goals? Based on what you know of this field of study, how would you rate this book? You also must provide reasons for your analysis. You cannot simply say, "The author did not clearly express her intentions." You may feel this way, but you must say how she did not express her intentions. What was missing? What would have made her intensions more clear? As with any other academic work you produce in sociology, simply writing your opinion is not enough. Since you were taking note of the various instances where the author did or did not support her intentions, you should be able to provide evidence for your opinion. If space permits, you should offer specific examples to illustrate your claims. Other questions you will want to address in your review might be,

- Is the book clearly written and laid out, or is the organization of the book confusing?
- Is the book filled with unclear terminology or jargon, or is it written clearly and straightforwardly?

- Does the book have a thesis?
- What is the author's methodology?
- What are the goals and aims of the book?
- Does the author achieve her goals in writing this book?
- What is missing from the book?
- What should have been included?
- What would have made the author's argument stronger?
- Do you recommend this text? If so, why? If not, why not?
- If you recommend this text, who would you recommend it to, why, and to what purpose?
- Would this book be useful for students in a college classroom setting?
- Importantly, as a sociologist, how do you think this book contributes to sociology as a field of study?

In the case of an anthology, you cannot write a review addressing all the issues in each essay or anthology contribution. You will, instead, focus on a few essays that you think stand out in the text, for both positive and negative reasons. If you are reviewing an anthology, you may want to note the following:

- Who is (are) the editor(s)?
- Who are the contributors?
- What institutions are they from?
- Do these essays complement one another?
- What themes do you find that are common among the chapters?

Although your review is opinion based, you cannot simply write, "I liked this book." You have to specify *why* you liked the book. *How* would you quantify "like"? *What* do you like about the book? You must be very clear and support all claims you make in your review.

ANNOTATED BIBLIOGRAPHY

Annotated bibliographies were already discussed in Chapter 3 as being an integral part of the writing and research process, but they are also written by sociologists as pieces of textual analysis and are often published in journals or sometimes on webpages run by social service organizations and agencies. Many of the same rules apply in writing an annotated bibliography as part of your writing process as in writing one for submission to a scholarly journal; however, there are some differences. This section will address how annotated bibliographies can be written as a form of textual analysis and can help increase one's understanding of a particular topic or area within the field.

Most annotations are very short, typically 150 to 250 words long—about the length of an article abstract. As a result, you will have to be as concise as possible in writing each annotation. Don't forget, the purpose of the annotated bibliography is to summarize, as succinctly as possible, a book or article and to evaluate its relevance to a particular topic. Since the purpose of your annotated bibliography is to find books/articles that pertain to one area of study, you do not need to summarize the work in great detail. Annotated bibliographies that are written for professors, or for inclusion in scholarly journals or other publications, should be written in a complete and clear but succinct manner, much like an abstract.

Introduction

Annotated bibliographies typically begin with a paragraph describing the purpose of the annotation. This introductory paragraph provides background information on your topic as well as a discussion explaining the parameters of your literature search and why certain similar topics were omitted from your search.

Citation

Citations are typically written in full American Psychological Association (APA) or American Sociological Association (ASA) format. Similar to ASA and APA reference sections, the citations, with the annotations following, are listed in alphabetical order.

Annotations

Again, although overall annotations vary, most annotations contain the same information—a summary of the book/article and its connection to the larger topic. Annotations often answer the following questions:

- What is the author's subject?
- What is the author's main focus?

- What is the author's scope?
- What do you think the author hopes to accomplish by writing this piece?
- What is the author's background?
- What are the author's qualifications? Do you find his work credible?
- Who is the intended audience?
- What relationship, if any, does this work have with any other works in this field of study?
- What conclusions are reached by the author?
- What is your assessment of the reading? How does this book/article compare to the other books/articles included in your bibliography?
- Are there any limitations or biases in this work? If so, what are they?
- What are your overall conclusions concerning this source?

Conclusion

Many annotated bibliographies often contain a paragraph after the annotations with an overall review of all the books/articles discussed in the bibliography.

What to Avoid

It is important to stress that each annotation is very short. To make the most of your word count, avoid the following:

- Generalizations and/or imprecise modifiers (*really*, *very*, *bad*, *good*, and *excellent*).
- Beginning each annotation with, "This article . . ." or "This book . . . ."
- First person ("I").
- Referring to the article/book by its full name multiple times in the annotation. To save space, refer to the author's last name instead.
- Repetition of information that can be found in the title. For example, in a review of the book *Gender and the Social Construction of Illness*, you would not need to say, "This book explores the impact that gender has on the social construction of illnesses." That is implicit in the title, and it is a waste of space to repeat it. Since the topic of the book is already clear in the title, the space in the annotation should instead be used to describe the book and provide an evaluation.

LITERATURE REVIEWS

A literature review is a critical review and analysis of research on a particular topic or area of study. Literature reviews focus on different themes and arguments found within the research and are most frequently used to help the writer formulate a research hypothesis. Literature reviews are typically written as a research paper or included within research reports, master's theses, doctoral dissertations, and scholarly journal manuscripts (see Chapter 8). Where the literature review is included will often dictate its length and structure, with longer literature reviews found in dissertations and books and shorter ones found in articles.

Your literature review should be written as an essay in which you explain to the reader how you came to your research topic and hypothesis. Just like any essay, your literature review should contain an introduction, body, and conclusion. We suggest creating an outline first, similar to the one created in Chapter 3, with a focus on the literature. This outline should trace the development of your argument based on the literature you found. If you are hypothesis testing, the annotated bibliography you compiled to prepare for your study will greatly help you in writing an outline and, ultimately, your literature review, as the annotated bibliography doesn't just provide a summary of relevant articles and books but, importantly, also contains your review of each individual article and how it relates to the other articles you collected. In your annotated bibliography, you should have made note of what theories or methodologies may be problematic or missing in previous research. Again, this can help give you possible ideas for research projects. As mentioned in the previous chapter, this saves you from having to go back and read the articles again to decide what to include in your manuscript.

We mentioned in Chapter 3 that you should concentrate on scholarly articles and books, and this is also what you should include in your literature review. From the annotated bibliography, select the articles and books that informed your research. What omissions from the literature inspired your research? Is there something in the literature that your study refutes? How could the literature be combined in a new way to support your theory? Again, the purpose of your study should determine which literature you select to include in the review.

Once you have selected the literature from your annotated bibliography, think about how you plan to structure the body of the review. The structure of the review will likely be determined by your research question(s) or assignment. Reviews are typically structured in one of three ways: chronically, methodologically, or thematically.

Chronological Review

As the name suggests, chronological reviews are arranged in chronological order by either date of publication, time period analyzed, or how a topic or area of study has changed over a given time. For example, articles and books published during a particular time period would be grouped and discussed together in different subsections of the body of the review. If you were examining the history of education reform, you could categorize the changes according to time period, such as examining changes in access to education before and after the 1954 *Brown et al. v. Board of Education* ruling.

Methodological Review

A methodological review is organized not by the research topic but by the methods used to conduct the research. For example, if the literature review examined the different approaches to studying religiosity in the United States, research that utilizes a quantitative approach would be grouped separately from research that utilizes qualitative methods.

Thematic Review

Thematic literature reviews are usually organized by the themes or concepts found within the literature on a given topic. How is the topic discussed or analyzed within the literature? What ideas or themes do you find emerging from the literature? For instance, a project studying literature on civic engagement might focus on the various forms of civic engagement and then on the demographics of those who would most likely participate in these activities.

Regardless of whether the literature review is thematic, methodological, or chronological, reviews should be organized by like concepts presented in the literature, such as trends in time periods or themes found in the literature on your topic. Do the articles or the research on your topic have a similar methodology, theory, or population type? What work do you feel is relevant to your project? Are there studies that you want to refute or support with your research? What research enhances your theoretical framework? You don't want to select too many different themes or subtopics, as it will confuse the reader. Instead, stick to the ones that most informed your research.

Keep in mind, the purpose of the literature review is to give the reader an idea of the journey you took through the literature that helped you develop your research project and hypothesis. If your research project explores the rates of asthma among the urban poor, for instance, you will probably find many articles and books on the overall topic of asthma among the urban poor. These articles/books address a number of issues or subtopics, also known as themes, within the literature that tackle this issue from a variety of perspectives. These subtopics range from what causes asthma within this group, such as second-hand smoke or pollution, to the increasing rates of asthma within this population. Research may examine the work done to reduce these rates. Research may also explore the difficulty in reaching subjects to participate in studies on asthma rates. You will find articles that focus on a particular age demographic, such as children or the elderly. You will also find articles that will address how the rates influence a particular racial/ethnic group within urban populations. Keep in mind that one article could cover several themes and also that different articles will address the same themes. Once subtopics are identified, organize the literature or sections of the literature into those subtopics. Remove the annotations you did not use.

As a next step, we would suggest creating another annotated bibliography that selects and summarizes the pieces of literature most relevant to your work and explains how these selected articles relate to one another and what is missing from the literature. As you present your analysis of previous research, you should also focus on relating these articles/books to one another. What do these articles and books have in common? Do they contradict one another? What is missing from the literature? Are there important methodological or theoretical concerns that should be addressed by the literature that aren't? How will you do it in your research? Make note of *how* this literature supports your argument. Organize your findings by subtopics—as the example below demonstrates with asthma—which can address a particular methodology, theory, or finding.

    I. Subtopic 1 (increasing rates)
- Article 1
- Article 2
- Article 3
- Article 4
- Article 5

   II. Subtopic 2 (reducing rates)
- Article 1
- Article 2
- Article 3

- Article 4
- Article 5

III. Subtopic 3 (difficulty reaching subjects)

- Article 1
- Article 2
- Article 3
- Article 4
- Article 5

The number of subtopics you include or address in your literature review will depend on your topic and your research project. You may address only two or three subtopics, or you may have several. However, be certain that the literature you include in your literature review informs your project, contributes to the discussion on this topic, and explains to the reader how you arrived at your topic. Again, be sure to focus the new annotated bibliography you create around the subtopics you find in your literature as opposed to going article by article, summarizing each one. As mentioned above, you may find that some of your articles fit several of your subtopics. You can include them in discussing multiple subtopics, but if you find that you are referring to the same article in every subtopic, pick the strongest point or two that the article makes and find other articles for your other subtopics. After your subtopics have been identified and the literature has been arranged by subtopic, you can then begin the process of fleshing out your annotated bibliography and molding it into a literature review essay.

You will begin the essay by introducing the reader to the review. In the introduction of your literature review, just like in the introduction to an essay, you should provide the reader with an overview of the types of literature you examined for your research, the way the review will be structured, and, importantly, the themes or reoccurring issues you found in the literature that pertains to your topic. You can also provide any definitions for terms found and examined in the literature you will present. For example:

This research concerns how a social problem is framed (Spector and Kitsuse 1987) and how issues relating to health and health care can be framed based on themes and ideas that resonate with its target population (Kolker 2005). The idea of "framing a problem" is quite relevant to the social sciences. This concept can be applied when addressing a number of social issues, such as missing children (Best 1987), labor disputes (Babb 1996), and even understandings of White separatism (Berbrier 1998);

furthermore, it holds great relevance to the development of health social movements. The use of frames is especially important in the case of the Black Church, whose congregants were not targeted by mainstream AIDS awareness campaigns. (Harris 2010:338)[15]

Once you introduce the literature review to readers, you should then move into the body of the review. Regardless of whether you organize the body of your review chronologically, methodologically, or thematically, you will have to present your literature in an organized manner based on concepts or subtopics found in the literature. To make your literature review more organized, we suggest providing subheadings for some of the larger subtopics you found in the literature that informed your project. These subheadings provide a very clear visual breakdown of the literature review and the topics you will cover in the review. If you do not want to use subheadings, you should still be sure that you have constructed clear transition sentences so your readers can follow your discussion as you move from one topic to the next.

After your introductory paragraph, you will present the research in order of subtopic. Again, you are writing a literature review, not an annotated bibliography, so you do not want to go article by article in your analysis and summation of the literature. You are going one step further in your literature review than you would if you were writing an annotated bibliography. Explain how these articles relate to one another and *omit* the summary of each article. If a number of articles make the same point, you should summarize or put their overall point or argument into your own words and cite the authors whose points were included in this summation. In the example on pollution provided above, the author could state under the "Increasing Rates" subheading:

Rates of asthma have been increasing among the urban poor (Jones, Collins, Smith 2009; Martin 2006; Williams 2005).

The rest of that section of the literature review should examine what the literature says about increasing asthma rates. As opposed to describing what each of the three articles says about pollution, this example summarized a common point about asthma rates among the poor. Since they all provided the same overall finding, you can cite the work together. You can break your subtopics up by paragraph or you can provide separate subheadings within your literature review. If your paper is on pollution, your subheadings could be race, class, increasing rates, etc.—whatever subtopics informed your project. Again, your literature review is based on what you learned from the overall literature, not necessarily what each piece of literature says. As a result, you do not go source by source but, instead, write an essay and use the literature to support your claim or argument. There will be a lot of citations throughout your literature review. Don't be worried if it seems as though every other sentence has a citation. This section is called a literature review for a reason. Ultimately, the argument you present in your review of the literature demonstrates to your readers, reviewers, and yourself the need for your research.

After you have gone through your various subtopics and referenced the pertinent literature, you will inform your audience of how it led you to your research topic. This is where you will discuss your hypothesis. Again, the purpose of the literature review is to place your research into a particular research area. You should use this section to talk about the ways the holes in the research that has been conducted directed you to take on your project the way you did. What was missing from previous work? What subtopics did you synthesize to develop your hypothesis? This discussion of your hypothesis also serves as a conclusion to your literature review. You want to be certain that you provide enough information in your literature review so that the reader can clearly see how you arrived at your hypothesis.

ENCYCLOPEDIA ENTRY

Encyclopedias are a collection of articles or entries that explain and summarize a particular topic. These entries are not necessarily considered textual analyses, as they are not written to analyze a topic. However, as encyclopedia entries are a presentation of summarized information on a particular topic—like book reviews and annotated bibliographies—we've decided to include a discussion of them here.

There are a variety of different types of encyclopedias, ranging from well-known online publications such as Wikipedia to old classics such as *The Encyclopedia Britannica*. In recent years, there has been an increase in the number of encyclopedias published on cultural and social science topics. Many of these encyclopedias are compiled and edited by sociologists and other social scientists. This section will focus on writing encyclopedia entries for inclusion in social science encyclopedias. As described in Chapter 3, specialized encyclopedia entries can be a great starting point when conducting research on a topic, in particular, one you know little about. Encyclopedia entries are also great writing pieces for beginners and provide a publishing option for sociology graduate students.

The prospect of publishing an entry in an encyclopedia may seem daunting for many, but writing it is actually quite straightforward, significantly more so than much of the writing you may have become accustomed to while in college or graduate school. However, there are still a few steps and things to remember in writing an encyclopedia entry.

Call for Contributors

As social science encyclopedias can have anywhere from several dozen to a few hundred encyclopedia entry topics, editors usually send out a call for contributors to social science graduate program and department listservs (electronic mailing lists), as well as to listservs consisting of members of sociology associations and groups. The call for contributors will be sent via e-mail or posting and will consist of the name of the editor as well as the publisher (if the encyclopedia is already under contract), the intended name and focus of the encyclopedia, and its target audience. The contact name of the editor is also provided for those interested in contributing to the encyclopedia. If you decide you want to write an entry, you should send the editor your CV as well as a brief paragraph explaining your research and writing interests and what you feel you can contribute to the volume.

Topics

Some calls for contributors contain a list of available encyclopedia topics that need to be written. Sometimes potential or interested contributors must contact the editor for this list. When you get the list of available entry topics, look through it and make note of the ones you may be interested in writing. Think about how many entries you might want to write and which topics and areas you feel you know a lot about. Some encyclopedia entries may vary considerably in terms of word count. As you review the topics, make sure to note the word counts required for the different entries. Take note if there are any specifications in terms of the entry's due date as well as what to include in it. Depending on the word count of each entry, your time constraints, and your level of expertise on the topic, you may want to select more than one entry to write. This means more publications (and more lines on your CV), and, in the event that the topics you are interested in are already taken, you will have "backup" entries.

Format

As each entry is part of a larger edited volume, it is important that they all follow a particular format. Editors will send out instructions with the specified word count of your entry. It is vital that you stay within the word count and include all required information. Some entries must include particular subheadings, such as the history of your topic. Others may require you to list a few books or articles for further reading on the topic.

To ensure that you are following the correct format, obtaining a sample entry from the editor could be very helpful. This will give you an idea of the style and format of your entry.

Research

The research you conduct on the topic for your entry should be exhaustive, but it will not be the same level of research you would conduct if you were writing a book or dissertation. As encyclopedia entries are generally short and only introductions to a topic, your research will primarily consist of library research to create an overview of the important facts and issues concerning this topic. For example, if you were to write an entry on political conservatism in the United States, you would start with an overall introduction to the topic itself, followed by a brief history of its rise in the United States, and then discuss any important figures in this movement.

If you would like to include statistics on your topic, obtain them from reputable sources such as government websites or other research or university projects and studies.

Writing the Entry

Entries should be clear, to the point, and jargon free. Remember, most of the people seeking out encyclopedia entries on these topics will have little experience with this topic or field. You should avoid direct quotes or citing other work. Since the purpose of the entry is to give the reader a general idea about the topic, it is appropriate to be general in your writing. You are not analyzing the topic but simply explaining what the topic is and pointing out any important issues concerning the topic.

In selecting the suggested readings you plan to include in your entry, pick the books or articles that provided you with the most insight on the topic and what you found to be the most helpful. List these readings in the appropriate citation format (ASA, APA, or Chicago).

Once the entry is completed, submit it to the editor. Depending on the size of the volume, it may take a few months for the editor to get back to you with any required revisions or edits to your piece. Once the entry is completed, you will receive a contract from the publisher. You are often compensated with a volume or issue of the encyclopedia, or you may receive some other form of financial compensation.

SUMMARY

The ability not only to analyze written text but to explain your analysis through your writing is important for emerging sociologists. An analysis of various texts was discussed in this chapter, along with the following topics:

- How to write a literature review
- How to write a book review
- How to write an annotated bibliography
- How to write an encyclopedia entry

The "Writing in Practice" piece for this chapter is written by Richard E. Ocejo. Dr. Ocejo teaches at John Jay College, City University of New York, and has authored a number of encyclopedia entries as well as book reviews. In this essay, Dr. Ocejo explains how he goes about writing both.

WRITING IN PRACTICE

by Richard E. Ocejo

Book reviews and encyclopedia entries require unique approaches and writing styles that you may not be familiar with from just coursework. They are also great intellectual exercises that challenge you to think about how to address a specific topic while taking into account audience, voice, and concision. Let's start with book reviews.

A book review was my first publication, when I was a graduate student in 2005. I have since published three others and plan on writing them regularly as my career continues. Probably what most fuels my desire to write book reviews is my love for reading books: academic, nonfiction, and fiction. Like other book aficionados, I lament that there is never enough time to read everything I want, and my literature queue is quite long. I therefore regularly read book reviews—in academic journals as well as more popular sources, such as newspapers and magazines—to see what's out there, learn a bit about a subject, and get a flavor for a field or genre. When I get a chance to write a book review, I rely a lot on the reviews I read as models and guides. But writing a book review for an academic source is, of course, much different from writing one for a publication such as a magazine.

(Continued)

(Continued)

First, if I am not familiar with it already, I read up on the journal I am publishing in. This plays an important role in determining your audience. For instance, I have published book reviews in the journals *Contemporary Sociology*, which is a journal of reviews and essays, and *City & Community*, which is a themed journal of mostly articles. Since *Contemporary Sociology* covers a wide range of topics, it has a more general readership that may not be familiar with certain subfields. But *City & Community* is a specific journal with a narrower audience that is likely already familiar with the book's main themes (in this case, urban sociology). I kept these facts about audience in mind as I read these books and wrote the reviews.

It may sound obvious, but how I read the book is also significant when writing a review. My approach to a book differs depending on why I am reading it: for a review, for my own research, or for pleasure. When I read for a review, I focus on the elements that are pertinent to the book's thesis, rather than to my own work or personal interests. This way, I judge the book on its own terms, not mine. I find this to be a difficult task, since we usually review books that are within our field of study, close to our own work, and have the potential to incite intellectual and even emotional reactions in us. I think the worst reviews are the ones by people who are upset that the author did not write the book on the topic they would have written on. I avoid this mistake by carefully locating the author's thesis statement, figuring out how she situates herself in the literature, and learning how she intends to address her problem (sociology books do not always have these basic elements of the research process conveniently laid out in the introduction, but they'll be in there somewhere). From there, I'm ready to determine whether or not the author's data analysis and conclusions work (i.e., fit the theoretical framework, support the concepts, contribute to the literature, etc.).

For instance, my most recent book review (2009)[16] was of David Grazian's (2008) *On the Make: The Hustle of Urban Nightlife*.[17] From my reading, I discerned that Grazian's thesis statement was that

> downtown entertainment spots . . . function as aggressively competitive environments in which participants are forever *on the make*, challenging each other for social status, self-esteem, and sexual prestige in a series of contests, attacks, and deflections that fill the evening hours. (5)

He used the Chicago school's classic notion of anonymity among urbanites and Erving Goffman's "dramaturgical" approach (1959)[18] to argue that both urban nightspot owners and consumers engage in a series of "hustles," or forms of impression management, to put on convincing performances. To support this argument, Grazian primarily relies on the accounts of his University of Pennsylvania undergraduate students. Because his thesis statement and framework set the book up to make a statement on urban nightlife revelers, I found his sample to be problematic and used this observation to make the following assessment in the review:

> Relying on Ivy League undergraduates limits the ability to generalize from the data in order to understand the meanings of urban nightlife interactions.... It would be interesting to have another social group in nightlife spaces depicted here besides undergraduate students. (2009:723)

In this quote, I wanted to call attention to an issue that I saw in the book while also bringing up a direction the book could have gone in to address some of its central concerns. Without calling attention to the issue, I would have just been talking about a book on urban nightlife consumers that I would have preferred to read (or to have written myself).

If book reviews inform readers of what's new in the field, encyclopedia entries inform readers of what has already been said about a term, concept, or theory in a short essay. I wrote an encyclopedia entry for my second publication, and I've since written one more. I often refer to encyclopedias to refresh myself on a subject or to learn its key literature, and I often refer my students to them when they first start researching a topic. Like book reviews and book review sources in general, encyclopedia entries and encyclopedias vary in size and theme. Academic encyclopedias can be general (e.g., *Blackwell Encyclopedia of Sociology*) or specific (e.g., *Encyclopedia of Gender and Society*), so knowing who your audience is will be just as important.

But an important point to keep in mind when writing an encyclopedia entry is that you should always assume that the reader is coming to the subject for the first time. Encyclopedias are references that people use to get a basic primer on a topic. Pretend readers are unfamiliar with the subject, the relationships it has to other subfields, and the debates surrounding it. At the same time, you cannot cover everything that has been written about your topic. The key to encyclopedia entries is synthesizing what the literature has said about it—including any arguments and controversies—into a coherent and concise statement while remaining neutral.

I approach writing an encyclopedia entry in a way that may sound like cheating: I look it up in other encyclopedias. Chances are, someone has already discussed your

(Continued)

(Continued)

topic in a concise way in some publication, and chances are it is in an old encyclopedia. When I do this, I try to find it in a general sociology encyclopedia (if there is an entry on it), as well as in an encyclopedia with a more specific theme, to compare the two. The reason I do this is to see how others have gone about approaching this difficult task, what has been said about this subject since the entry was published, and how I can discuss the subject with a different focus, perhaps a focus that helped me understand it.

For instance, my most recent encyclopedia entry was on Pierre Bourdieu's concept of "cultural capital" for the *Concise Blackwell Encyclopedia of Sociology* (2011).[19] To start, I found the entry in two older encyclopedias, both of which were fairly general. While neither entry required significant updating (i.e., no major "breakthroughs" had radically changed scholars' thinking on the subject), I felt there was an area of the literature I was familiar with that these entries neglected and that could help clarify the term for someone unfamiliar with it. This was the subcultural literature, in particular the work of Sarah Thornton (1996) on subcultural capital.[20] In her book, she makes a nice, clear explanation of cultural capital's relationship to other forms of capital—"High levels of income and property often correlate with high levels of cultural capital, but the two can also conflict" (10)—and cites academics as examples of people with high cultural capital but low economic capital and professional football players as people with low cultural capital but high economic capital. When I first read this, as a graduate student, it really helped me understand what the concept was all about and how it related to a few of Bourdieu's other concepts.

To sum up, book reviews and encyclopedia entries are unique forms of academic writing that are valuable for scholars at all points in their careers. For students and young scholars, they are a great way to learn different writing styles and how to engage with literature and subjects in a clear manner. In addition, they are great additions to one's CV early in a career while also being intellectually stimulating and challenging. Both types of publications are fairly easy to get into. Journals that feature book reviews (most do) usually have a book review editor (if not, the managing editor handles it). I suggest contacting this person, telling him your interests, and asking if he has any books he would like reviewed. The editors I have encountered are usually very willing to give review assignments. Encyclopedia entries work a bit differently. Usually, the editors announce that they are putting together an encyclopedia on sociology or a more specific topic and are searching for contributors (they may send such announcements around through listservs, academic departments, and sectional websites and newsletters, so keep your eyes open for them). They usually provide a list of available topics, along with their lengths and due dates. If an available topic interests you, simply e-mail the editor and request it.

—Dr. Richard E. Ocejo, PhD, is assistant professor of sociology at John Jay College, City University of New York.

NOTES

1. Lucal, Betsy. 2004. "Review of *Intersex and Identity: The Contested Self.*" Review essay of Sharon E. Preves's *Intersex and Identity: The Contested Self. Gender and Society* 18(3):254–55.

2. Preves, Sharon E. 2005. *Intersex and Identity: The Contested Self.* Piscataway, NJ: Rutgers University Press.

3. Ehrenreich, Barbara. 2001. *Nickel and Dimed: On (Not) Getting By in America.* New York: Henry Holt.

4. Mills, C. Wright. 1956. *The Power Elite.* New York: Oxford University Press.

5. Alford, Robert R. 1998. *The Craft of Inquiry: Theories, Methods, Evidence.* New York: Oxford University Press.

6. Melville, Herman. 1967. *Moby Dick.* New York: Bantam Books.

7. Marable, Manning and Leith Mullings, eds. 2009. *Let Nobody Turn Us Around: Voices of Resistance, Reform, and Renewal.* 2d ed. Lanham, MD: Rowman & Littlefield.

8. Gates, Henry Louis, Jr. [1992] 2009. "Black Anti-Semitism." Pp. 566–70 in *Let Nobody Turn Us Around: Voices of Resistance, Reform, and Renewal*, 2d ed., edited by M. Marable and L. Mullings. Lanham, MD: Rowman & Littlefield.

9. Truth, Sojourner. [1851] 2009. "Ain't I a Woman?" Pp. 66–67 in *Let Nobody Turn Us Around: Voices of Resistance, Reform, and Renewal*, 2d ed., edited by M. Marable and L. Mullings. Lanham, MD: Rowman & Littlefield.

10. Pattillo-McCoy, Mary. 1999. *Black Picket Fences: Privilege and Peril Among the Black Middle Class.* Chicago: University of Chicago Press.

11. Davis, Mike. 2001. *Magical Urbanism: Latinos Reinvent the U.S. City.* London: Verso.

12. Harris, Jerry. 2002. "Magical Urbanism (Book)." Review essay of Mike Davis's *Magical Urbanism: Latinos Reinvent the U.S. City. Race and Class* 43(4):73–78.

13. Logan, John R. 2002. "Magical Urbanism: Latinos Reinvent the U.S. City (Book)." Review essay of Mike Davis's *Magical Urbanism: Latinos Reinvent the U.S. City. International Journal of Urban and Regional Research* 26(3):647–48.

14. Milian, Claudia. 2000. "Magical Urbanism (Book Review)." Review essay of Mike Davis's *Magical Urbanism: Latinos Reinvent the U.S. City. Journal of Hispanic Policy* 13:109–12.

15. Harris, Angelique. 2010. "Panic at the Church: The Use of Frames, Social Problems, and Moral Panics in the Formation of an AIDS Social Movement Organization." *Western Journal of Black Studies* 34(3):337–46.

16. Ocejo, Richard E. 2009. "As It Seems: Producing and Consuming Nightlife in the Postindustrial City." Review essay of David Grazian's *On the Make: The Hustle of Urban Nightlife. Sociological Forum* (24):3.

17. Grazian, David. 2008. *On the Make: The Hustle of Urban Nightlife.* Chicago: University of Chicago Press.

18. Goffman, Erving. 1959. *The Presentation of Self in Everyday Life.* New York: Anchor Books.

19. Ocejo, Richard E. 2011. "Cultural Capital." In *Concise Blackwell Encyclopedia of Sociology*, edited by G. Ritzer and J. M. Ryan. Oxford, UK: Blackwell.

20. Thornton, Sarah. 1996. *Club Cultures: Music, Media, and Subcultural Capital.* London: Wesleyan Press.

CHAPTER 5

WRITING FOR THE INSTITUTIONAL REVIEW BOARD

Although the pursuit and dissemination of knowledge is important to researchers, it is also important to ensure that the participation of our human research subjects is voluntary and that participants are not placed at unnecessary risk throughout the duration of, or as a result of, our research. Therefore, before we are allowed to conduct research on human subjects, our proposed project must first be reviewed by a board of researchers and scientists known as an institutional review board, or IRB. IRBs are charged with ensuring that human study participants, or research subjects, are treated ethically and fairly, which entails informing participants of their ability to withdraw from the research study at any time for any reason and safeguarding against adverse effects on human participants.

The purpose of the IRB is to examine the proposed methodology, the handling of the participants' informed consent, the protection of confidentiality, whether there is a high amount of risk or controversy involved with the research, and, importantly, that any benefits associated with the research outweigh the potential hazards. IRBs also conduct annual reviews of research that has already been approved.

IRBs are made up of a minimum of five individuals with a variety of disciplinary perspectives. There is usually at least one social scientist on an IRB committee. All faculty, staff, and students affiliated with an institution that receives federal aid and where members are conducting original research on human research subjects are required to submit their work for review. This means if you, as a student, plan to engage in original research on human research subjects, you will likely have to present your work to your institution's IRB.

The prospect of having your research reviewed by a board of researchers may seem intimidating, yet, as researchers, we want to make certain that those who are providing us with valuable data and information are not harmed as a result of our research. In fact, most journals and grant applications require authors or applicants to indicate whether or not they have obtained IRB approval prior to data collection. As a rule of thumb, you should not speak to any potential respondents without IRB authorization, because without this authorization, you are typically not allowed to report any data obtained from participants.

To obtain IRB approval, you will first have to submit an IRB application describing your project. This application typically includes a consent form, sample interview questions or protocol, and the results of a test on the ethical treatment of participants that most institutions require you take. Not all IRB offices are the same, and, as such, not all IRB applications will be the same. However, since these offices must adhere to federal guidelines, IRB offices generally require the same information of all applications. They want to be sure that the researcher doesn't place her participants in harm's way and that if there is potential harm, participants are aware of it and of their right to withdraw from the study. This chapter will explore how IRB applications and ancillaries—what is generally included with these applications (consent/assent form, test results, and sample interview questions)—are written, as well as the application process. First, we will provide a brief history of the IRB and examine two well-known projects that likely would have benefited from an IRB review.

BRIEF HISTORY OF THE IRB

There are numerous examples throughout medical and scientific (including social scientific) history where advances were made in research at a grave expense to the participants. Well-known examples include experiments on Jews and other groups in the years leading up to and during World War II, as well as the Tuskegee and Guatemala syphilis experiments. As sociologists, we typically don't have to worry that our research will place our study participants at risk for physical harm. Unlike medical researchers, chances are we are not testing drugs and other pharmaceuticals on our study participants. Also, our work is not likely to run the risk of causing extreme mental or emotional harm to study participants. However, there are some prominent examples of social scientists conducting research that inadvertently harmed their study participants.

The Milgram Study: An Example of Deception

In July of 1961, Yale professor and psychologist Stanley Milgram, fresh from his research on the six degrees of separation, wanted to find out why so many

German soldiers and civilians followed the orders of Adolf Hitler. Milgram was particularly interested in discovering why these people willingly participated in the experimentation on and extermination of Jews, Gypsies, homosexuals, the disabled, and the other groups Hitler deemed problematic and/or expendable. Milgram placed an ad in the local paper recruiting volunteers for his study. When potential participants showed up to Milgram's office, they were informed of the "project," which they were told examined how physical pain influences one's ability to learn. In reality, the project examined if people were willing to harm another person on orders from an authority figure. For this experiment, the authority figure was Milgram and his team of researchers.

When study participants arrived at Milgram's laboratory, they were "randomly" assigned to one of two categories—teacher or student. In reality, all study participants were assigned as teachers, and "confederates," or research assistants, were assigned to the role of student. Milgram instructed the teachers (actual participants) to increase the intensity of electrical shocks that students received every time they provided a wrong answer. In many instances, Milgram reported that respondents seemed anxious and uneasy but still continued to shock the students, even when the students begged the teachers to stop. There were many instances where the teachers wanted to stop but Milgram instructed them to continue, and they did, causing what they believed to be great physical and potentially fatal harm to the students. Some of the students were told to complain to the teachers of heart problems, and yet the teachers continued to shock the students past the level Milgram informed them was dangerous. Several of the students being "electrocuted" fainted, but a substantial number of respondents (65 percent) turned the dial to the highest level, administering the highest levels of pain. When the teachers or study participants were debriefed and informed of the study, many were extremely distressed and upset that they were willing to harm a person based on a simple order.

The Stanford Prison Experiment: An Example of Manipulation

Ten years after Milgram's project, Stanford psychology professor Philip Zimbardo conducted what became known as the "Stanford Prison Experiment." Zimbardo randomly assigned students to the roles of prisoner and prison guard to examine how people acted out these roles. Zimbardo turned the basement of the psychology building into a makeshift prison in preparation for the 2-week research experiment. However, because of the issues that arose, the project had to be terminated after Day 6.

After the first day, Zimbardo reported that prison guards had become sadistic and were abusing and unnecessarily punishing the prisoners. Tensions grew in Zimbardo's experimental prison to the point where the prisoners initiated a hunger strike, and Zimbardo had to end the project to prevent a potential "prison riot." Zimbardo reported that those in the role of prisoner felt vulnerable and fearful throughout this project, whereas his prison guards thrived on the power they were given. Respondents from both groups were not only upset by their behavior but by what they were exposed to while in their "prison."

Although both Milgram's and Zimbardo's studies yielded valuable results, debate exists about whether the harm and deception to which the respondents were exposed was worth the benefits of the study findings. It is important to note that both Milgram and Zimbardo did not intentionally place their participants in harm's way, as the responses of the participants were unanticipated, but the research clearly had a negative effect on many of the respondents. IRBs have been devised to protect participants from some of the adverse negative consequences that may arise as a result of the pursuit of knowledge.

The National Institutes of Health (NIH) began to issue policies on the protection of human subjects in 1966. Following this, between 1974 and 1978, the National Commission for the Protection of Human Subjects of Biomedical and Behavioral Research met to devise a set of guidelines for dealing with human subjects in both behavioral and biomedical research in a report that became known as "The Belmont Report." This report outlined three basic ethical principles that researchers should keep in mind when conducting research on a human subject: respect for persons, beneficence, and justice. Respect for persons means that researchers must allow for all participants to participate willingly in the study and must protect their identities and the study results obtained from them. Beneficence means that all study participants should be treated in a respectful and ethical manner. Justice refers to the idea that research should not be conducted to the sole benefit of the researcher and that researchers should not take advantage of study participants.

As a result of "The Belmont Report," the Federal Drug Administration and the Department of Health and Human Services created a set of rules and regulations for working with human subjects. These rules were most recently updated in 1991 and now include the Federal Policy for the Protection of Human Subjects. This most recent update requires that all agencies or institutions receiving federal funds ensure the protection of their human subjects. To ensure participants' protection, NIH issued Title 45, Part 46 of the Code of Federal Regulations, which provides the rules and regulations for IRB boards, as well as rules and ethical guidelines for conducting research.

IRB PROCESS

While not all IRB committees are the same, this section offers advice on what to think about and the types of information you may need to include in your IRB application and consent forms. For more specific questions and concerns about the IRB process at your institution, you should consult one of your professors or your advisor as well as seek advice from your institution's IRB office. IRB offices are typically housed in university or company research administration departments.

First, be certain that your project is well defined and can clearly be articulated to a board of researchers who are not necessarily social scientists. Students are typically required to work with a faculty advisor on their projects, so you should review your project with your advisor or professor and ask him for any advice he may have on submitting an application to your institution's IRB. After you speak with your advisor, we suggest visiting your institution's IRB office and website for information on the IRB process.

Once you have spoken to your advisor and visited the IRB office/website, you may want to ask a few people who have gone through the process at your institution to find out if they had any difficulties or have any advice. Every institution has its stories of researchers submitting and revising their IRB applications numerous times before approval was granted, possibly delaying research funding and/or even graduation dates.

Although required application materials vary across institutions and review boards, you will likely be required to submit the following:

- Proof of your knowledge of ethics in research
- An IRB application
- Consent forms
- Sample interview or survey questions (if any)

Ethics in Research

Before researchers apply for IRB approval, evidence must be shown to the committee that the researcher is aware of and understands the rights of the human subject and the role of the IRB. IRBs often require that researchers submit the results of a test, or some other documentation showing that their knowledge of research ethics has been evaluated. Many institutions require that researchers complete an online tutorial on research ethics followed by an online test, both found on the institution's IRB website. This tutorial's certificate of completion should be included in your application packet.

Types of Reviews

All research that involves human subjects must be submitted for review. The nature of your project will determine the type of review you will have to go through. Typically, research used for a class project or for teaching or evaluation purposes does not need to comply with federal guidelines or to go through a full review, as the risk of harm is minimal. This type of research is exempt from full IRB review and is reviewed only by the IRB chair. However, a majority of your other projects will likely be subject to either an expedited or a full review.

Expedited reviews involve the review of projects that are typically uncontroversial and do not contain any deception. Data collection in these projects will place study participants at minimal risk. Research that goes through expedited reviews typically requires little revision, and only the IRB chair and one or two other committee members, rather than the entire committee, review the project.

Research that is submitted for a full review by the IRB is research that can place the study participants at increased levels of risk. This requires that all members of the board review the research, and, often, at least one person in the researcher's area will review the work as well. Approval is achieved by a majority vote from the board. Full reviews are often conducted on research that uses sensitive respondents or potentially controversial projects. For instance, if a study were to investigate illicit drug use among currently incarcerated prisoners in a federal penitentiary, the project would have to go through a full review process. Examples of sensitive respondents and controversial subjects are provided below.

Sensitive Respondents

- Incarcerated subjects or parolees
- Pregnant women
- Minors (anyone under the age of 18)
- People with physical or mental disabilities
- Recovering or current drug/alcohol addicts

Potentially Controversial Projects

- Questions that pertain to suicide
- Research protocol related to controversial issues

- Blood samples
- Potential physical/mental harm of subjects
- Controversial behaviors—sexual, violent, illegal in nature, drug/alcohol use/abuse—of the subjects

APPLICATION

IRB committees often require that applicants submit the following information about themselves and their research projects.

Contact Information

Provide the name and contact information of the principal investigator—the person in charge of the project and data collection. If you are a student, you will need to identify your faculty advisor and provide her contact information as well.

Project Title

Be sure to provide a very clear and descriptive title. Unlike the title for a grant proposal or a journal article/book, the application title does not have to be catchy or even that interesting. You are not trying to draw people to your article to get them to read it. Those reading your IRB application are required to read it, title included. Your article is not under review—just how well your proposed project and data collection methods comply with federal guidelines. The title should show that you have an obvious idea of what you intend to examine in a clear and straightforward manner.

Purpose of Project

Identify the nature of the project and the purpose for data collection. Are you collecting data for a thesis or dissertation? Data collected for a class or for teaching typically do not have to be reviewed as closely since the data collection is used as a learning tool. Importantly, chances are the research collected for a class or for teaching will not be published. As a result, IRB committees tend to be more lenient in reviewing these projects. However, this situation can become more complicated if the project you would like to conduct began as a classroom exercise. Different institutions handle this differently, and you should speak to someone on your IRB board to find out how you should deal with this.

Research Protocol/Project Description

Identify your research protocol. How will you collect your data? Explain, in detail, your proposed methodology. Will you be administering questionnaires? Conducting an oral history? Reviewing medical files? Vising historical archives? If you are using secondary data that have already been reviewed by an IRB committee, you may not have to submit your project for review.

Project Time/Location

Identify when you think the proposed data collection will begin. To make an informed decision about this, you should already have an idea of how long the IRB review process typically takes at your institution. You should also know whether or not your project will likely go for a full review or expedited review. The research period at most institutions is a year, which means you have 1 year to collect your data. This doesn't mean you have to analyze your data within this time, just that the data have to be collected within this time; however, you can always apply to renew your IRB application for another year.

You will also need to describe the setting where the data collection will take place. If you are administering surveys, where will they be administered? On your campus or another location? Online? Make sure you are clear in your explanation, as where the research occurs can change the way permission is granted.

Study Participants

Explain the recruitment and selection criteria of your sample population. Information on your study participants and the potential recruitment method will typically be described in a longer narrative. Describe who your ideal study participants will be and the process by which you plan to recruit them. You will need to identify if employees or students at your institution will participate in the study.

Will your research be focused on one particular racial/ethnic group while omitting others, or will you focus on men while omitting women from the sample? If so, you will have to explain why. To ensure that scientists adequately research issues facing women, children, and people of color, federal regulations specify that researchers must explain to the committee why a particular racial/ethnic group, age category, or gender was excluded from the study.

Special Populations

These are populations that consist of sensitive respondents whose vulnerability may not allow for them to participate willingly and freely in the research study. As such, these populations of people typically receive additional protection from the IRB. Please see the list of sensitive respondents above for examples.

Harm

As social scientists, we typically do not have to worry about protecting our study participants from physical harm, as we are not testing drugs on them and are unlikely to expose them to any physical or mental harm. However, if you believe that your research could potentially harm your subjects or place them in harm's way, you will need to notify the IRB on your application.

Deception/Manipulation

You must notify the IRB committee if your project involves deception of any kind or you do not plan to identify yourself as a researcher to your participants. In these cases, the researcher often feels that the subjects' knowledge of the project will influence the data collection. Are you examining the subjects' participation in illegal activities? Will the subjects' employment standing or finances be impacted by their involvement in the project? Will you be manipulating your study participants' behaviors or potential responses? If so, why? You will have to explain how this manipulation is important to your project.

If you do plan on deceiving your study participants or manipulating their responses in any way, you will need to debrief your subjects, or explain to them the nature of the project, after the research has taken place. If you deceive your study participants, discuss whether or not debriefing is part of your research protocol; if it is not, you will need to explain why.

Risks and Benefits

Explain any risks the study participants may potentially face and how the risk involved in participating in this project is a necessary part of your data collection and may yield important findings. Identify any benefits of your project. Will your project benefit study participants in any way? Will it advance a particular area of knowledge? Will your data potentially provide a valuable resource and, if so, to whom?

Again, the potential benefits of your project to society or to the advancement of knowledge must outweigh the risks it may place on your study participants. If your project is relatively straightforward—for example, conducting an ethnography exploring how college students prepare for exams—it will typically yield fewer risks for your study participants. As such, you can simply say, "The risks to participants involved in this project are minimal." You should not say there is no risk, as you don't know for sure how your project will turn out since you have yet to collect the data. What if it turns out that some of your college student study participants prepare for their exams by creating crib sheets to cheat? Both participants and IRBs may fear that your findings may potentially influence their academic standing. We don't expect you to foresee every potential problem that may arise as a result of your data collection, but the committee wants to know that you are prepared for any possible risks to your participants.

Compensation

Will your study participants be compensated for their time and participation in your project? Compensation can consist of anything from money to course credit to free T-shirts and food. Explain what the compensation will be and if all your subjects will receive the same level of compensation. Some IRBs will allow you to include general information about your compensation, but others require you to be specific. This can be the difference between saying you will provide a gift card to respondents and saying you will provide a $40 Amazon.com gift card to respondents.

Informed Consent

You must report to the IRB the point at which you plan to inform your participants of the nature of the project and of their right to withdraw from participation at any time. You will need acknowledgment from your participants that they have been informed of and understand their rights. You can get this in writing on the consent form or verbally in a script that you prepare, in which case documentation of informed consent is waived. You will also need to inform the IRB committee of who will be obtaining the consent from the participants, when, and how. For example, in some cases, the principal investigator may have research assistants to handle this task. The IRB review committee still must ensure that the person obtaining the subjects' consent has thoroughly informed the participants about their rights as study participants.

If no one under the age of 18 will be participating in the study, you can simply say, "No minors will participate in this study." However, if there will be minors participating in this project, you will need not just to seek out the consent of the minors participating in the study—called assent in this case—but also to gather the consent of a parent/guardian. It will be necessary for you to prepare a separate consent form or verbal script for the parent/guardian and an assent/verbal script for the minor participant. Minors and those with limited cognitive capabilities sign assent forms because they are not legally able to consent to anything or enter into contracts. However, these participants should still be informed of the project and their right to withdraw from it. Parents/guardians are able to consent to minors' participation in the project, but the minors still have to agree as well.

Funding

You will need to explain whether or not the project is funded at the time of the IRB application. If the project is funded, you will need to identify the funding agency, and, in some cases, you may even have to identify how much money you have received from the agency. This is done to ensure that there is no conflict of interest in the data collection process.

Confidentiality

Confidentiality refers to ensuring the privacy and protection not only of your subjects' identities but of your data as well. It is vital that researchers keep data confidential. More often than not, you are required to remove names and all identifiers, such as telephone numbers or addresses, from the data. Researchers will often hear or be privy to people's personal feelings and opinions, and study participants will be much more likely to be honest if they feel their responses will be kept confidential. It is important that participants understand that although you know their identities and their responses, you will keep that information private. However, you may not be able to protect their responses if you are forced to hand over your data to a law enforcement agency or court. There have been instances where researchers have been forced to give up their data to law enforcement officials because their respondents had participated in an illegal activity, such as selling narcotics or robbery. This is particularly important to sociologists and criminologists, as we often observe and are privy to illegal activity. We are not lawyers or priests, and it is important that our participants are aware that we can protect their identities or responses only to the extent allowed by law.

You should also consider if others would be able to identify your study participants from your data. Although confidentiality is ideal, you may be unable to ensure the confidentiality of your study participants in some instances. For example, if you are interviewing the president of a large nation in North America with a population of a little more than 300 million, chances are you are interviewing the President of the United States, and it will be virtually impossible for you to protect the identity of this subject. If you don't think you can ensure the confidentiality of your study participants, for whatever reason, inform the IRB committee.

Anonymity

Anonymity is achieved by removing anything that can be used to identify individual study participants. Therefore, the researcher does not know the identity of the person supplying the information. This can be accomplished by using surveys and questionnaires, where the consent form is kept separate from the questionnaire and the respondent is often assigned a number. This ensures that all data are separate and almost always ensures the privacy of the respondent, as the researcher herself doesn't know the respondent's identity. The data cannot be connected to the respondent in any way, so no one can trace the responses back to individual respondents.

Data Protection, Storage, and Disposal

Describe how you plan to protect your data. Where will your data be stored? Where will your consent forms be stored? Will you store your data on a password-protected computer or in a locked file cabinet in your locked office?

After data collection and analysis takes place, you will be responsible for ensuring that your data and all consent forms are destroyed after a particular period of time. Inform the committee of how long you will wait before destroying the data.

Audio/Video Recording

Explain whether or not you plan to record respondents or their responses for later data analysis through either audio or video means and why this recording is necessary. For sociologists, recording participants' responses is commonplace. We often use digital voice recorders or even photographs to capture responses or moments for accurate review. You will need to inform the review committee whether or not your project will involve audio or video recordings and, if so, how long these recordings will be kept, in what manner they will be stored, and when they will be destroyed.

OBTAINING CONSENT

IRBs need to be assured that researchers will adequately inform their research participants about the project and that their participation in the study is voluntary. Prior to data collection, consent must be obtained from all participants over the age of 18 or from the legal guardian of any minor or subject with limited cognitive capabilities. Consent can be obtained in writing or verbally. Assent must be obtained from all respondents under the age of 18 as well as from respondents who are unable to sign into legal contracts, such as those with limited cognitive capabilities. To obtain consent, you will need to be certain that the potential respondent is provided with information about the project in a very clear and jargon-free manner, a manner someone with a sixth-grade education could easily comprehend. In the event that your respondents may not be fluent English speakers, this information will need to be presented in a language that they can understand. For example, if some of your potential study participants speak English and others speak Spanish, you will need to prepare consent forms in both English and Spanish.

Written documentation of consent is almost always required before research is allowed to commence. However, there are some instances where written documentation can be waived, as in the case of online surveys or phone interviews/surveys. Written consent obtained in a form prepared by the researcher is referred to as a consent form. Consent forms should be about one page in length (this will vary depending on the nature of your project, but you don't want to scare off potential respondents with a long and complicated consent form) and are often written in letter format addressed to potential respondents. Again, this should be written in a manner that a typical sixth-grader could understand. Preferably, the consent form should be typed on department or university letterhead, as it makes the IRB form appear more professional. In fact, some IRBs will allow only consent forms printed on letterhead.

Consent forms should contain the following information:

Researcher Information

Introduce yourself to the reader. If you are a student, you should explain that you are a student completing this project as part of your master's thesis project, for example. As a student, you will also need to include the name of your university, department, and advisor. You should also provide your contact name, e-mail address, and phone number, as well as the contact information of your faculty advisor in case respondents need to reach you after participating in the project.

Project Description

Briefly describe the study and its purpose. If deception is at all involved in your study, you will need to be careful how you word your project description as not to reveal too much information to your potential respondents. The project description is important because it explains to your participants what they are signing up for and what you will need from them. Explain what the study will entail. Will they be completing a questionnaire? Will they be interviewed? What types of questions will you ask? How many times will they be interviewed? How long can the interviews be expected to last? Will the interviews be audio or visually recorded? If so, why are you recording the interview? Explain that this will allow for the details of the conversation to be more accurately recorded.

Be upfront about anything that may be problematic for respondents. Are there any potential conflicts of interest for the potential participant? Will respondents be asked to answer questions they may feel uncomfortable answering? It is always better for participants to learn about potential risks or problems they may experience as a result of your project before participating rather than once they have already begun. Also, the IRB committee will be looking for evidence that you are going to do what you said you would in your ancillary documents. Your consent and assent forms will be one of the places they will look.

Risks/Benefits

Just as you had to explain the potential risks or benefits of this project to the IRB committee, you will also have to convey this information to your respondents.

Risks

As previously mentioned, almost all research contains some sort of risk. Respondents need to be aware of even the most minimal risks, such as feeling uncomfortable answering questions because they relate to some contested subject matter, such as religion or sex. They should be assured that any possible risk they may experience will be outweighed by the benefits obtained from participating in your project.

Benefits

Describe any benefits to participating in your project. The benefits could be some sort of compensation, monetary or otherwise, that respondents receive in exchange for their participation. Respondents should also be made aware that their own community or the larger society could benefit from their participation in your study, as their responses could yield valuable findings for yourself or the field of study. If it will be available to them, participants should be informed that they can view the results of the project once the project is completed.

Confidentiality

Explain how the data and information obtained from respondents will be treated and stored. Potential respondents should be made aware that you will not disclose their identities or the information obtained from them as a result of the study in any way other than what the respondent originally agrees to. Inform your potential participant of the manner in which the data will be stored, as well as how long the data will be kept before being destroyed. Make sure they realize that if you are aware of their identities, you can protect them only to the extent allowed by law. As mentioned above, this may become an issue if you plan on interviewing a subject about her participation in some illegal activity. Again, confidentiality means that, as the researcher, you are aware of the respondent's identity as well as responses but will protect her identity from others.

Anonymity

If the data will be collected in a manner that removes all identifiers linking the participants to their responses, not even the researcher will know the identities of the respondents and responses will not be traceable back to respondents. Projects cannot be both confidential and anonymous, as *confidential* means the researcher knows the participants' identities but keeps them hidden, and *anonymous* means the researcher does not know the identities of the people providing the responses.

Right to Refuse Participation

You must clearly convey to respondents that they are in no way obligated or required to participate in the study or to answer any questions. They should also be informed that they can withdraw from the study at any point without any negative repercussions.

Possibility of Publication

One of the main reasons why we conduct research is to publish our results and let others in our field know about our findings. It is important that your respondents are aware the results of the study may be published. Although we are required to keep our work confidential, as we mentioned before, it is sometimes difficult to promise complete confidentiality to respondents when publication occurs. This is especially important if respondents waive their right to confidentiality. Students may not necessarily think about publishing results, but you always want to make sure the option is available, especially if your study yields important findings.

IRB Office Contact Information

You should provide the contact information of the IRB office at your institution in case the respondents have any concerns about their participation in your project. You can simply provide the name, e-mail address, and phone number of the IRB office or IRB chair.

Acknowledgment

After you have explained the project and addressed confidentiality as well as all risks and benefits, you will need to be certain that your respondents acknowledge and understand what they are consenting to. They should also acknowledge and agree to a recording of the interview, if applicable. This will usually include a spot for them to sign and/or check off that they have read and understood the information and give their consent.

Once the above information is included in the consent form, your form is ready to submit with your IRB application and any other requested information from your institution's IRB. Once your research application is approved, the IRB committee will return your written consent form with their stamp (often a literal stamp) of approval. The stamped consent form should be copied and distributed to your potential respondents to read and sign. They should also acknowledge, in writing, that the conversation may be audio recorded or that their real names may be used (if applicable). After written consent is obtained, ideally, you should photocopy the signed consent form and immediately return it to your respondents. If that is not possible, we would suggest having your respondents sign two copies—one for you to keep and the other for them. An example of a consent form is provided in the Appendix of this book.

Not all research requires written documentation of consent. IRBs sometimes waive proof of written documentation of consent for researchers. This typically occurs when data are collected online or via phone. Written documentation can be waived in these instances, as anonymity can be guaranteed and this research contains little risk. Nonetheless, the acquisition of verbal consent is common in research that utilizes phone interviews/surveys, and some IRBs will require a type of digital signature to prove online consent.

Regardless of whether you intend to waive written documentation, you will still need to explain the project to potential respondents and make them aware of their rights as respondents and any risks involved in participating in your project. This information should be provided in a script that you read to each respondent prior to data collection. This prepared script should contain the same information as the written consent form and should be read to the respondents prior to research. The respondents will need to agree verbally to participate in your study and to an audio recording of the conversation or use of their real names, for instance. If you plan on waiving written consent in your project, you will need to prepare a script to include with your IRB application. See the example of a verbal script in the Appendix.

Assent

Assent is obtained from study participants under the age of 18 or those with limited cognitive capabilities who are unable to enter into legal contracts. Whether you are working with a minor or a person with limited cognitive capabilities, the assent form must be prepared in a way the respondent can easily understand. In the case of minors, assent forms are usually prepared for respondents age 7 and older, as most 7-year-olds have developed reading and comprehension skills. To obtain consent from parents/guardians to allow their children to participate, a separate parent/guardian permission form must be created. This form should provide similar information to that on the consent form. See the samples of the assent and parent/guardian forms in the Appendix.

Once the application is completed, along with any consent/assent forms/script, sample survey questions, and proof of your completion of the tutorial on ethics in research, you are ready to submit your application packet to your institution's IRB office. After a review of your work, IRBs can accept your application, deny your application, or require revisions to the study protocol before the research will be approved. A well-thought-out and detailed IRB application for a project that doesn't place the study participant at too much risk will increase your chances of obtaining IRB approval.

SUMMARY

Institutional review boards (IRBs), as well as the IRB application process, are discussed in this chapter. This chapter also addresses the following topics:

- The history of the IRB and the impact of both the Milgram and Zimbardo studies on the IRB process
- The various types of reviews conducted by IRB committees
- The IRB application process
- Various terms and concepts used by IRB committees to describe the project and potential study participants
- The steps needed to obtain consent from potential respondents

In this "Writing in Practice" essay, Carter Rakovski describes her experiences going through the IRB process on her own and her perspective and advice about the process based on her experiences as a former IRB committee member.

WRITING IN PRACTICE

by Carter Rakovski

Before I became a professor in sociology, I worked as a research consultant. One of my consulting jobs was at a private, business-oriented university in New England where I helped faculty with their research projects. My day-to-day work included installing and trouble-shooting software, getting data ready to analyze, coauthoring manuscripts, listening to professors' research hypotheses, and suggesting appropriate statistical tests. My supervisor suggested I volunteer for the university's institutional review board (IRB) as a staff member on the committee, which was composed of faculty members, another staff member, and a person from the community. By having people with different perspectives at the table, the board is better positioned to protect potential research participants. I was also sent to a conference regarding IRB practices and issues. I was impressed by the gravity of the ethical issues being discussed, especially in medical research. Is it ethical for a researcher to spend time testing a drug that is already well known to be effective? Who is paying for this research (e.g., drug companies), and does that influence the results? All researchers studying people have ethical decisions they must make, starting with what research projects they choose to undertake. Often the public is supporting research either directly through government funding or through the support of a state-funded university faculty position. Do researchers have an obligation to undertake research that can benefit the public? What happens when something goes wrong and someone is hurt?

After receiving my PhD in sociology and starting my first faculty position, I again served on a university IRB. This time it was in a large, public university in the Southwest. We met in a large conference room once a month on a Friday morning for 2 hours. Prior to the meeting, I would receive a large packet in the mail with all the protocols that would be reviewed at the upcoming meeting. Each protocol was also assigned to a specific member of the board who would lead the discussion of that protocol at the meeting and make a recommendation to the board. I would usually have one or two assigned to me. Before the meeting, I would scan the large packet of protocols and then read carefully the one assigned to me. A protocol is the IRB

(Continued)

(Continued)

application from a researcher and any supplemental materials, such as consent forms, survey instruments, and letters of support.

At my first meeting, the chair of the IRB called the meeting to order, and the members of the faculty (usually about five), one community member, and two staff members sat around the conference table, reviewing the protocols. When it was my turn to lead the discussion of my first protocol, I was nervous. What if I missed something important? What if they disagreed with my recommendation? To my relief, the board chair and another member had also read my protocol carefully. They agreed with my assessment, but they also pointed out some things that I missed, such as the lack of a letter of support from the school. The researcher proposed to observe students in an elementary school classroom. She needed to obtain a letter of support from the principal agreeing to give her access. I recommended that the board approve my protocol with the provision that such a letter would be submitted. And they did. After that, I felt comfortable and enjoyed reading and discussing research protocols from all over campus for the next 2 years.

Most of the concerns I had with protocols in sociology were when researchers wanted to ask participants about sensitive, embarrassing, or illegal behavior. The IRB wanted to make sure that a researcher had solid research objectives that could be met only by the methods proposed. For example, is it necessary to include survey questions regarding behavior that could be damaging to participants' personal or professional lives if known publicly? If so, what safeguards are the researchers employing to keep that information secure? Some research involves asking subjects about painful memories. The emotional toll of completing the survey or interview must be anticipated. The researcher must have provisions for how she or he will handle cases where someone displays signs of depression or suicidal thoughts. Benefits can be introduced that might offset risks, such as giving participants helpful literature or contact information for mental health providers. Monetary incentives, such as a grocery store gift card, are sometimes used. Researchers collect data in a variety of formats: paper surveys, online surveys, audio or video recordings. The IRB proposal must specify how this data will be stored, who will see it, and when it will be destroyed.

From my participation in those 2 years of meetings, I learned what to look for in writing my own IRB proposals and the importance of being clear and following the guidelines. Now I start writing a new IRB proposal by downloading the proposal form provided by the university. I complete each section of the form in a clear, precise, and succinct manner. Just like when explaining statistical results or research methods, this is not the time to be creative or poetic. The emphasis is on clarity and giving the relevant answers to all questions. Remember your audience. The IRB committee member who reads your proposal only wants to understand the proposed research to assess the potential risks and benefits to the participants. To write this, you must also be clear about your project.

In addition to the research proposal form, other materials should be included—namely, the survey instrument or interview guide and letters of consent. If you are collecting data in an organization, such as a school, a letter indicating support for the project by a leader in that organization should also be submitted. Letters of consent are letters given to potential participants (subjects) that explain all the risks and any benefits of participation in the research. Many IRBs provide sample letters that you can use as a starting point for your letter of consent. They also provide help through websites containing short videos, PowerPoint slides, and links to more information. Students should proofread their proposals for any typing or grammatical errors and have a faculty advisor review their proposals prior to submission.

Do not be scared by the IRB process. Most universities have an IRB officer, who can answer any questions faculty and students may have about the submission and review process. The faculty assigned your protocol can also be a resource by suggesting edits or requesting more information. Some people see the IRB process as a hurdle standing in the way of starting their research, but it is a necessary safeguard for the public. The IRB process forces researchers to articulate their plans prior to involving the public. Maintaining the public's trust in scientific research is the responsibility of all researchers. Without the willingness of people to participate in scientific studies, we would not be able to move forward with our quest to understand the social world. The IRB provides oversight to be sure we continue to earn that trust.

—Dr. Carter Rakovski, PhD, is associate professor of sociology at
California State University, Fullerton.

CHAPTER 6

WRITING AND THE RESEARCH GRANT APPLICATION PROCESS

One of the ways social scientists obtain funds to do research is through the monies distributed via grants. A grant is a monetary award given to an individual or organization to accomplish a particular goal. Submitted applications are reviewed and scored for awards by a committee consisting of other scholars and researchers within the discipline or organization. When grants are scored, a certain number of points are applied to various sections of the grant proposal. Those with the highest number of points receive the grant award. Learning to write an effective grant will help you score high and acquire the funds you request.

Grants are awarded to pay tuition, for travel to conduct or present research, and even to provide funds to run nonprofit organizations or agencies, such as clinics and schools. Grants are particularly valuable for social scientists, as they fund our research projects. This chapter examines the grant application and submission process and how to develop a budget. As with any papers or applications you submit for review, you must remember that detail, organization, clarity, feasibility, articulation, and, importantly, following instructions are key.

DEVELOPING A RESEARCH PROGRAM

Scholars approach the grant search process in two main ways. Some scholars decide to structure the project they are embarking on around the call for grant applications or proposals. They first search for grants based on their overall research interests. If they find a grant for which they fit the eligibility criteria, they develop a research project based around it and then apply. Others—and this is far more common—search for grants to fund their already established research projects/ideas. For these sociologists, the development of their research program consists of the following steps.

Develop a research idea based on a topic of interest. Research topics were discussed in Chapter 3. Ask yourself, is this topic something that sociologists or other social scientists would be interested in? Would the potential results of this project have important social and policy implications? Do you have a personal interest in this topic?

Conduct a thorough review of the pertinent literature on your topic. Is there already research on this topic? What has previous literature said about this topic? How have other researchers studied this topic? Have these previous studies been funded? (Typically, you can find out if studies were funded, as authors often thank their funders in the acknowledgment section of publications.)

Based on your review of the literature, what do you propose to do differently than previous research? If you propose to conduct a study on the impact of after-school programs on the grade point averages of junior high school students and a similar article has already published on the topic in a reputable journal, you need to indicate what you will do differently. This is your opportunity to expand on a theory or provide an alternate theory or reason for a particular behavior or societal occurrence.

Based on your review of the literature, as previously addressed in Chapters 3 and 4, you will develop your thesis. From this, what can you expect to find? Furthermore, based on that research, how do you expect to go about gathering data to support or refute your thesis? This is usually where the grant comes in. Researchers can obtain grants to help them in the pre-research phase, such as in compiling a literature review, but most often, grants are obtained for data collection and analysis.

You want to make certain that you have a well-defined project and that you can clearly articulate your intentions on paper before you even begin to search for a grant.

SELECTING A GRANT

Before you can write a grant application, you must first select a grant appropriate for your project. As the purpose of this chapter is to learn to write a grant application, we will not go into too much detail on how to search for a grant. It is important to note, however, that it is ill advised for students, particularly undergraduates, to search for grants without first seeking advice from professors and advisors who are already well aware of the funding opportunities in their field of study or at their institution. In addition, colleges and universities typically have a grant, or sponsored programs, office. These offices aid faculty, staff, and often students in the search for new grants, fellowships, and award programs and opportunities to help fund research. Grants offices also aid the researcher in the distribution of any grant funds received.

In the social sciences, many grants are provided for work that explores social problems and issues, such as education and health care. For example, currently, the rates of HIV/AIDS are quite high within communities of color—highest among African Americans. Research and programs designed to address AIDS rates among African Americans would likely be funded by organizations such as AIDS service organizations, governmental organizations, and other nonprofits and universities. Additionally, the increasing rates of poverty among youth and Islamophobia in America are timely topics. The more timely your project, the more grant opportunities likely to be available. On the other hand, consider that the more timely the project, the more competition there will be from other people seeking funding.

Countless organizations provide grants and funding to researchers. It is important to make sure that your research project or proposal is appropriate for the grant to which you want to apply (see Chapter 3 for advice on writing research proposals). There are a number of ways to go about finding a grant, including through websites and other resources. Typically, the three types of places that fund research are universities and colleges, government organizations such as the National Institute of Mental Health and the National Science Foundation, and foundations and organizations such as the Russell Sage Foundation and the Robert Wood Johnson Foundation. Grants can also be intramural or extramural. An intramural grant is one researchers can apply to from within the organizations or agencies for which they work or the schools which they attend. An extramural grant is one researchers apply to or receive from an organization to which they do not belong.

Organizations, especially large ones such as the Ford Foundation, provide smaller grants as well as some large-scale, multimillion-dollar grants. In addition, they do not provide funds just to academics or those within the social sciences. These grants are made available to people in the general public. The applicant pool can be quite large for many grants. This means that a lot of people will probably apply for the same grant, which decreases your chances of getting it. You will have to spend a great deal of time on your grant application to be confident it is well written and as clear as possible to earn you the highest possible score.

APPLYING FOR A GRANT

The first rule in grant writing is, if you see a grant that you qualify for, apply, apply, apply! The more grants you apply for, the more likely your project will be funded. Make sure to apply to as many grants and funding opportunities as possible. Plus, applying to multiple grants allows you to get your name "out there." If the review process is not blind—when your name is removed from your grant application—reviewers, often scholars in your discipline, will read through your grant applications and will get to know you, your research interests, and your proposed project.

Now that you have gone through the various organizations' websites and information and found the perfect grant for you and your research, you will want to ask yourself a few questions.

What Is the Purpose of the Grant?

Keep in mind that organizations offer grants to fund particular projects. They tend to have a specific agenda in mind and a direct objective for each grant. Be positive that whatever project you are proposing fits well within the organization's call for applications. A call for applications is what an organization issues when it is searching for applications for its grant awards. The call for applications, also known as a call for proposals, typically consists of a description of what the organization is looking for as well as instructions on how to write the grant application, what information your application should include, and how the application should be formatted (this will be addressed in more detail below).

Am I Eligible to Apply for This Grant?

If the organization is seeking grant proposals and applications from sociology doctoral students whose areas of research include crime and deviance, are in the final stages of the dissertation writing process, and are interested in teaching at a liberal arts college, make sure you fit all the requirements. If you are a first-year master's student, you should not apply for the grant. Additionally, if you have just accepted a tenure-track position and your dissertation is already completed, you should not apply for the grant. In general, you want to make sure you fulfill all the eligibility requirements for the grant. One way to do this is to create a chart or table and write out all the eligibility requirements for applicants or principal investigator(s) (PIs) on the chart. As the lead researcher on the grant, the PI is the person who actually receives the grant funds, and the grant will typically be in that person's name. After you list the qualifications, note how you fulfill each criterion. For example, say an organization is seeking applications from master's students in the social sciences and humanities who attend state schools and have spent at least 5 years working in social services. As you can see in Table 6.1, this applicant fulfills the eligibility criteria for grant applicants.

An applicant who did not attend state school and has no work experience in the social services (see Table 6.2) has little chance of receiving the grant. In fact, the grant application may be disqualified before even getting to the review stage, as this applicant does not fit the search criteria.

Once you complete these tables and can see the ways you fit the organization's criteria, you can move forward with the application process.

Table 6.1

Grant's Requirements	My Qualifications
Master's students	I am a first year MA.
Social sciences and humanities	I am a sociology student.
Attend state school	I am attending New York State University.
Spent more than 5 years working in social services	I spent 7 years working as a social worker.

Table 6.2

Grant's Requirements	My Qualifications
Master's students	I am a first year MA.
Social sciences and humanities	I am a sociology student.
Attend state school	I am attending a private university.
Spent more than 5 years working in social services	I have no work experience.

What Is the Grant Looking For?

In addition to eligibility criteria, grants also include a detailed description of what they are looking for in the applications. For example, a university intramural grant's call for applications may specifically state that it is looking for junior faculty, or assistant professors. This call may also require that the applicant complete an application that responds to the following prompts:

- Provide a 200-word abstract or a short summary of your project.
- Provide a longer, 1,500-word, description of your intended project.
- Provide a discussion of the significance of your proposed project in 1,200 words or less.
- Provide a budget justification, a reason for why you are requesting the funds, in 750 words or less.

In the grant writing process, it is imperative that you are clear in your understanding of what the organization is looking for and that you can clearly explain how your research deserves the grant award. This brings us to our next discussion—what actually goes into the grant writing process.

WRITING UP THE GRANT

If the first major rule in grant writing is to apply, apply, apply, the second rule is to make sure you follow *all* instructions exactly as listed. Grants often contain very explicit instructions that must be followed for the grant application even to make it to the review process. These instructions often include a specific format. In fact, many organizations that distribute grants employ a person whose sole job is to make sure applicants follow all instructions on the grant.

Organizations, especially large foundations and government organizations, can receive thousands of applications for grants, and including specific formatting instructions allows for uniformity and ease in the review process for the applicants and the organization. For example, a call for applications may require that the applicant submit a proposal in Veranda, 10-point font with 1½-inch margins. You may be accustomed to writing your papers in 12-point, Times New Roman font with 1-inch margins, but if you want the grant to make it to the reviewers, you will have to abide by the format required by the organization. Not following these instructions will often result in disqualification of your application, and you will either have to edit the grant proposal in adherence to the specifications or wait to apply during the next application cycle

Table 6.3

Grant's Requirements	My Application
Veranda	✓ - Yes
10-point font	✓ - Yes
1½-inch margins	✓ - Yes
ASA format	✓ - Yes

(organizations typically release grant applications in annual or biannual cycles). Again, it is also important to remember that the organization is offering you money to conduct a research project; so if you are instructed to complete your grant application in Veranda, 10-point font with 1½-inch margins, make sure to complete the application in Veranda, 10-point font with 1½-inch margins.

Similarly, you will also likely be instructed to use a particular format for your references and in-text citations. In the social sciences, this will usually consist of American Sociological Association (ASA), American Psychological Association (APA), or Chicago style. Make sure to reference your work properly in the correct citation style throughout your grant application (see Chapter 3).

To make sure you remember to follow all instructions, create another table, similar to those shown in Tables 6.1 and 6.2, but focus on instructions instead of qualifications.

Grant Sections

Funders want to know what you plan on doing, what previous literature has said/found about your topic, and your qualifications.

Most grant organizations request the following information from applicants.

List A

- Literature review (Literature reviews are often included as part of the description of the proposed project. Other times, they are their own separate section.)
- Description of the proposed project (What issues will you address?)

- Significance or impact of your proposed project
- Budget justification

Grant applications typically have a number of different sections and selection criteria on which they base their evaluation. We will discuss the types of writing involved in each section. However, it is important to note that not all grants ask the same questions of their applicants. The purpose of the grant will typically dictate the types of questions the application asks. If a grant is designed to help doctoral students complete their dissertation research and writing, it may include the following prompts.

List B

- Describe your dissertation.
- Describe the current stage of your dissertation project, and outline the remaining steps that must be completed before your project will be submitted.
- Provide a budget justification.
- Provide a letter from your advisor or dissertation chair.

As you can see, the prompts and requirements presented in List B are somewhat similar to the ones presented in List A. They are asked a little differently because the structure of the research is a little different. The following will address how the other sections of the grant application, using the example provided in List A, are typically written.

Literature Review/Background

This section of a research grant proposal is similar to the literature review you would write for a research paper. Since we go into great detail on literature reviews in general in Chapters 4 and 8, the focus in this section is specifically on writing literature reviews for grant applications. Since a review of the literature can be formatted in different ways, the literature review within a research grant proposal will often be its own separate section; however, it can also be incorporated into the introduction. Instead of asking for a separate literature review, this section may also be called "background" and encompass a review of the literature.

As with any review of the literature, the purpose of the literature review in the grant proposal is to show the committee that you have done the appropriate amount of background research on your topic and that you know what previous research has been conducted. You are also presenting to the committee an idea of what previous researchers have found and an introduction to the overall topic. Some of the reviewers may not know a lot about your topic; therefore, you want both to make sure you provide enough information to show them you know about the topic and to provide them with enough information about your topic that they appreciate the importance of your proposed project.

Your literature review not only adds justification for your project but also shows the committee you are well versed in this area and they can trust that you are going to know how to use the funds. A clearly written literature review shows the review committee not only that you know a lot about the topic but where the deficiencies within previous research lie and, importantly, how your research can contribute crucial knowledge to a particular area of study.

As with any literature review, make certain to properly cite the literature referenced. This is where you need to find out what the citation requirements are for the grant application. Does the organization require that you cite your sources in ASA, APA, or Chicago format? Be very careful in your citation style. Again, you are asking for your research to be funded. The least you can do is make sure you properly cite the material. If no citation style is required, you can typically cite the way you would in your discipline, which is ASA for sociologists.

Importantly, at the end of your literature review, as you would at the end of any literature review, you will include your hypothesis or thesis statement—a quick and simple statement about what you believe you will find. Based on the research you have conducted on the literature, what have you learned? What do you plan on doing? What do you expect to find? A well-formulated thesis is vital to a well-proposed project.

Description of Proposed Project

You will need to describe and justify a need for the research project that you plan on conducting. Be certain that your description of the project is well articulated. Explain the following to the review committee:

- What you want to do
- Why you want to do it
- How you plan on going about it

The description of the proposed project contains a number of different sections. Some grant applications require a review of the literature in your description, but since we discussed that above, we won't discuss it here. The basic literature review will be the same. The description of the proposed project also comprises the following points.

Your Thesis

This is the result of the analysis you performed on the literature you amassed for your review. Expand on the one- or two-sentence thesis statement you included at the end of your literature review. Depending on the grant, this could also be a research question, problem, or hypothesis.

Methodology

Here you will present a methodology that will allow you to explore the research idea you developed as a result of your review of the literature. In this section, you will clearly explain how you will go about conducting your research. Reviewers want to be certain that you are aware of the different ways you can go about collecting data and of the benefits and pitfalls of the different methodologies. They also want to be certain that you have selected the best possible methodology for your project.

We cannot stress enough that you should be certain to have a professor or colleague review your research proposal and methodology to confirm that what you are proposing is feasible. Ask yourself this: Given your time, skill set, and resources, can this project be accomplished in the manner you propose? If you are planning an empirical study, would it be best to gather the data using qualitative methods, quantitative methods, or both? Once you have determined which you will select, you will need to figure out what qualitative or quantitative methodologies you will employ. What will best allow you to explore your thesis? Will you use interviews, focus groups, surveys, etc.? Remember, selecting an inappropriate methodology could result in your grant application being rejected.

As you write your methods section, be as specific as possible about what, exactly, you will do to gather your data. If you are using surveys, how many surveys do you think you will need to analyze to yield the most accurate results? If you are proposing ethnography, where exactly will you be going? How long will you be in the field? If you plan on utilizing focus groups, how many participants will be in each group? Where will they be located? How many focus groups will you have? You will need to spend some time explaining why this is the best way to go about gathering your data.

If you are using a sample population for your study, try to describe your potential population in as much detail as possible. Explain how your potential sample is necessary for your research. Provide reviewers with a general description of your potential respondents. Who are your subjects? Will you be seeking respondents from a particular demographic—age, gender, race, ethnicity, sexual orientation, etc.? If so, you will need to describe who you are looking for and why. You should also explain where you plan on finding the subjects, as this may be integral to your research design. What if you want to explore the response of high school students to a particular safe-sex campaign? You will need to explain how you will gather your subjects, as you may need to get permission from a high school or a state or local Department of Education before being able to select students from that school to incorporate into your study. Are you sure the high schools will grant you that permission? Be sure that you have access to your sample population before writing the grant. Reviewers may be cautious to give a grant to someone who does not have definite access to the intended study population, so this can reduce your chances of receiving the grant.

Some grants specify a time period from the date of the receipt of funds to the completion of the project or data collection. Be confident that you can complete your project within the time allotted in the grant description. Explain in your description how you plan to complete the project in the time allotted.

You will also need to explain clearly the feasibility of your project. It would be nice for a single researcher who wants to examine obesity among Latino youth to be able to conduct in-depth interviews with 5,000 Mexican American families within a year; however, the chances of accomplishing that feat are slim. That is far too many interviews to be conducted, transcribed, and analyzed within a year's time. A review committee may see that this is quite an ambitious feat and not believe the researcher would be able to accomplish it. This may result in the researcher not receiving the funds.

Be sure to mention whether or not you have the approval of the institutional review board (IRB) office at your college or university (see Chapter 5). Review committees are often hesitant to provide funding for research that has not yet been approved by an IRB committee. What happens if the IRB application for your research project is rejected but you have already received grant funds under the assumption that you would obtain IRB approval? You can try to reapply for IRB approval and fix your application; however, organizations typically require that the funds be used within a year of receipt. What happens if you don't get IRB approval within that time? The funds won't be used and could have gone to fund someone else's project.

While writing up this section, it is important to remember that your research has not yet been conducted. So, as opposed to writing in past or present tense, you want to write in future tense. For example, "I propose to gather interviews from 100 undergraduate students," rather than, "I gathered interviews from

100 undergraduate students." This section is focused on what you *plan* on doing, not what you will actually be able to do. You do not necessarily have to do everything exactly as listed in your proposal, but once you receive the grant award (and have IRB approval), you may be limited in how much you can change about your proposed project.

Significance of Research

This is sometimes a separate section within grant applications, but it can also be incorporated into your description of your research project. You should be able to express to the review committee why your proposed project is worthy of the organization's funds. What are you doing that is different from what previous research has done? How does your project expand knowledge within a particular area of study? Does your project contribute to society? If so, how? You should be able to answer all these questions. This is a key section of your research proposal, as it justifies to the committee why your project is worthy of funding.

Budget

Since you have described your research project and why it is important to the review committee, you must explain how much money is needed to conduct your research. Every grant application has a section that requires applicants to list their proposed budget. You may also be expected to provide a justification for the cost of each item. Reviewers will want to know what you plan on doing with the money you are requesting. If they find that your budget is well thought out and well explained, you will earn more points toward your application score. Different grants will require different levels of detail in the budget section. Some grants will require that you provide a very detailed budget, while simple estimates will suffice for others.

Travel-Related Costs

Research grants often provide travel money to do your research. Examples of travel-related costs include the following:

Flight—Do you need to fly to your research site? If so, how much would a flight cost? Go to a travel website and put in your estimated dates of travel to get an idea of how much a ticket would cost. Don't forget that flight costs vary depending on time of year, time of day, length of stay, and even day of the week, so be sure to do your research. For example, it is more expensive to travel from New York City to Paris on a Friday in May than on a Tuesday in January.

Ground transportation—Do you need to pay for a ride to and from the airport? Do you need to pay for transportation once you arrive at your destination? Will you be taking public transportation or paying for taxis? How about your study participant(s)? If you are conducting interviews, how will you meet with your respondents? Will you compensate them for their travel? You should also estimate how much it would cost for ground transportation (rental cars, gas, taxis, trains, and public transportation) and provide this estimate in your budget.

Conference-related travel—Funds can be requested to pay for conference-related travel. As a researcher, you want to share your findings and get feedback from your colleagues. Find out from the conference's organizing committee what the conference fee will be as well as the cost of membership, as many organizations allow only members to attend conferences. If they allow nonmembers, they often charge them a substantially higher conference fee. Most social science organizations, such as the Society for the Study of Social Problems and the ASA, encourage student attendance and participation.

Accommodations—Where will you be staying while you conduct your research? Will you be staying in a hotel? How much do hotel rooms cost? You will, once again, want to figure in the different costs of the seasons. Often, if you stay in the conference's "host" hotel, you are able to receive a discount on the cost of the hotel room.

Per diem—Grants that will fund travel will also usually fund per diem expenses. It costs money to be away from home, and you will have to pay for every meal, snack, etc. A per diem is the amount of money used to pay for these expenses. Different institutions, organizations, etc. pay out a set per diem. This can be determined by where you are going or what you are doing. Others allow you to provide your own estimates. If you are allowed to provide your own, estimate how much it would cost you for each meal. Try to be conservative but not too conservative. For instance, an estimate of $8 for breakfast, $15 for lunch, and $25 for dinner should suffice. This would come to about $50 per day.

Data Collection and Analysis Costs

Examples of data collection and analysis costs include the following:

Respondents—Will you be using human subjects in your research? This could be for interviews, surveys, focus groups, etc. If so, will you be compensating your study participants for their time? The level of compensation researchers typically provide to their participants is often based on the level of demand the researcher places on the participant (and the researcher's level of funding). Participants often receive either monetary compensation or gifts for their participation in a study. Gifts could include movie tickets, T-shirts, gift bags, gift cards, candy, etc. Will you be feeding your respondents? If so, include the cost of food for your study participants.

Reference materials—Grants can cover the cost of the reference materials needed to conduct the research. Do you need money for books, journal articles or subscriptions, newspapers, etc.? How much will photocopies cost? Write and explain your estimate of these items and how they will aid your research.

Software—Computer software can be used to help develop, disseminate, and analyze surveys. Do you need software your campus does not already have access to? Find out the cost of the program you need, and explain how it will advance your work. Software can also be used to analyze qualitative data and even transcribe interviews.

Equipment—Most grants do not cover computer equipment such as laptops or desktops. But you can get the cost of other equipment covered, such as voice recorders, tapes, CDs, USB flash drives, batteries, transcription machines, headsets, microphones, calculators, and office supplies.

Your methodology will determine the amount of office supplies you will need. Will you be using paper surveys? Think about everything you will need for the respondent to complete the survey. First you will need the survey itself. How long do you think the survey will be? How many surveys will you need? How much will you need for paper, ink, and photocopies, as well as for pens and clipboards for your study participants to use? Do you need staplers, paperclips, envelopes, highlighters, etc.?

Shipping/telephone costs—How are you going to collect the data? Will you be mailing out surveys to respondents? How much will postage and envelopes cost? Will they be returning the surveys to you? How much will return postage cost? Will you be conducting telephone interviews? How much will it cost you to make the telephone calls?

Research assistants—Will you be able to conduct all your proposed research yourself or will you need help? Research assistants can be used to help gather and analyze data. If you will be using a research assistant, how much will you pay him? Whether you pay him by the hour or by the job, in calculating your research assistant's pay, you will want to make sure you pay at least minimum wage. You may also have to consider accompanying costs required by your institution.

Compensation for the researcher's time—It takes a great deal of time and energy to conduct research, and some funders compensate the researcher for her time. If the grant allows for PI compensation, write a statement considering the amount of time you will spend on this project and your salary, or how much your time is worth. Calculate it and include this in the budget. These funds are not typically available for student researchers.

Before you write out your budget, create a chart to help you itemize your potential expenses. This will help keep you organized and help you see if you forgot to include anything.

Table 6.4 Transcribing Interviews

Pay Per Hour	Number of Interviews	Approximate Audio-Tape Length	Total Cost of Transcription
$15	22	29 hours and 30 minutes of interviews, about 1 hour per interview	$442.50

Table 6.5 Cost of Conference Presentations

Total Conference Registration	Hotel	Flight	Total Cost
$70	$300	$200	$570
Total Amount Requested			
$1,012.50			

Remember to be as clear as possible in explaining your budget. You will not want to provide simply the monetary value of the item; you will also need to provide a justification for all your intended purchases. Funders want to know where their money is going, and justifiably so. These organizations want to be certain that you have done your research and are realistic about the possible costs of your project. In terms of costs, you want to be as specific as possible while still allowing for a bit of wiggle room. You also want as little out-of-pocket expense as possible.

Furthermore, provide as close an estimate as possible to what the call for applications is awarding without requesting more funds. If the grant is awarding $10,000, make sure you request as close to $10,000 as possible. If you need only $300 to conduct your research, you should not apply for that particular grant (nor would you likely receive the grant), as other researchers could utilize those funds completely.

In presenting your budget, keep similar information together. In your budget justification, don't start with a discussion of your accommodations and how you will compensate your respondents and then go back to the cost of your flight. Discuss all travel-related information together. Remember, detail, organization, *and* clarity (in addition to a very impressive project) are the keys to a well-written grant application.

SUBMITTING THE GRANT

Before you submit the grant, organizations frequently require ancillary items to be submitted along with the grant application.

Cover Sheet

Grants will often require the applicant to complete a cover sheet that consists of the applicant's name and contact information, the title of the project, and information about the grant. It may also include information about the PI's institution or university. If the grant must be submitted in hard copy, the cover sheet will typically be the first sheet of the grant application. If the grant is to be submitted electronically, then the cover sheet must also be completed electronically and submitted along with the grant. See the sample cover sheet in Figure 6.1.

Abstract

Abstracts (described in further detail in Chapter 8) are a brief summary of your research project. Grant applications will often dictate the length of the

Figure 6.1

> **Grant Proposal Title:**
> *The Impact of After-School Programs*
> *on Students of Color*
>
> **Submitted to:**
> **A. Dassler Gumbs**
> **and Cincinnati Jake Educational Foundation**
>
> **Principal Investigator:**
> Jane Doe
> 111 University Ave.
> State University
> City, State
> Tel: 111-555-1111
> xxxx@email.edu
>
> **Project Abstract:**
> This project will examine . . . [typically 250 words]

abstract. However, most abstracts tend to be 150 to 300 words in length. Your abstract should be concise and summarize the various aspects of your proposal. Since you have likely not yet done the research, your abstract will provide the following information:

- Overall introduction to the project
- What previous literature/research has said about the topic/issue
- Methodology (what you propose to do and how you plan on going about it)

This is different from an abstract you would write for a research report, as that would also include a short mention of the results and analysis. Some grants will provide explicit instructions on the exact format of the abstract. For example, abstracts are often centered, single spaced, and italicized.

Researcher Qualifications

All grants require the researcher submit a description of her qualifications and research experience. Review committees want to be assured that applicants are actually qualified to conduct the research they are proposing.

Review committees typically want to know where applicants have gone to school, what special training they may have, what their publications are, and where they have presented their research. Some grant applications require detailed researcher narratives or autobiographies. Others require simply a curriculum vitae.

Final Review

Before submitting the grant, make sure you have followed all instructions. Again, if you don't follow all instructions on your grant proposal, it will very likely be rejected without being thoroughly read and evaluated. Ideally, you have paid attention to the word count and other formatting instructions. You have answered all questions in their entirety. You have provided a well-detailed and clear budget and justification for your budget. You still may want to go over the numbers one more time. Make sure you have included the cover sheet, abstract, and your curriculum vitae. Now that you are ready to submit the grant, show it to at least one other person to be certain you have followed the instructions and you have a readable proposal. Send your grant off, whether electronically or via standard mail, well before the deadline. Do not wait until the last minute.

ACCEPTANCE AND REJECTION

If your grant application was accepted, congratulations! Keep in mind that some grants may require a final report where you explain exactly what you did with the money and what costs changed. You may be asked to submit receipts or even a sample of the research you collected with the funding. We provide the same advice for the final report as we did for the rest of the grant. Be sure to answer all questions clearly and completely. We know that once you have received the money, this may seem less important, but keep in mind that you may want to apply for money from the same organization again or you may need to include that organization as a reference, and you want to make sure to leave a good impression.

If your grant was rejected, do not despair. The opportunity remains for you to learn from your experience and continue to apply for other grants. The feedback reviewers provide, if applicable, can consist of everything from suggestions on readings to ways you can enhance your research project. Their suggestions are designed to help you enhance your project. In the event that a researcher does not receive the grant, she can often use the suggestions to make her application stronger when she applies for the grant again the following year (make sure that is within the grant's regulations, because some organizations do not allow you to apply for a grant 2 years, or two calling cycles, in a row). The researcher can also take the comments and incorporate them into another grant application for a different organization's call for proposals.

SUMMARY

The importance and need for grant writing are highlighted in this chapter. We discussed the development of a research program, along with the grant application process. The following topics were addressed:

- Searching for and selecting grants to which to apply
- Writing literature reviews and explaining the thesis, proposed methodology, and potential significance of the project
- How to develop and explain the budget
- The grant submission process
- How to handle a rejected grant proposal
- What to do if your grant has been accepted

In this "Writing in Practice" essay, Dr. Juan Battle, a professor of sociology, urban education, and public health, discusses how he became aware of the importance of grant writing in the beginning of his academic career. Dr. Battle considers the four key "ingredients" needed for success in the grant writing process.

WRITING IN PRACTICE

by Juan Battle

Combining my time as a student and a faculty member, I've been in higher education for almost 30 years. Therefore, my response to the testimony that "publications and grants are the currency that purchases favor in the academy" is AMEN.

Without question, the largest deficit in my graduate career was grantsmanship. During graduate school, I was employed by professors and worked on their funded projects. However, I never even saw a physical grant during my entire graduate school career.

When I started as an assistant professor, I quickly learned that the freedom and infrastructure available to many of my graduate school professors were not the products of simply being faculty members. Instead, they were the benefits of having their research funded. Thus, I began to explore how to get my research funded.

The first thing I learned was that relatively few faculty actually get external grants . . . and for good reason. In short, they're hard to get and sometimes even harder to manage. Be that as it may, I persevered.

I first contacted my grants administrator and asked him for the names of the top five funded faculty members in the social sciences at my institution. I scheduled a meeting with each of them and was very transparent about my intentions: I wanted to learn how to write and then run grants—two very different but very necessary skill sets. In the end, I started working with one of these professors. Over the past nearly two decades, he has become a great mentor and friend to me. We've worked on several projects and have even taught graduate courses together. I have no doubt that my career would not have been as successful had it not been for that relationship.

During my tenure as a professor, I have been fortunate to have had local, statewide, national, and international research funded. So what are the four key ingredients to successful grantsmanship? Precision, Patience, Persistence, and Partnerships.

Precision

If you're going to ask someone for money, you must be clear about what you're going to do with it. In some form or another, four basic questions really need to be answered:

1. What do you want to know? What's the research question?

2. Why do you want to know it? What's the contribution to the field, or how will your findings matter or make a difference?

3. What do you think the answer is? What are the working hypotheses driving the research?

4. How do you intend to find out? What methodology are you going to use . . . and why?

As a rule of thumb, spend one third of the proposal addressing Questions 1 through 3 and two thirds addressing Question 4. In other words, one third should discuss what *others* have done, while two thirds should describe what *you* are proposing to do.

(Continued)

(Continued)

Patience

My first million-dollar grant to get funded was the sixth million-dollar grant that I wrote. The first five never got funded. And higher education does not reward your effort, only your product.

Similar to producing publications, producing grant proposals involves writing and then collaborating and then rewriting and then thinking and then rewriting and then wading through and incorporating comments from colleagues and then rewriting and then wading through and incorporating comments from blind reviewers and then rewriting and then . . . I think you get the idea.

However, as with walking, tying your shoes, driving, or speaking a foreign language, the more you do it, the easier it gets.

Persistence

In higher education, most graduate students and junior faculty start out writing articles. If we submit an article for review and it is rejected by a journal, we typically look for another—more appropriate or lower-tiered—venue for publication. And for many of us, we'll keep shopping that article (or book proposal) around until some journal says "yes." Even if the journal is *Ladies' Home Journal*, we press on.

Unfortunately, if a grant is rejected, far too many academics scrap the research idea and/or move forward without any or adequate funding. In short, we are more committed to the project/research than we are to getting it funded.

Well, just like a dissertation takes commitment and persistence, so too does a grant.

If your first externally submitted grant gets funded on the first submission, you probably didn't ask for enough money, knew someone on the review committee, or were so lucky that you should immediately start playing the lotto . . . and please buy me a ticket (smile).

There is a difference between the producer (you) and the production (your grant). Therefore, don't take negative comments personally. Hang in there; it gets easier.

Partnerships

Ever wonder why people say that misery loves company? Well, because it's true. As I shared above, one of the first things I did when I decided I wanted to write grants was to partner with someone else more experienced and successful than I was.

I found that collaborating with colleagues who were also writing and running grants was and still is an invaluable experience. The multiple aspects of successful grantsmanship—the joy of getting funded, the agony of getting denied, the quagmire of hiring and managing staff, the stress of meeting deadlines for submissions and reports, and more—should not be endured alone. Like a dissertation defense with a bitter committee, it can never be adequately described . . . it can only be experienced. You never get over it; you only get through it.

But in the end, it's worth it.

Finally, remember, it gets easier . . . and at times is actually fun and exhilarating. Money gives autonomy—and, to me at least, that's a good thing. If I could have done anything differently, I would have started and learned to manage discouragement earlier in my career.

Either way, it's been well worth the journey. So get in there and, as Nike says, "Just Do It!"

—Dr. Juan Battle, PhD, is professor of sociology,
urban education, and public health at the Graduate
School and University Center, City University of New York.

CHAPTER 7

WRITING AND THE DATA COLLECTION PROCESS

Most of the writing we have examined in this book has focused on a final product—book reviews, grant proposals, institutional review board (IRB) applications—but this chapter examines the writing that is part of your progress toward these products. To complete an article or grant, you need a research project, and to complete that project, you need to select and use a methodology.

We include this chapter here not to provide a complete overview of research methods but to explain to students who are conducting survey research, focus groups, or interviews, or recording fieldnotes the types of writing they will have to create and some strategies for completing them. This chapter will not replace a book or course on research methods; however, the writing you produce within the methods is an important aspect of writing for sociology, and to discuss it properly, we begin with some background on the selection and use of research methods.

As mentioned previously in this book (see Chapter 3), your project will begin with a topic and library research on that topic. Once you have selected the topic of interest and formulated research questions and a hypothesis and/or thesis, you must figure out exactly how you will collect the information you need to prove, disprove, or answer them. In sociology, we divide our research into the general categories of qualitative and quantitative methods. Some social scientists would also include experiments as a category, but, as this category is more common in psychology, we will not include it here.

Qualitative research allows for an in-depth analysis. Rather than gathering general information on a variety of different subjects, qualitative research tends to focus on a small sample of people and provides detailed information on that group. Qualitative methods are also useful if the research question or hypothesis is not immediately apparent and you would like to explore a particular issue, person, or location in more detail and allow the direction to emerge as the research progresses. This is called grounded research. Qualitative research generally involves speaking to, or collecting data on or from, several individuals, events, or aspects of culture. Whether you collect this information on an individual level or from groups of individuals at the same time, writing must occur to complete the work.

When we examine something quantitatively, we generally begin with one or several hypotheses about the relationship between two or more measureable characteristics (variables). Since quantitative research consists of placing individuals and their responses into certain predetermined categories and relies on statistical analysis, the samples are often much larger than those that would be collected through qualitative methods.

The type of method you choose for your research depends on the questions of interest to you. If you are interested in questions about how an organization is structured or how a society functions, you will probably focus on qualitative methods. If you want to look at a relationship between variables or understand how certain characteristics affect others, you are more likely to use quantitative methods.

When thinking about methodology, you also want to keep in mind your plans for the results. If you are trying to tell a story by sharing the lives of individuals, you will want to use qualitative methods. If your intention is to run a statistical analysis on your data to examine an interesting relationship, your responses are going to have to be closed-ended quantifiable data. You may also choose to employ a mixed-method approach, in which you might use quantitative research for a general perspective and qualitative for a more in-depth view.

QUESTIONS

While there is a distinct line between qualitative and quantitative methods, there is writing within both areas that includes asking questions of those who play a role in the group, society, or organization of interest. Therefore, this section of the chapter will discuss questions in general and then will specifically examine the ways questions differ depending on your method. Included in this examination are the types of questions used in surveys or questionnaires (generally quantitative) and interviews and focus groups (qualitative).

Preparation

If you enter this stage of your research unsure about which specific methods you will use, you may want to begin by thinking about the types of questions

Figure 7.1

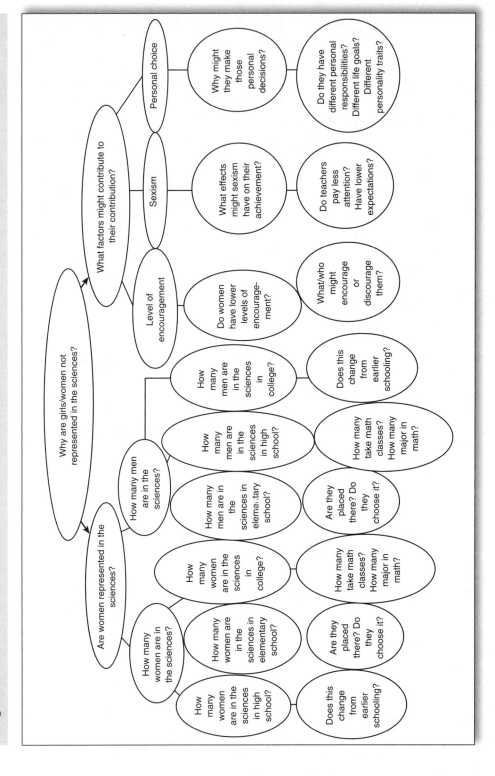

you would like to answer with your research. Consider your larger research questions or thesis. To answer those questions or address those ideas, what do you need to know? Try building a question tree. Start with your first question and ask yourself what information you need to answer it. Then, look at that second level of questions: How do you answer them? As you work your way down to the roots of your question tree, continue to break down each question into more questions. Once you reach questions that can be answered with a simple "yes" or "no" (or another one-word response), you should stop.

Examine the questions on the top levels of your tree: Which questions can the participants of your research answer directly? Separate these questions from those you will need to research through document analysis, observation, or other methods—for example, what is the high school graduation rate for New York City? You may find that some questions can be answered through multiple methods, and, if the resources are available, you should try as many of those methods as possible. This process is called triangulation, because you collect data through the use of different methods to attempt to find the true value.

Next, you may want to categorize your questions. Which questions deal with cause and effect? Which are exploring a setting, people, or organization? These will help you think about whether your research is qualitative, quantitative, or mixed. Additionally, once you create and refine your questions, you may find that they serve one method better than they do the others.

Before getting into the detail work of refining your questions, as described below, you should think about the objective of each question. What is the purpose of the question? How does it serve that purpose? If you haven't used the question-tree method, you might instead consider creating questions to serve particular objectives. For example, if your objective is to find out the effect of age on attitudes about technology, you will need to know how old your respondents are as well as how they feel about technology.

Each of the "better" questions in Figure 7.2 focuses on technology in a different way and is more precise, as is the question about age. In writing your questions, you should carefully consider what you are looking for and which questions best fill that need. Consider that in the first question, you are asking your respondents to define both *feel* and *technology*. Does a microwave count as technology? Or are you just referring to more recent technology? Does *feel* refer to their use, their dangers, or more general attitudes?

If you are attempting to conduct quantitative research, you will want your answers to be in an easily analyzable form. However, if you had an idea that age might lead to differing attitudes, for example, but you are unclear what exactly those attitudes might be, you may want to conduct a qualitative study with members of different age groups.

Figure 7.2

Objective:	Find out the effect of age on attitudes about technology	
Needed questions:	[age]	How old are you?
		What year were you born?
	[technology]	How do you feel about technology?
Better questions:	[age]	How old were you on your last birthday?
	[technology]	How useful is a cell phone in your daily life?
		How often do you use the Internet?
		How important are air conditioners in your community?

While the research we conduct in college and graduate school does not always provide us the time to pretest our questions, if you have the time and the resources, pretesting is ideal. Even if you cannot fully pretest, trying out your questions on different types of people and seeing whether their responses fit your goals can help you adjust your objectives and/or the questions that fulfill them.

Understanding the specifics of the types of questions you might use to create survey, interview, and focus group instruments that fulfill your research needs is important. However, there are some general considerations you should take into account while writing your questions.

Categories of Questions

We have spoken generally about the different types of questions that tend to distinguish qualitative and quantitative methods. Closed questions ask respondents to select their answers from several choices. With closed questions, the form of the response is already determined. This is most useful for quantitative, especially survey, data since responses will have to be in a particular form for you to analyze them. Open-ended questions leave the form of the response up to the respondent. These questions provide the opportunity for unintended answers that can open up new avenues for research. For both interviews and focus groups, make sure you use open-ended questions. A question to which someone can respond with a couple of words will not give you quality interview data, and a survey would better serve your purposes. The types of answers you are interested in can help determine how you frame your questions.

Figure 7.3

[open-ended]	1) What is your impression of your children's school?
[closed-ended]	2) What is your impression of your children's school?

             (1) Very   (2) Somewhat   (3) Neutral   (4) Somewhat   (5) Very
                  positive   positive   negative   negative

             3) How would you rank your children's school?

             (1) High quality   (2) Neutral   (3) Low quality

Each of the questions in Figure 7.3 will give you a slightly different answer. The second one, for example, is called a Likert item and asks you to choose a level of agreement or emotion on a scale generally made up of five or more options. Often, Likert-item questions are clumped together and, as a whole, create a Likert scale, which has been shown to be more representative of an attitude about a particular topic than is an individual question. For example, if you simply ask Question 2, you will get one answer. But if you break the question down as shown in Figure 7.4, you can put this information together on a scale and gain a more detailed understanding of your respondent's overall attitude about the school.

With a question like a Likert item, you may also want to consider the utility of a neutral response. Without it, you will create a Likert item with a forced response, and, for this reason, many researchers will leave off the neutral option. Too many respondents, when given the chance, will choose to remain neutral rather than taking a stand in one direction or another. Unless the neutral answer is really important to you or is a valid answer in your research, it may be best left off. However, some people will skip a question if they feel none of the answers fits their true feelings. You should think deeply about the neutral option before deciding whether to include or exclude it.

In addition to the general category of closed- or open-ended questions, other categorizations are used to organize questions. Demographic questions often start or end a survey or interview. These questions refer to facts about the respondents, their lives, or the context within which they are addressing your questions. These questions usually start or end research because they are considered easy questions. Someone can much more easily and quickly tell you his birthdate than tell you what he thinks is the most important part of his community. However, some demographic questions are considered more personal

Figure 7.4

What is your impression of your children's teachers?

| (1) Very positive | (2) Somewhat positive | (3) Neutral | (4) Somewhat negative | (5) Very negative |

What is your impression of your children's classmates?

| (1) Very positive | (2) Somewhat positive | (3) Neutral | (4) Somewhat negative | (5) Very negative |

What is your impression of your children's school building?

| (1) Very positive | (2) Somewhat positive | (3) Neutral | (4) Somewhat negative | (5) Very negative |

What is your impression of your children's homework?

| (1) Very positive | (2) Somewhat positive | (3) Neutral | (4) Somewhat negative | (5) Very negative |

What is your impression of your children's classroom assignments?

| (1) Very positive | (2) Somewhat positive | (3) Neutral | (4) Somewhat negative | (5) Very negative |

than others. For example, many see income as being quite personal. Age can also be an uncomfortable topic for respondents. Some researchers will move these questions to the end of the instrument. Additionally, similar but less personal questions can be asked in their place. For example, asking respondents about social class and year of birth is considered less intrusive than asking about income and age. Be forewarned, however, that while year of birth will give you the respondent's age within a year, social scientists consider social class to be an objective measure. Not everyone has the same idea of the boundaries of social class, and individuals may have political or personal reasons for placing themselves in one category or another.

Your research will also include other factual questions that are not demographic but may ask a respondent to calculate, recall, or even guess some information where there is a "right" answer. In these situations, you must recognize that you have to take your respondents' word on the accuracy of their answers. Your assumption is that they have answered the question to the best of their ability. Sometimes, it is their ability to recall that you are interested in. If you ask a parent for the name of her 6-year-old child's teacher, and the parent does not know (or gives you an incorrect name), that can tell you something about her relationship to the school. On the other hand, if you ask a teenager how many hours he spends watching television, an accurate response is more important, and you lack the ability to validate his response (except by asking his parents to estimate as well). As with demographic questions, you rely on your respondent to know the answer but also recognize that he may not even realize he does not know it.

In asking factual questions, it is important to create questions you believe your respondents can answer. If you intend to find out the size of the national debt, it makes more sense to look it up than to ask the average American. While some may know a number, few are likely to provide an accurate one. Recall that your objective for asking a question (even when the objective is in the form of a question) may be different from the question you are actually asking your respondents. For example, if you are interested in whether the average American knows what the national debt is, you might ask respondents to tell you what the debt is. You would not be asking them because you wanted the factual information but because you were interested in whether they knew it. You should avoid using the survey as a way to collect facts about American government, of which your respondents may have limited knowledge.

In addition to factual questions, you can ask opinion questions. Often, this and the second category of factual questions overlap somewhat. Some may also rephrase factual questions in the form of an opinion. For example:

Thinking about all the time you spend in communication with doctors, nurses, pharmacists, and other medical professionals, how many hours per week would you say you spend talking about your health with experts in the field?

This question is both attempting to collect factual information and recognizing that the information you collect is the respondent's opinion. Opinion questions are usually the meat of your work—be it qualitative or quantitative. Generally, you are trying to use your research to capture an attitude, an opinion, or a perspective from your respondents. You want to know if they enjoy the park in their neighborhood or think the local shops sell quality items. You want to know *how* people feel, *what* their opinion is, and *why* they think a certain way. It is through these types of questions that you find those answers.

Compound Questions

You should avoid compound questions at all costs. They come in several different forms. For example, consider this question:

Do you think your mayor is a good person and an effective politician?

If you believe both of those statements are true or false, then you can give a simple yes-or-no answer. But how do you answer if you believe your mayor is an effective politician but not a good person? The solution to this is to make sure that each question asks *one* and *only one* question. The compound question above would more accurately represent the opinions of your respondents if it were divided into two questions:

Do you think your mayor is a good person?

Do you think your mayor is an effective politician?

Keep in mind that both of these questions ask the respondent to use her own definitions of *good* and *effective*. If you wanted to use your own measure, you would either define *effective* and *good* or break these two questions into even smaller questions that would represent a good person and an effective politician for you. For example:

Do you believe that your mayor cares about the environment?

Do you believe that your mayor always puts the welfare of your city's residents first?

Do you believe your mayor is organized?

Do you believe your mayor works hard?

Do you believe your mayor accomplishes his goals?

This similar example of a poorly worded question might lead respondents to give an answer to a question you did not intend to ask:

Is the mayor someone with whom you would like to go to a football game?

Consider what a "yes" answer actually means. It could mean that the mayor is someone you think would be fun to hang out with. It could also mean that you love football enough that you would go with anyone who asked. Maybe you think the mayor would pay and that would make it worth your effort. A "yes" answer to this question may not accurately provide the information you were hoping to gain from it. A better question either would refer to an activity you are sure the respondent finds enjoyable or would directly ask if the mayor seems like someone the respondent might want to spend time with at a social event.

Biased Questions

Also keep in mind that you do not want your questions to lead the respondent in one direction or another. Respondents can often feel as though the questions, even the opinion/attitude-based ones, have a right or wrong answer. When you are acting as an interviewer or focus group moderator, a participant may try to read your face for evidence that he has said the right thing. With a survey instrument, he may try to use the questions that surround the question he is answering to find out if he is giving the "right" answers. The respondent may ask himself, is the person who wrote this survey asking the questions in favor of the mayor or opposed to him? Does she think this is a good educational policy or a bad one? If your questions are continually in support of a person or policy, your respondent will react to that slant. For example:

Do you believe that this mayor has done more good for the city than any other mayor?

Do you think that this mayor was justified in taking over the schools because he has done so much good work in other endeavors?

Instead, you may want to consider mixing up your questions so the respondent does not know your perspective or what your previous research has already shown you. Explain that critics of the mayor have said particular things, and ask him if he agrees; then tell your respondent that supporters have said other things, and ask him for his level of agreement. This should present a more balanced perspective to your respondent, which will give you more representative answers.

Additionally, bias can sometimes come from the organizations, companies, or individuals conducting the research. Participating in a survey sponsored by a neighborhood organization that has helped gentrify a neighborhood may automatically get more favorable responses from one group and more negative reactions from another. If you can eliminate that kind of biased information from your research, it can allow your data to be less influenced by it.

Reliability

The reliability of a question refers to the results of the replication of the question. A reliable question elicits the same response from different people, and, therefore, any differences in the answers would be a result of differences between respondents. This is the type of question you want to create. If your questions are not reliable, you may be measuring something other than what you are interested in, such as your respondents' understanding of the question. Reliability cannot be completely ensured, but it can be maximized.

Writing clear, well-defined questions can increase reliability. Asking only one question at a time as well as including the other methods we suggest in this chapter can also help. This will increase the likelihood that all your respondents will understand the questions in the same way. For an interview, including options for your interviewer to personalize questions (such as using the correct personal pronouns *he / she / them*) can also increase the reliability of your questions.

Validity

A valid question is one that asks the question you are trying to have answered. Reliable questions are also more likely to be valid. Additionally, asking the same question in several different ways can ensure that the structure of the question will not be a barrier between you and your research goals. While it may not have an immediately analyzable effect on your question, including a space for your respondents to explain their answers can help you see whether they are responding to the questions you are asking.

Question-Based Methods: Survey

A survey instrument is the survey document, whether on paper or in digital form (surveys viewed on a computer or other electronic device), that includes all the questions. In addition to the questions, you may provide specific instructions to introduce a question and/or methods for dealing with questions that do not apply to a particular respondent. Keep in mind that unless the survey is conducted online and a help option has been made available, the respondent has no one to whom she can go if she comes across something she does not understand. Any questions a respondent has must be answered by the survey, and any survey directions must be clear, as there is no one to explain problems or fix issues that might arise. If a respondent is confused and has to hunt down the researcher every time she has a question, she is likely to become frustrated and not complete the survey.

As we discussed in the beginning of this chapter, survey questions are generally closed and use particular quantitative responses. Closed questions are those that include response categories. These refer to the different answer choices available to the respondent. The structure of the response categories is how we define the question's "level of measurement." At the "lowest" level, we have nominal questions. Nominal answer options give the respondent the choice of categories represented by text and/or non-meaningful numbers.

Figure 7.5

What is your sex?	How would you categorize yourself? (check all that apply)
☐ Female ☐ Male	☐ White American
	☐ Black American
	☐ Latino/a
	☐ Asian or Pacific Islander
	☐ Native American
	☐ Caribbean
	☐ European
	☐ African
	☐ Other

When a question's answer choices have a particular order and can be organized from highest to lowest or smallest to largest, it is an ordinal question. However, the distances between the different categories for such a question are not necessarily the same, and you cannot perform mathematics on them.

Figure 7.6

What is your mother's highest level of education?

- [ ] Less than high school
- [ ] Some high school
- [ ] High school graduate
- [ ] Some college
- [ ] Associate/junior college degree
- [ ] Bachelor's degree
- [ ] Graduate degree (MA, PhD, JD, MD)

Please specify: _____

Levels of agreement (*strongly agree, agree, neither agree nor disagree, disagree, strongly disagree*) are another example of ordinal answer categories. While the order is meaningful, you cannot average *strongly agree* and *neither agree nor disagree* and come up with *agree*.

Finally, the categories of interval/ratio variables include numbers with values that can be placed in a meaningful order. A response category that represents the respondent's number of children as *1, 2, 3, 4*, and so on is interval/ratio. Someone with four children has twice as many children as someone with two.

Figure 7.7

What was the first grade you spent at this school? (Check one)

[ ] 7th	[ ] 8th	[ ] 9th
[ ] 10th	[ ] 11th	[ ] 12th

While there are ways to treat nominal and ordinal data as interval/ratio, much of the higher-order statistical analyses use interval/ratio-level data. This should not preclude you from using data measured at the other levels, but it is something to keep in mind.

Instrument

Generally, a survey must begin by recording the permission of the respondent to conduct the research. IRBs differ slightly from institution to institution, but, for many, the first page of your survey will have to be a copy or two of the consent form you created during your IRB proposal process (see Chapter 5). Recall that this form should explain the research, how you will protect your subjects' privacy, and how they can get in contact with you should they need to. The final version you receive from the IRB after acceptance will display your institution's official seal or stamp as well as the date when permission to conduct your research expires. There should also be a place for both you and your respondent to sign. Your respondent keeps a copy and returns the other to you.

The second sheet of your survey will often be a contact information sheet. Again, you may have informed the IRB that you would not collect contact information (in which case, you should skip this step), but contact information is generally useful in case there is a problem with the survey or you have compensation to award once the research is complete. Whether you can gather respondents' actual names is something you decided during the IRB process, but other information you may need is a phone number and a home and/or e-mail address. In most cases, this form is disconnected from the survey following verification so that individual responses remain anonymous.

The survey should begin on the third sheet (if we count both copies of the consent form as one sheet). Because of the level of anonymity most IRB agreements require, surveys can include an identification (ID) number that connects the consent form, contact information, and survey. They should all be kept separate from one another to prevent accidental identification.

Survey questions should be numbered consecutively, as should the instrument pages. Some surveys also include section headings so the respondent has a reference for what types of questions she will be responding to. For example, a survey that connects high school classroom environment to college experiences might use headings such as those shown in Figure 7.8.

Depending on the structure of your survey, you may also want to use introductory sentences as a road map to lead respondents through your survey's subsections. Your section headings can also fill that role. In addition, you may want to include other information before a question or section as a prompt to stimulate your respondents' recall and further explain the individual or group of questions. For example:

In thinking about all the time you spent in high school, how many hours in a typical week did you spend engaged in any of the following activities?

Figure 7.8

Demographic Information: This is where the respondent is asked about race, gender, age, location, family type, etc. Social science surveys generally include the big three variables (race, class, gender), since these categorizations can lead to some similarities in experience. It is important to know—whether subjectively or objectively—where people position themselves or are positioned by others. Choosing not to include these variables is a valid personal choice, but one must be prepared for the possible response from the academic community.

Pre-High School Experiences: Your respondent's life before entering high school could be important to your research. These questions might allow you to examine whether the effect on college experiences comes from high school or something previously in the respondent's life.

High School Classroom Environment: These are the questions that begin the essential aspects of your research. Here you would collect as many questions as possible that examine classroom environment from different perspectives. What are the aspects that make up classroom environment as you understand it? Teachers? Students? Paint or pictures on the walls? Clean desks? Private lockers or bins?

College Experiences: Similar to the previous section, these are the other questions that are important to answering your research questions. You should make sure to be clear in writing your questions and consider the connections between these and the previous questions. Are you looking for a change? Similarities? A new perspective? These should all be considered here.

Conclusion/Completion: This is not necessarily a heading in your instrument, as you might not have a concluding page/section. If you feel your respondents would not answer an income question before other questions, it might be included here. You may also have some concluding remarks about incentives, contact information, or where they could go to find out more information.

Since the respondent must be relied on to read and understand the instrument you have created, you should make sure to use language the respondent can understand. The above question could be rewritten if you believe your respondent may read or understand the question differently. For example:

When you think about all the time you spent in high school, how many hours a week did you spend doing any of these activities?

The format of your instrument should be consistent throughout your document. If you ask respondents to check boxes, you should not ask them to fill in circles or circle the correct response later. If you include open-ended questions, decide whether you will use a blank space or underlines, and continue to use that convention.

One place where the opinion on consistent questions may differ is the use of reversed questions. While switching the direction of a question (for example, placing strongly agree at the bottom of a scale after you have used it at the top of the scale in a different question) can help ensure that your respondent is reading your questions and not just filling out the same answer for each question, it can also confuse people who are legitimately trying to answer the questions. The best way to judge whether your respondents are reading the questions is to change the direction of the questions rather than the response categories. For example, instead of phrasing the statement this way:

My child's math teacher does a great job educating my children.

[strongly agree, agree, neither agree nor disagree, disagree, strongly disagree]

Use this statement:

My child's teacher does an inadequate job teaching my children math.

[strongly agree, agree, neither agree nor disagree, disagree, strongly disagree]

If you do choose to reverse or change your response categories, be sure to let the respondent know that his level of agreement may be represented differently in those questions. You could write,

Please read carefully, as the response categories have changed.

A good survey also prepares for the possibility that some respondents will not need to answer some questions. To deal with this, we implement branching or skip techniques—rules that tell respondents which questions they should answer and which they should ignore. When you ask a respondent whether he has any children, his answer determines whether he should go on to answer questions about his children's ages or the schools they attend. Be sure that the skip instructions are clear and that page or question numbers accurately reflect the instrument. Explain both what the respondent should do if he does have children and what should happen if he does not.

Do you have children?

If so, please continue with Question 2.

If not, please continue the survey with Question 7 (Page 2).

Utilizing skip techniques saves respondents from reading through questions that do not apply to them. It streamlines the process and personalizes the survey to some extent.

Once you have created your instrument, you will use it to collect data, which you will then analyze. We will talk briefly about analysis following a discussion on the writing that occurs when working with qualitative methods.

Question-Based Methods: Focus Groups

As the name of the method suggests, focus groups are groups of people who focus on a particular aspect, definition, or understanding of an issue. Rather than concentrating on only one perspective, focus-group moderators (those who lead and organize focus groups and are most often also researchers on the project) are interested in a range of viewpoints, are trying to understand the difference between groups, or want to see how people interact around a particular topic. Focus groups are often used to pilot questions for other research or to assist in understanding the data already collected. Focus groups generally include fewer questions than would a survey or interview. Consider that, during a survey or interview, one individual answers each question. In a focus group, your hope is that one question will lead to a conversation with several participants. So a question that might take a single respondent 10 minutes to answer could take a focus group a half hour or more. For this reason, a 2-hour focus group can include as few as 4 but should not include more than 12 questions. Keep in mind the following characteristics of focus-group questions.

Open-Ended

First and foremost, like other qualitative methods, focus-group questions should be open-ended. If you ask your respondents a yes-or-no question, you will get a yes-or-no answer and discussion will be difficult. You do not want to ask, "Do you like your job?" as respondents can immediately answer with a simple yes or no.

Instead, think about what you are truly interested in discovering and what type of discussion would elicit that kind of response. You can find out whether your respondents like their jobs by asking them, "How do you feel about your job?" or "What do you enjoy about your job?" Both of these questions will probably give you the answer to the question, "Do you like your job?" but can also provide your research with additional information that could be invaluable even if unplanned.

Easy to Understand

Remember in writing your questions that focus-group questions are meant to be spoken and are often spoken by someone other than the person who wrote them. Focus-group questions should be written in a way that is easy for the group to understand, as well as for the moderator to say. For example:

How would you categorize the relationship between your children and social networking websites?

This is a little wordy, and what you are trying to say may not necessarily be clear to your group. Instead, try writing the question in a more conversational manner using words that are familiar to your respondents. Also, remember that you are not asking for a single word or a quick sentence, you are trying to initiate a discussion. A prompt such as "Describe how your kids use Facebook" might elicit more useful responses.

Instructive

Since focus groups usually include a moderator, you will also want to write clear instructions. If your focus group involves only answering questions, your directions to the moderator need only include the length of time for the entire group and, potentially, instructions for different types of questions. You may also want to include directions for the moderator to read to the group, which could include how long the focus group is going to last, how questions from participants will be handled, any issues regarding privacy and record keeping (see Chapter 5), and who will be in charge of making sure the conversation flows smoothly. Make sure to distinguish the focus-group creator's directions for the moderator from those directions intended for the entire group. Once you decide on a text format (bold, italics, underline) to indicate each type of direction, remain consistent throughout.

You can also include more involved activities in a focus group, in which case you will need to write more-detailed directions to introduce each activity. If you would like the group to rank problems in the neighborhood and come to some agreement, you will have to explain whether they are creating their own list of issues or you are giving them a predetermined list, as well as whether you want the group to agree on the most problematic or the least problematic issue. If you would like the group to draw a representation of their neighborhood, you may have to explain that they are allowed to use their imaginations and that artistic skills are not necessary.

Short

Focus-group questions should also be short. The amount of information the group has to remember should be limited. It is much better to ask your group a series of short questions than to create a question so long that your respondents have to take notes or ask you to repeat it. For example:

> What do you see as the goals of education, and how good of a job do you feel the school your children attend has done in obtaining those goals?

This question could be divided into several smaller questions. First, you could ask a question about the goals of education. You could follow with questions about the school's role in reaching those goals and whether it has been successful. As this series of questions draws on previous answers, you or the other moderators may want to jot down notes or write answers on poster board so the group can refer to them during the later questions. Be sure that writing notes for the group does not become a central activity, however. If you find that your respondents are pausing to wait for you to finish writing or adjusting their responses to fit your paper, you are likely writing too much. It may be a good idea to write their words down but keep them to the side, bringing them into the conversation only when you need them for later questions.

The "Why" Chromosome

While much of what makes sociology interesting is the questioning of the world through the word *why*, it is important to avoid this word in your focus-group script as much as possible. Consider these examples:

"Why did you do that?"

"Why did you think that was right?"

"Why don't you like that?"

These questions, while perfectly valid for understanding a situation, can come off as accusatory when used as a follow-up to a respondent's answer. For many respondents in a group setting, the question "Why?" leads them to feel that you are questioning the validity of what they just did or said or that you think they need to justify their behavior. Instead of using *why*, find other ways to ask the same question. Ask respondents to tell you more or explain further. You can even ask them to describe their motivations for a particular act or response.

Start on the Bright Side

Since a focus group relies so heavily on the interactions among members, it is important to keep the group feeling positive while they are still growing accustomed to one another. Therefore, in the beginning, you should try to phrase your questions in a positive manner so your respondents are encouraged to continue telling their stories. Once the group has established a rapport, they are more likely to be comfortable sharing the tough times with the group, especially if they believe they will get support from people going through similar problems.

Once you have created a list of questions, you should go through and edit them, ensuring you have followed all the guidelines in this chapter and are serving the purpose of your research. This will likely include the winnowing down of a long list of questions into only a few. This final list will then become the basis of your focus-group script.

Creating the Script

Your focus-group script should begin with a descriptive title and a number— for example, Math Education (#1). In this way, you can distinguish the focus-group scripts on different topics from one another, as well as from earlier drafts. You should also include a quick note that gives some indication of the amount of time needed for the entire session and whether there will be a break. It is also helpful to the moderator if you include a sentence or two reminding him of the overall purpose of the focus group. What are the questions you are hoping to answer? What information are you trying to access?

Before you move into questions, you should include a short introduction for the moderator that introduces her as well as the project, organization, or company. If there is a reason not to introduce the group behind the work (be sure you have listed that in your IRB application), you can still give your participants a brief overview of the project, including as much information as necessary without damaging your project or taking too much time from the group itself. For example:

> Good afternoon, everyone. My name is Jiani, and I am a student at the University of New York. We are conducting a study on workplace environments. We hope that the research conducted here can lead to changes in employment for many Americans. This is a safe space. For this work to be effective, we ask that you be as honest as possible. This session will be recorded, but your names will not be used in any publications created from this focus group. The whole process should take about 2 hours.

A large part of what makes a focus group work is the group members' interactions with one another and with the moderator. It is therefore helpful to build your questions gradually toward the main goals of your research. By working your way through different types of questions, you should be able to create a good rapport among members of your group.

Opener

To create a comfortable environment for your focus-group participants, you should start with some opener questions. The opener is an opportunity for you and your respondents to get comfortable with each other and for you to begin to hear everyone's voices. However, the development of animosity between group members is also a risk in the beginning. During this time, you should ask people to talk about factual information rather than going in-depth about feelings, explanations, and memories. Learning a little about the group and allowing the respondents to connect based on their commonalities is the ideal product of the opener. As previously mentioned, questions about age, income, religion, or prestige can be problematic and can lead to jealousies or biases. These questions, if needed for your work, may be better answered by a questionnaire or later in the process. On other occasions, these questions may be more appropriate. If you have a relatively homogenous group, some of those types of opener questions will be less likely to cause problems.

Think of the opener as that "get-to-know-you" task a college professor might have had you do on the first day of class. You were not necessarily expected to provide detailed information about your life. Instead, your professor asked for your name, year (e.g., sophomore, junior, first-year graduate student), major or area of expertise, and maybe something interesting about yourself. This task does not require a lot of thought or opinion but provides your professor with some information about you, and it works similarly for the focus-group participants and moderator.

Introduction

As distinct from the opener, the questions in the introduction section are meant to get the group comfortable with the topic of your research. If you are interested in problems in public schools, you might begin this section by asking about what education means to the respondents or by asking them to describe the daily schedules of their school-aged children. If you are interested in their negative experiences with particular data analysis software, your introductory section might include questions on how they understand the software: What does it do? What is it most used for? Why do they not use something else?

Primary Questions

These questions are the essential part of your research. This is where you get to the primary focus of the group. The majority of your time and energy should be put into both writing these questions and having your focus group answer them. The script should indicate which questions are the primary questions so the moderator knows how much attention should be paid to them. If you used the question-tree method, these are the questions closer to the top of your tree. These questions should represent the essential parts of your research.

Conclusion

Finally, you may want to include a couple of questions at the end to conclude the group. You might simply ask your respondents if you have forgotten something or if they have any questions. You might also consider asking for a final evaluation or conclusion of the topic or group.

Question-Based Methods: Interviews

The basis of good qualitative research is good interview questions. To collect the data you are interested in and to elicit the information you require from your respondents, you need to write quality interview questions and be, or train, a good interviewer. We will not discuss the training of interviewers here, as that is outside this book's scope, but we will examine the creation of your interview instrument.

Informal or Unstructured Interviews

The first decision to be made is how structured your interview will be. For an unstructured interview, you should begin with broad or general questions to generate responses you can build on. Unstructured interviews are most often used as part of a larger ethnography, as they allow the respondent and the context to dictate the frame of the interview. Unstructured means you are going into the interview with fewer prepared questions and you allow the interaction between the interviewer and the respondent to determine the follow-up questions.

Informal or unstructured interviews are difficult to do well. If you go into your interview looking for particular answers, it can be hard to find them productively in this format. However, it is the easiest kind of interview to conduct. The best way for an informal interview to occur is during the course of a conversation. It provides a comfortable, safe environment for respondents to tell you about themselves and their lives while providing you with valuable information.

Generally, an informal interview will occur early in your research process. At this point, you are trying to understand the unique perspectives of your respondents. If, for example, you are interested in charter schools, your first unstructured interview might consist of a walk with a teacher or student around a charter school. You would take note of what she found important, what she avoided, and what she returned to, either physically or in conversation.

Because of the informal nature of the interview, there is not a lot of writing to be done beforehand. For the most part, your respondent leads you through the conversation. However, you may have some particular questions you are interested in trying to weave into the conversation. Early in the process, these questions are probably "survey" questions where you ask informants for a "tour" of their world (e.g., "Show me your school"; "What does your neighborhood look like?"). Later in the process, the questions become more specific—focusing on particular structures, people, or ideas.

It is important to remember not to force the informal interview. An interview is not the same as a conversation, as you go into it with at least a vague questioning scope, but you should do your best to allow your questions to emerge naturally. Part of this is being aware of the context. If, in the course of your tour around the charter school, your respondent has a negative reaction to entering an algebra class, that will likely be a good time to ask your questions about math education at the school. If you are sitting down to enjoy lunch, your questions about the nutrition of the lunch program will make a smooth transition.

Finally, similar to focus groups, you should begin your informal interview with general questions before moving on to more personal ones. Ethnography works only when you build a strong relationship with your respondents, and jumping right into extremely personal information can block that relationship from forming. Wait for the invitation to delve deeper into their lives, and then move slowly and cautiously.

Structured Interviews

As an interviewer in your post-secondary or early graduate career, you will likely start out with a structured interview. The difference between structured and unstructured interviews is similar to the difference between interviews and surveys. While surveys ask respondents to choose from a predetermined set of answer categories, a structured interview asks respondents to answer a predetermined set of questions. An interview provides more freedom in responses than a survey does, and an unstructured interview provides that freedom in the questions asked.

For many researchers, the biggest problem with the unstructured interview is that it is often unreliable (see above) because each interview is different and built from each respondent's answers to her or his particular set of questions. Reliability is more important in statistics, as it is needed for accurate analyses, but is still considered with interviews. Structured interviews have a premade interview frame, which ensures that each respondent will answer the same questions and allows for comparability.

In ethnography, you would most likely use structured interviews as you moved further into your research. Specific questions are more likely to develop as you work with your respondents and learn more about their worlds. If you are using interviews as their own methodology or as a companion to surveys, structured interviews may be ongoing throughout the research.

Similar to the focus group, you should include directions for your interviewers (especially if you will not be conducting all the interviews yourself) and instructions to read to your respondents. When you begin a new topic in your interview, it is beneficial to explain the purpose the next group of questions will serve. For example:

These next questions will address your attitudes about mathematics education.

Interviews should also begin with introductory questions. As mentioned previously, these could be demographic questions covering age, race, or location. Income, again, is a question many respondents do not feel comfortable answering and, even if other demographic questions are not, is often placed near the end of the instrument.

Semi-Structured Interviews

A semi-structured interview combines the freedom and adaptability of an informal interview with the organization of a structured interview. In preparing a semi-structured interview, you should begin the same way you would for a structured interview. The difference lies in your ability to be flexible and change, modify, or add questions as needed. In a structured interview, one of your goals is to ensure that each respondent is given the same interview instrument and that any potential interviewer effect is controlled for. With a semi-structured interview, you recognize that each situation is different and some people may require further information, a rephrasing of the questions, or something else entirely. Semi-structured interviews provide a place for that.

Semi-structured interviews are often conducted after informal interviews because the interviewer has developed a few particular questions from observations or informal interviews but may still have some information that has not been revealed. Respondents engaging in a semi-structured interview are able to elaborate and discuss things that are perhaps only tangentially related to the questions, which would not be allowed in a structured interview.

OBSERVATION

Rather than the question/answer format of the methods discussed above, fieldnotes are, very simply, your observations of a place, area, person, or interaction. Fieldnotes, like the unstructured interview, are most commonly associated with the larger method of ethnography but may also be created through the observation that might be conducted when scouting a location for research, getting some background information on an event, or doing a class assignment for a methods class.

Fieldnotes have a built-in scaffolding process leading to the final product (usually the excerpts included in your paper, report, thesis, or dissertation). The process often begins with jottings or scratch notes. These are quick notes you take while on the scene. This is followed by the expansion of these notes, which should occur as soon as possible after the jottings to ensure little data is lost. Finally, the "final" fieldnotes are written. Reflections and analyses of the data may happen concurrently with jottings, may occur during the expansion of the fieldnotes, or may be done as analysis through the creation of themes and collections of thoughts, images, and documents. Although some researchers publish or make their fieldnotes available, fieldnotes generally act as data and are not an end in themselves. However, if you are conducting research for an organization or company, it may require the submission of both your fieldnotes and your analysis of them.

What to Write

The purpose of fieldnotes is to capture a detailed written "video" of a scene, accompanied by your own external monologue or your internal voice-over. You want to depict the feel of the scene on a paper and share it with your audience. Anyone who reads your notes or, more likely, the excerpts included in papers, articles, or books, should feel as though they are there—they should see the people and places you describe and hear the conversations you record.

Your fieldnotes should be filled with thick description. Rather than simply saying the neighborhood is suburban, describe what you see that leads you to that conclusion. Perhaps you know that the city of White Plains is a suburb of New York City. You can begin by noting that information, but you also need to include a description of how it is illustrated in front of you. Are there single-family houses? Neatly trimmed grass? Children playing outside? Individual garages? What in your observations led you to the suburban classification?

The purpose of your fieldnotes is not just to describe how an area might be categorized as wealthy or poor, suburban or rural but also to paint a picture of where you are, and where your informants and respondents are. What does the neighborhood look like? Are there parks? Stores? Apartments? Houses? What is the weather like? How does it affect the environment? What time of day is it? What happens in this neighborhood at this time of day? What might you have expected to happen that is not happening? Do you notice particular sounds or smells? Some researchers take a moment to close their eyes and "get a feel" for the place before taking notes.

Thick description does not end with the setting. Your jottings and eventually your fieldnotes should also include descriptions of the people in the setting. You want to notice how people interact with each other or avoid interactions with each other. What are the community members saying to each other? What gestures are they sharing or hiding from each other? What is the context within which they are interacting? All this information provides a vivid image of where you are, which is ripe for your analysis but also serves as the evidence that brings your readers to the people you are studying in a way that other methods may not.

Fieldnotes also can include conversations or informal interviews that you have with respondents.[1] Accurate representations of their words are important. If you change their vocabulary or the order of their words, you are changing their meaning. You will need to be careful in transcribing your conversations with others, and if recording is not possible, you will likely need to take detailed notes of what respondents are saying. Make sure also to take note of your respondents' body language and other reactions to your questions or their answers.

How to Write

The actual writing of fieldnotes eventually becomes a matter of personal preference. You will know how much you can write down without disrupting the scene, how much you need to write to remember it later, how quickly you need to flesh out your notes, and even what types of notes you need to take.

Jottings

For many, the notes taken in the field are distinct from the eventual product. You have only so much time in a community, household, or organization to take notes, and every moment you are looking down at your notebook, computer, smartphone, or tablet is time you are missing something occurring in front of you. Obviously, you cannot be expected to write nothing and remember everything. Instead, you have to teach yourself to take quick notes that will remind you of what you didn't have time to take down in full.

You will be recording several types of information in your notes, and you will want to distinguish among them. You should begin by indicating time, place, and date. You may want to add a title, the number of the observation, and the name of the observer if you will have multiple people or multiple observations at a particular site. Some people put this at the top of the first page as a header, while others might use the title page format and place it on a separate page.

Setting descriptions are one type of data you will collect in your fieldnotes. These are descriptions of the community, people, and activities. If you think of this in terms of a play, movie, or television script, this would be the piece that tells you how to create the scene or the background action. The setting should include the place, as described above, but also what the people look like and what they are doing.

The content of the notes can also include description. More often, this is where you describe the conversations and activities people participate in. You will likely want to create codes for yourself to indicate the people you have observed or interacted with so you can separate out different people's behaviors and speech. You should also skip lines between different people and/or activities to make it easier to distinguish them from each other. Your notes can also include other information you might have gained from interviews or conversations about what you are observing.

Finally, you might also record the less objective reflections. These are the ideas you have about what you are observing. While much of this will happen as you are rereading or rewriting your notes, there may be a few reflections you make on the spot that you would like to record. You will want to make sure your reflections and analyses are distinguishable from your observations. When you incorporate your notes into your final document, your reflections are often written within the body of the text, while your observations are slightly offset. Your reflections should also include any particular effect you, as the researcher, might have had on the environment. You will not always be able to tell what your effect is, especially if you have no comparison, but other times, your impact may be easier to discern. Additionally, if questions arise or your observations contradict or change previous conclusions, you may want to include that in your reflections as well.

How you choose to distinguish or separate these types of jottings is up to you. You might want to put them on separate pieces of paper or in separate files. You could also divide your paper horizontally or vertically so each type has its own location. What is important is that when you read it later (or when someone else reads it), you are able to recognize each element.

Fieldnotes

For some, the jottings are just an earlier draft of the fieldnotes. For others, these are two separate processes. Those who separate the two consider the process of creating fieldnotes also to be a process of synthesizing the jottings with additional reflections, ideas, observations, and analyses you wrote down during your note-taking session. You might also find that you have a gut feeling about something or a general overview of a situation. Some of these will remain in your head for years, separate from what goes down on paper, but you will want to include others to ensure that your fieldnotes are as complete a representation of the field as possible. Since your notes are a shorthand version of what you observed, part of what you are writing is a more fleshed-out version of your notes. In addition to this, you will find that your notes will remind you of things you had forgotten or misunderstood.

You may have also written to friends or family members or kept a journal or diary. These likely include a lot of reflections but will also include descriptions and content. Be sure to look back at these other forms of record keeping when compiling your fieldnotes. You may discover something you missed that develops a new perspective on something you had previously thought of in a different way.

The transition from jottings to fieldnotes should happen as quickly after "leaving the field" as possible. You will know how much time is too much, but we would suggest not leaving it for more than 24 hours and not sleeping before writing it up. If you wait too long, you will find that data will be lost, as you will not be able to remember what your symbols mean or many of the thoughts that were important to understanding your jottings.

Your fieldnotes can also begin to integrate the different sections of your notes. Make sure to keep the distinction clear between your observations and your reflections because, as you analyze your fieldnotes, you will need to refer to the places that led you to draw the conclusions you did. To assemble the story your fieldnotes create, you will want to set the scene (with your description), present your evidence (with the content), and share your analysis (using your reflections).

Since they are intended to create a feeling of intimacy and presence on the scene, fieldnotes should be written in the present tense. What are your informants *doing* and *saying*? How does the community *look*? Even as time goes by, readers will remain in the field with you and will connect with what is happening.

Unless you have been told or decided otherwise, the audience for your jottings and fieldnotes is you. They should make sense and build a scene you can understand. Eventually, they become a part of your larger qualitative product, though, so your fieldnotes should include enough information to create a distinct picture for others as well. These are your data and will be for many years, so they must be clear and informative. If you pick them up 10 years from now, you should still be able to see the people and places described.

TRANSCRIPTS

During your qualitative research, you will likely find you need to record your respondents—either during interviews, conversations, or focus-group discussions. While the actual recordings are of use in themselves, as they provide context and tone, it is best to create a transcript of the recording as well. A transcript is a written copy of the recording that makes analysis, especially when done with data analysis software, more simple. It can also make your interviews and focus groups clearer to those who did not participate in them, because the readers do not have to battle with background noise, language, pauses, or interruptions.

To keep your transcript records clear, you may want to include some information about setting at the beginning of the transcript. You could include where you were, who was in the room, and the date and time of the interview or focus group. You might also include who conducted the interview. You might decide to use codes rather than names if you are eliminating names from final documents.

A transcript is generally written in a format similar to what you might find in a script, with some kind of identifier followed by the respondents' exact speech. Some people bold, italicize, or capitalize the name of the person speaking. Others may use a hanging indent, which indents the conversation but sets the name of the respondent or interviewer slightly to the left.

Figure 7.9

Interviewer:	What was your childhood neighborhood like?
Harden:	I was in a quiet neighborhood . . . pretty average. You know, not a lot of noise or problems.
MARK (Interviewer):	What is your strongest memory of that neighborhood?
Respondent (#0010):	I remember my bike. I spent hours riding it between and around the houses.

Similar to fieldnotes, your transcript is not just capturing your respondents' words but their meanings and voices as well. Therefore, you should write the respondents' words exactly as they have spoken them. This also means determining how much of the scene and their speech you need to record to re-create the interactions between you and the respondent or among respondents. For authenticity, many social scientists believe that every utterance should be included in your transcript. Utterances include verbal fillers such as "uh" and "um" or "like" and "you know." Often, these utterances are edited out when you include excerpts in the final document you produce, but they can provide information about the respondents' mood, confidence, or attitude. Background distractions such as a ringing phone or a crying baby can provide you additional data about how focused the respondents are on your questions and what other things are occurring in their lives. Pauses in conversation and restarts can also be important in creating your complete transcript. Generally, we use a dash [—] to indicate a stop/restart in conversation and ellipses [. . .] to indicate a fading out or a pause. Transcribers will often use brackets [ ] to note background information, such as a phone ringing. If words are unclear in places or you cannot hear what your respondent is saying, you should use a question mark in parentheses or use ellipses.

Because of the high level of detail involved, completing a word-for-word transcription can require a lot of time. Depending on your equipment and ability, it can take 3 to 4 hours to transcribe a 1-hour interview and will likely take longer if the interview includes multiple people, background noise, or interruptions. For this reason, some people opt to create a summary of the important moments of the interview or to index the important themes or codes instead of fully transcribing. If you keep a record of where in your recording certain themes are discussed, you can go back to them later and transcribe the particular conversation of interest without having to transcribe the entire conversation.

For those who plan to analyze their qualitative data with data analysis software (see below), a full transcript makes more sense. An abridged transcript means you may miss out on important information because you didn't see it as important the first time you went through the interview, analyzing as you transcribed. Having access to your full interview can make omissions less likely.

As transcription can be a lengthy and arduous process, you will likely want to find transcription software (if you are dealing with digital recordings) or a transcription machine (if you recorded on tapes). There are free and low-cost options to help with this, as well as more expensive options. You may also want to purchase a pedal, which will allow you to start and stop your recording without taking your hands off the keyboard. Be sure to research the options and select the best for your budget and your needs.

TECHNOLOGY

Because of the changing nature of technology, more researchers now are turning to computer-based methods for their research and data collection. While the foundation of writing the questions doesn't change, there are some important considerations to keep in mind when thinking about computer-based research methods. Many of the concerns about questions in general are also valid for research using a computer. You must consider your population: Are they a group that has familiarity with and access to computers and/or the Internet? If they are an older or less wealthy group, they may not be able to properly use the technology you have made available.

For others, the lack of portability (the ability to take questions with them in the car or on a commuter train, for example) might keep the work from getting completed. The possibility for variation in structure is also greater on a computer because people have different-sized screens, operating systems, and web browsers. This leads to a lack of control on the part of the researcher over what the questions look like once they are in the hands of the respondent.

However, computerized surveys do have some advantages:

- **Immediate data collection.** Because the data are entered into a computer, they can be immediately coded and entered into a database in preparation for analysis. Calculations can also be completed during the process. If a respondent says that he visits the library four times a week, the computer can ask, "During the 16 times you visited the library this month, how often did you check out a book?" Previous answers can also act as data for later questions. If a respondent tells you she went to Oberlin College, when you ask about her major in a later question, you can specifically refer to her time at Oberlin College.
- **Immediate response validation.** Depending on the sophistication of your computerized survey, you may be able to decide the appropriate form for each response. If you ask how many children a respondent has and you are looking for a numeral, you can program the computer to not accept an answer from the person who wrote "too many" or "not enough." A computer can be programmed to tell respondents to change their answers to something that fits the rules you have defined.
- **Creativity in structure.** The use of a computer allows for creativity in the way your survey is received by your respondents. A computer can randomize questions so you can eliminate the order bias. When a survey or interview is programmed, you can also include complicated skip or branching techniques. It is much easier for a computer to send respondents who have said they are married with more than four children to your survey section on "large two-parent families" than it is for an interviewer (or a paper survey) to find or direct respondents to find the appropriate section.
- **Potential portability.** While a survey on a computer may be more difficult for some of your respondents, others will find that they can take and

work on their survey anywhere. Those people with laptops, smartphones, or tablets may be able to continue to answer your questions whenever and wherever they have the time.

- **Supplements.** If you are creating an unstructured or semi-structured interview on a computer, you have the opportunity to add links to other information, definitions, or rephrasing of the questions. You can also add access to visual aids or extra space for longer answers.

In composing your instruments for computer, there are several possible revisions to keep in mind. Similar to a paper survey, instructions need to be clear. The individual is responsible for navigating away from problematic pages, so understanding what kinds of answers will be accepted is important. Respondents also need to know whether they can select more than one answer or whether they should enter a numerical value or text.

Since the actual paper can be seen and held by your respondents, a paper survey does not need to indicate its length. But your online instrument should begin by giving your respondents some indication of how long it will take and should also include a progress bar with page numbers or percentage complete so respondents can track how much farther they must travel before they reach the end.

As mentioned above, screen sizes differ, especially with respondents' access to mobile phones, tablets, laptops, and desktops, but you want to maintain as much control as possible over what your respondents see. Pages should not require too much scrolling. You will not be able to fit every type of monitor, but you can create a survey that does not overwhelm a page. About 50 percent of computer monitors have resolutions between 1024 × 768 and 1366 × 768, with 45 percent of monitors larger than that. However, if your population is part of a generation that may use smaller, more portable devices, you may not want to create your survey to fit a very large screen. You will likely want to include at least 50 percent of the page on the screen at once so your respondents will not have to scroll farther than one additional page when responding to your survey. If the resources are available, you may want to check your survey on several screen sizes or use a program that will optimize the screen for the device being used to access it.

Finally, because of the nature of a digital research method, you may need to get special permission from your IRB to use some kind of digital signature rather than a pen-on-paper signature. You may also have to create a digital version of your consent form so the school's stamp will be visible to respondents. Be sure that each survey entry still has its unique number and that the consent form and contact information are separate from the bulk of the survey.

DATA ANALYSIS

While instruction in data analysis is outside the scope of this book, we would like to take a moment to briefly discuss the technology used for qualitative and quantitative data analysis in the social sciences. As undergraduate or graduate students, you may not have a choice in software. Often, your school will have a license for one type of program, and you will have no recourse other than to use it. However, if you are in a situation where multiple options are available or you are able to choose, please keep the following information in mind.

Sociologists generally choose between ATLAS.ti and NVivo (this program replaced QSR N6 and Nu*dist) for their qualitative data needs. Both programs will allow you to code data—highlight particular themes—which is essential for analyzing qualitative data. However, they both deal with data slightly differently, and one may be more useful than another for your research. Unfortunately, several data analysis programs are exclusively for PC. Both of these programs fall into that category.

ATLAS.ti is generally considered easier to learn, and it also allows for relationships to be illustrated between the various codes. Additionally, ATLAS.ti keeps the text within its original conversation (rather than creating an excerpt), which preserves the context as you work your way through your transcript. NVivo is much more useful if you are dealing with very large databases and if you want to integrate qualitative and quantitative data, and it has a version available for managing a larger project with multiple workers.

Your choice of statistical software will also be influenced by the type of project you are working on but may be more influenced by price and availability than will your choice of qualitative data analysis software. Statistical Package for the Social Sciences (also known as PASW and IBM SPSS, although most researchers still refer to it simply as SPSS) has been a staple of many social science departments. It is generally user friendly and produces easy-to-read results. However, even the basic package can be expensive, especially for an individual, and many researchers find it limiting for some more complicated analyses. Some sociologists also prefer Stata, although it is more widely used in economics. Stata has also been favored for more complicated or less common statistical procedures. Both SPSS and Stata are available for Mac.

In addition to these two software options, researchers also consider several others. SAS has been around for a long time and can be good for very large databases (it is also available for Mac). R is very heavy on the amount of programming required but is open source, which means it is readily available online. Finally, Excel does not have the complex statistical support of most of the others, but it comes with most copies of MS Word and is therefore usually immediately accessible on PC and Mac.

If available, demonstration, trial, or student versions of the software may allow you to get a better idea of which software package you prefer, and, over time, you will develop your own feel for data analysis. Some of the student versions (such as SPSS) will actually give you a limited version of the software for a lower price. Some software will expire after 4 years, while others will remain limited but not expire.

Chapter 8 provides instruction on the proper ways to integrate your written data into manuscripts. Recall that quantitative data are generally more about the summary of information, and you will therefore use percentages, tables, and diagrams to represent them. Qualitative data tell the stories of individuals or groups, so you are including quotes, descriptions, and reflections based on your interactions with or observations of others.

SUMMARY

This chapter provides you with the information to create most of the instruments you will use in social science research. With this as your foundation, your research can address the hypotheses or research questions you are interested in and the chapter can continue to provide important advice as you work your way through the process. This chapter highlights the following:

- Writing questions for surveys, focus groups, and interviews
- Compiling fieldnotes
- Creating transcripts
- The use of technology in data collection and analysis

The "Writing in Practice" sections for this chapter are written by qualitative and quantitative researchers, both currently professors in California. Thurston Domina shares his experiences with quantitative methods, and Randol Contreras describes his thought process in trying to write up his ethnographic research.

WRITING IN PRACTICE

by Thurston Domina

I started crunching numbers and writing about statistics because nobody else wanted to. I was fresh out of college, working as a research assistant to a bunch of lawyers who were investigating the legality of a set of proposed changes to admissions policies at a large, public, urban university. The lawyers were interested in the equity questions the admissions changes raised. But to really address these questions, they needed a quantitative social scientist.

Admissions decisions at big public universities revolve around a sort of regression equation. A student's admissibility is a function of high school grades, scores on college admissions tests, and other extracurricular activities. The university wanted to increase the weight it placed on test scores. My bosses, the lawyers, worried that such a change would have disproportionate negative consequences for students of color. In response, the university released a series of tables designed to show that the consequences would be small and equitable. My bosses didn't believe these tables, but they knew the media and the judges would—and they didn't have the methodological skills to refute them. And that's where I came into the picture. I had no training in statistics, and my math background was mediocre (I just barely squeaked through calculus in high school and again as an undergraduate). But my bosses wanted me to make sense of the university's estimates of the effects of the proposed admissions changes. If the estimates were wrong, they wanted me to figure out why and come up with an alternative set of estimates.

In the weeks that followed, I got a crash course in quantitative sociology. I learned about sampling, weighting, multivariate modeling, and confidence intervals. But, more important, I learned that numbers have great power in our society. When the university released its estimates, it framed the debate around the proposed admissions changes. If my bosses couldn't convincingly refute the university's estimates, their legal arguments would fall on deaf ears. It occurred to me that learning how to produce compelling social statistics and communicate them effectively might provide me with an opportunity to change the world for the better.

The intuition that numbers are powerful continues to motivate my work and guide my thinking about writing in the social sciences. And it's this potential for social influence that makes quality writing so important. To be influential, quantitative sociology must be relevant and accessible. The easy way to be relevant is to answer a question that others are asking. The harder way to be relevant is to convince others to start

(Continued)

(Continued)

asking a new set of questions. But regardless of its relevance, quantitative research will have little influence if it isn't accessibly written. Our research is often complex and highly technical. But our writing doesn't need to be. The quantitative social scientists that have changed the world have done so by finding a way to communicate their research to readers who aren't quantitative social scientists. Doing so requires direct and relentlessly clear writing—writing that avoids jargon but seeks out revealing examples and illustrations.

But clarity doesn't mean simplicity. In fact, it seems to me that the primary responsibility of the quantitative sociologist is to make the process through which we draw our conclusions as transparent as possible. We can be wrong—everybody is from time to time. But if we've articulated our methods, assumptions, and findings with meticulous precision, we're less likely to be wrong. Furthermore, if we write carefully and thoroughly, our errors are likely to be identified before they cause harm. Since numbers convey authority, writing that is muddy and ambiguous is potentially dangerous. Like the judges and reporters that my lawyer bosses worried about, many consumers of quantitative research are willing to take our conclusions on faith. Quantitative writing that fails to fully articulate the compromises and decisions that underlie any statistical conclusion enables sort-of reading. By contrast, good quantitative writing makes that sort-of reading impossible, since it takes the reader by the hand and leads her or him through the entire scientific process.

—Dr. Thurston Domina is an assistant professor of education and sociology at the University of California, Irvine.

WRITING IN PRACTICE

by Randol Contreras

After writing fieldnotes, then finding themes and doing data analysis, there comes a point when I, as an ethnographer, have to make some serious writing decisions. I must choose a writing style, or voice, and decide on the amount of analysis and description. I realize that with whatever decision I make, there will be advantages and drawbacks in terms of academic recognition and reader satisfaction.

For instance, in writing up my research on Dominican drug robbers in the South Bronx, I chose to write in a clear and jargon-free style, which general readers would appreciate. I wanted my audience to easily understand the everyday lives of the study participants and not have to decipher complicated ideas in complicated sentence structures (which is the hallmark of most academic literature). And this took lots of work. I spent weeks, and sometimes months, ensuring that I simplified theories, concepts, and analysis while keeping the substance and complexity. It involved rewording and shortening sentences, shaving paragraphs, removing "filler" phrases and words, and replacing long words with short ones. Most of all, it took lots of rewriting. And then more rewriting. The payoff, I thought, was worth it, as readers would experience a memorable, smooth, and enlightening read.

However, I soon found out that there were drawbacks in writing both clearly and descriptively. After reading a part of my book manuscript, a colleague claimed that my research sounded too much like a "novel" and seemed as though I had "made it up." Then he grabbed two ordinary ethnographies from his office bookshelf and offered them to me as guides on writing up "real research."

Initially, I was offended, especially with the suggestion that my work was fiction or "made up." But later I realized that the simplicity of clear writing could put off academic readers who are accustomed to turgid, complicated expressions. Thus, they can interpret clear and simple writing as not being academically rigorous. Worse, they can liken it to journalism, which has no obligation to educate readers *sociologically* but mostly to tell stories of interesting places and people.

In the end, my challenge was to find a writing balance that incorporated description, analysis, and clarity. In other words, I knew I had to not only clearly describe what went on in the field but also noticeably explain it theoretically or conceptually. So in my book on South Bronx drug robbers,[2] I make the sociology obvious—I conspicuously uncover hidden social meanings and create new concepts to show that there is more than meets the eye. Also, I write *clearly* to avoid frustration on the part of readers, who may not have academic training. Last, I provide lots of description so readers have enough fieldwork data to challenge my analysis and also get a powerful sense of this South Bronx social world. In all, I realized that ethnography is just as much about the writing as doing the fieldwork alone.

–Dr. Randol Contreras is an assistant professor
of sociology at California State University, Fullerton.

NOTES

1. *Informant* is the traditional term for people who bring the researcher into the field. Because of the negative connotation of the word, many ethnographers have now switched to the term *respondent*, which we will use here.

2. Contreras, Randol. 2012. *The Stickup Kids: Drugs, Violence, and the Pursuit of Happiness.* Berkeley: University of California Press.

CHAPTER 8

WRITING EMPIRICAL PAPERS FOR JOURNAL SUBMISSION

As sociologists, we do not just conduct research to satisfy our own intellectual curiosities concerning a particular topic or social problem. We communicate and keep up to date about the current research in a field by submitting research reports and studies to scholarly journals for other sociologists to read. Research reports published in scholarly peer-reviewed, or refereed, journals are among the most highly respected types of writing within the academy. Each paper is read and reviewed by the journal's editor and, typically, by at least two other scholars in the area of study. These experts deem the papers to be new and important contributions to the field. The papers we write to submit to these journals are called manuscripts, as they are writings intended for publication that have not yet been published. This chapter will explore the writing involved in preparing your work for publication in a scholarly journal. We will review each section found within most scholarly journal manuscript articles. Although literature reviews were previously discussed in Chapters 4 and 6, we will revisit this topic again with an emphasis on how they are incorporated into manuscripts for scholarly journals.

JOURNALS

There are dozens of refereed sociology-specific journals, as well as journals that publish social science and interdisciplinary research (research on a particular topic from a number of different disciplinary perspectives). These journals vary by focus, range, readership, impact factor (how often the articles in the journal are cited, which shows how popular or respected the journal is among sociologists), acceptance rate (how many submissions they typically receive and how many they accept), and research methodology. Sociology-specific journals, as well as journals that publish sociological research, include the following:

- Acta Sociologica
- American Journal of Sociology
- Annual Review of Sociology
- British Journal of Sociology
- Deviant Behavior
- Electronic Journal of Sociology
- International Review of Social History
- Journal of Homosexuality
- Journal of Politics & Society
- Mobilization: The International Quarterly Review of Social Movement Research
- Rural Sociology
- Signs: Journal of Women in Culture and Society
- Social Research
- Sociological Insight
- Sociology
- Theory in Action
- American Journal of Economics and Sociology
- American Sociological Review
- Armed Forces & Society
- Comparative Studies in Society and History
- Economy and Society
- Ethnic and Racial Studies
- Journal of African American Studies
- Journal of Mundane Behavior
- Journal of Sociology
- Qualitative Sociology
- Science and Society
- Social Forces
- Sociological Forum
- Sociological Theory
- Symbolic Interaction
- Youth & Society

The discussion of the submission of papers to refereed journals may seem premature, particularly for undergraduate students and new graduate students. However, it's important to remember that journal articles are submitted under blind review, which means that as long as the paper fulfills submission requirements and is considered to be a contribution to the field, anyone can publish in scholarly sociology journals. There are, however, journals that specialize in publishing undergraduate research and work:

- Eleven: The Undergraduate Journal of Sociology
- Journal for Undergraduate Ethnography
- Perspectives, the Online Journal of Sociology
- SocialEyes: Undergraduate Sociology Journal
- Sociology—The Harvard Undergraduate Research Journal
- Student Journal of Latin American Studies
- Ideate: Undergraduate Journal of Sociology
- Midwest Journal of Undergraduate Research
- Reinvention: A Journal of Undergraduate Research
- Sociological Insight
- Sociology Undergraduate Journal

Manuscripts are often difficult to write, especially for students, as they may not know what kind of information, or even how much information, they should include in their papers. Your manuscript should provide enough information that someone else who reviews the same literature and conducts a similar project with the same methodology will find parallel results. The structures of these papers and often what is included in them depends on the nature of the project, methodology used (qualitative or quantitative), and the researcher's own style. Journal articles can be structured and written in a number of different ways, and the formatting style of the discipline will often determine that structure. Social science journals usually require that the author submit her manuscript in American Sociological Association (ASA) or American Psychological Association (APA) format.

The previous chapter examined the writing involved in research based on quantitative and qualitative data collection; this chapter will explore how to prepare a manuscript based on that data and the process of submitting it to a scholarly journal. We will also examine the differences between how quantitative and qualitative papers are structured and prepared.

General Structure

Social science research papers are structured to show the step-by-step process researchers used to study a social issue, from start to finish, but it is important to note that not all articles are written in the same format. Articles based on empirical research typically contain the following sections: introduction, literature review, methodology, results, discussion, and conclusion. Researchers use this structure to inform their audience of the research on a topic (introduction), how they developed their hypothesis (literature review), how they went about conducting their study (methods), what they found (results), their interpretation of what they found (discussion), and the larger implications of their project (conclusion). Most articles within the social sciences contain this information, regardless of the research method. However, depending on the nature of the qualitative project, it may be necessary to present the material in a slightly different fashion.

As you can see in Tables A, B, and C, the structure of qualitative and quantitative articles is relatively similar, as they both document the steps taken in conducting the research presented in the manuscript. Much of the difference lies in how the theoretical framework is developed and presented. Many qualitative researchers use grounded theory to analyze their data, and those who do focus on the process of developing a theory to explain the behavior they observe (or participate in). As a result, for many qualitative researchers, the presentation of the paper will vary, as these researchers are not testing a hypothesis, as is the case with most quantitative projects. Instead, these qualitative researchers are looking for the theory to emerge from the data

Table A:	Table B:	Table C:
Quantitative Paper Structure	Qualitative Paper Structure *(hypothesis testing)*	Qualitative Paper Structure *(grounded)*

• Introduction
  o Set the stage
  o State the problem/ issue
  o Respond to the problem/issue
 	
• Literature Review (this can also be incorporated into the Introduction)
  o Theoretical framework/ hypothesis
 	
• Methodology
  o Research plan
  o Participants/materials
  o Analysis
 	
• Results/findings
  o Describe major findings
 	
• Discussion
  o Restate hypothesis
  o Tie results back to literature
  o Larger implications
  o Limitations
  o Future research
 	
• Conclusion (which can also be incorporated into the Discussion section)
	• Introduction
	  o Set the stage
	  o State the problem/ issue
	  o Respond to the problem/issue
	
	• Literature Review (this can also be incorporated into the Introduction)
	  o Theoretical framework/ hypothesis
	
	• Methodology
	  o Research plan
	  o Participants/materials
	  o Analysis
	
	• Results/findings (some qualitative research combines this with the Discussion section)
	  o Describe major findings
	
	• Discussion
	  o Restate hypothesis
	  o Tie results back to literature
	  o Larger implications
	  o Limitations
	  o Future research
	
	• Conclusion (which can also be incorporated into the Discussion section)
		• Introduction
		  o Set the stage (this tends to be more detailed than in qualitative papers that test hypotheses)
		
		• Methodology
		  o Research plan
		  o Participants
		
		• Theoretical Framework (grounded—no hypothesis testing)
		  o Literature review
		
		• Results/Findings
		  o Describe major findings
		
		• Discussion
		  o Restate theoretical framework
		  o Tie results back to literature
		  o Larger implications
		  o Limitations
		  o Future research
		
		• Conclusion (which can also be incorporated into the Discussion section)

collected. As such, the manuscript is structured so that the emergence of the theory is examined and presented. That is why, as you see in Table C, the theoretical framework is presented after the methodology; the data must already be gathered before the theory can be examined to explain the behavior. The nature of your project will determine the structure of your paper.

Throughout this chapter we will explore the process of writing a manuscript, with a focus on the various sections found within manuscripts based on empirical research. Since most empirical studies within sociology tend to have the same basic structure, we will present our discussion of the manuscript section by section, including how qualitative research that utilizes a grounded approach is structured differently. However, there are several things you want to think about before you begin to write your manuscript.

Purpose

Social scientists write a variety of different types of articles. We write manuscripts based on research reports, empirical studies, literature reviews, theoretical articles, and case studies, just to name a few. We write this research for a variety of reasons. You should ask yourself a few questions to gauge your purpose before you begin to structure your manuscript:

- Does your research address a social problem?
- Do you have a solution to a particular social problem that you will address in your paper?
- Does your research address a disagreement or concern within the discipline?
- Is there some theoretical debate that you want to address?
- Does your research expand on what previous research has said about your topic, methodology, or theory?
- Does your research address a particular practice within a certain area or field of study?
- Does your project explore how an organization or a group operates?

Think about the common themes that emerge from your findings. What can you report from your findings? Once your purpose is established, you will then need to select a journal.

Selecting the Right Journal

As the purpose of publishing your manuscript is to ensure that your research is included in the literature or discussion on your research topic, it is vital that you select the right journal for submission of your manuscript. You want to make sure the right people (those interested in and informed about your topic) read your paper and learn about your research. This is imperative, because if your manuscript examines a topic or methodology inappropriate for the journal, the editor will likely not submit your work to reviewers (the review process will be discussed in more detail later in this chapter). This could result in your paper being rejected for publication in that journal before it even reaches other scholars in your field. For instance, if your manuscript explores the influence that religious ideology has on different racial/ethnic groups and does not mention the issue of gender, you probably should not submit your manuscript to a journal that specializes in gender studies.

It is also important to make sure you select the correct journal because by selecting a journal you are also, in essence, identifying your audience. Just because a journal may be a social science journal, sociologists are not necessarily the only ones reading it. Many of the journals we submit to are interdisciplinary. If you are planning to submit your work to an interdisciplinary journal, don't assume that your readers will know all the sociological terms and/or concepts. You may need to provide more detail and explanation, as the audience is not necessarily only sociologists.

There are a few guidelines that can help you select the right journal. You can ask your professors/colleagues for their suggestions on where your research might fit. You can also look through your literature review and your reference section. Do you repeatedly cite the same journal? If so, you may want to submit your work to that journal. The more journals you read, the more familiar you will become with the various journals and the writing styles involved.

Format

Once you have selected the journal to which you intend to submit your work, carefully read its *submission guidelines*. Submission guidelines vary by journal; some journals require that the paper be submitted in ASA format, others in APA. Some allow for submissions of up to 30 pages, not including tables and references, while others require that submissions be no longer than 20 pages, including tables and references. Journal submission guidelines can usually be found on the journal's website.

Instructions typically pertain to these areas:

- Word count
- Use of footnotes/endnotes

- Font size/style
- Margins
- Structure (format of title page, abstract, and instruction on how to organize text)
- Citations/references
- Tables/charts/pictures
- Permission (how to obtain permission to use another person's photography, excerpts from books, articles, etc.)

Some argue that it's best to construct the article first, find a journal that would be appropriate for it, and then restructure your article based on the journal's formatting requirements. Others would suggest that you find the journal for your article first and then structure your article from the beginning based on the journal's submission requirements. There are pros and cons to

Figure 8.1[a]

[a]American Sociological Association. 2012. "*American Sociological Review*: Manuscript Submission." Washington, DC: American Sociological Association. Retrieved April 2, 2012 (http://www.sagepub.com/journalsProdDesc.nav?ct_p=manuscriptSubmission&prodId=Journal201969&currTree=Subjects&level1=N00).

each method. If you write the article first, you are able to save the submission decision until the end, but you may find you have written something that requires significant revising to fit the subject area or format of your journal of interest. On the other hand, you could write something to fit a particular journal and then have to change it to fit another journal if it is not accepted. Either way, be sure to consult articles published in the journal you plan to submit your paper to as an additional guide on how to structure your paper, tables, references, etc.

Now that you are certain as to what type of paper you will write, who your intended audience is, and potentially what journal you plan to submit your manuscript to, the work of writing it up begins. We will discuss the sections of a journal manuscript in the order they typically appear (although the abstract, or a short summary of the paper, is generally placed before the introduction in the final manuscript, it is often the last section written, so we will discuss abstracts last). The length of each section will vary depending on the journal, nature of the project, methodology, etc. As you write each section, be sure to remember that you are entering into a scientific discussion on your topic and every aspect of your research will be held up to scientific inquiry. You will need to explain your project more than adequately and justify research decisions while also discussing any potential flaws in your project.

INTRODUCTION

The introductory section is typically only a few paragraphs long (although it can vary based on the length of the manuscript as a whole), as the primary purpose of this section is to provide the framework for your paper. Although not all journal manuscripts have a separate section labeled "Introduction," they all begin with a section where the author introduces the reader to the paper and the topic. In writing your introduction, it is useful to think of what drives us as social scientists to conduct research and report our findings. There is some issue out there that we, as social scientists, want to address, and some of us conduct research and report our findings with the hope that our work will influence some sort of policy or at least the way that issue is understood. As such, most of the empirical and even theoretical papers we write and publish reports on respond to a social problem or issue. In your introduction, you want to make sure you clearly state what your paper will address and how you will go about exploring the topic.

The introduction to your research has three main functions: setting the stage, stating the problem, and responding to the problem.

Setting the Stage

Introduce your topic and your reason for analyzing the topic. Although it is safe to assume that most of the people reading your paper will be somewhat knowledgeable about your topic and the issues surrounding it, you shouldn't build your paper on that assumption. Not everyone reading your work will be well versed in the issue(s) you are addressing and the theories and research methodology involved in examining this issue. To address this, you may need to set the stage for your readers.

You could do this by starting with a striking opening line. Think of a good book or an interesting magazine article you have read. They often start with an opening line or phrase that captures the audience's attention. In magazines or newspapers (see Chapter 10), this is referred to as a "hook." Below, you will find illustrations of some well-known opening lines from books you may have read:

> It was the best of times, it was the worst of times, it was the age of wisdom, it was the age of foolishness, it was the epoch of belief, it was the epoch of incredulity, it was the season of Light, it was the season of Darkness, it was the spring of hope, it was the winter of despair.
>
> —Charles Dickens, *A Tale of Two Cities*[1]

> It is a truth universally acknowledged, that a single man in possession of a good fortune, must be in want of a wife.
>
> —Jane Austen, *Pride and Prejudice*[2]

> It was a bright cold day in April, and the clocks were striking thirteen.
>
> —George Orwell, *1984*[3]

> I am an invisible man.
>
> —Ralph Ellison, *Invisible Man*[4]

Some of these lines are long and descriptive, while others are straightforward and to the point. Either way, these opening lines draw in the reader and set up the story. You want *your* opening line to do the same. Your introduction should grab the reader's attention. You may want to begin your paper with an interesting fact or statistic about the issue you plan to examine. A researcher exploring diabetes within Latino communities could start his introduction with the following:

The Centers for Disease Control and Prevention[5] estimates that the rates of diabetes among Latinos in the United States have increased dramatically in recent years.

Although not enormously striking, an opening sentence such as this not only would let the reader know what the paper will be about but also would highlight the importance of the issue you plan to address, as well as the importance of your paper.

You can also begin with a quote from a notable scholar or theorist. For instance, if you were conducting research on the response of a sample of residents to the high unemployment rates in their city, you could begin your paper with the following line:

More than 50 years ago, C. Wright Mills (1959)[6] wrote, "Nowadays people often feel that their private lives are a series of traps" (3); it would appear that today, very little has changed. Unemployment rates are increasing in both urban and rural areas throughout the country.

You can even begin with an interesting anecdote or story about your experience with the subject. This could be particularly helpful if your project is based on ethnographic research or some other firsthand account. For example, if you are writing about your experiences observing student–teacher interactions in a classroom, you could use a passage from your fieldnotes to start the paper.

Mr. Smith beamed as the students in his fourth-grade class raised their hands, both anxious and eager to answer his question: When did Columbus arrive in the Americas? Students jumped in their seats and called, "Oh, oh," as they frantically waved their hands back and forth, hoping they would be the one chosen to answer.

The author could then put this scene into context and explain to the audience how it is important to the work or representative of the issues pertaining to the research question.

These are just a few ideas for how you can start off your paper. The primary goal is to make sure you set the stage and provide enough background information about the issue for your readers.

Stating the Problem

Once you set the background or let the reader know a little about the over-all topic, your next goal will be to state the problem. Be clear for your readers (and reviewers) when you explain what the social problem is. Again, the pur-pose of writing the paper is to address a particular social issue or problem. You need to clearly define for the reader what this issue is and why it is important. You should be able to articulate clearly, in one sentence, the overall point of your paper. In fact, you can simply write:

This paper will address . . .

An opening sentence that is straight to the point not only informs your reader about the paper and topic but keeps you on track.

The nature of your project will determine how you state the problem. For example, if your manuscript is based on empirical research where one or more independent variables were manipulated, clearly explain to the reader which variable you tested. You could write:

This study explores the influence that the [independent variable] has on the [dependent variable].

Let's say you are studying the influence of fast-food consumption on the body mass index, or BMI, of teens. The independent variable in this case would be food consumption. The participants' BMI would be the dependent variable. The dependent variable is the variable influenced by (dependent on) the independent variable. For example:

This study explores the influence fast-food consumption has on the BMI of a sample of youth between the ages of 13 and 17.

The above example clearly explains to the reader the issue that the paper will address.

Responding to the Problem

Now that you have set up the background, provided the context for your reader, and described the problem, you are ready to explain how your research explores or responds to the problem. You are not necessarily explaining what the large-scale response to the problem *should be*, just how *you* respond to the problem with your research. This is the point in the introduction where you explain to the reader what your paper is about. In this last part of your introduction, you tell the reader why your paper is worth reading. In essence, you should be able to explain your theoretical premise and how your paper will address it. What do you think is contributing to this problem? How do you go about explaining it in the research you present in this paper? This is typically where the author would describe and introduce readers to her hypothesis if she were hypothesis testing. If your paper were to explore the influence of fast-food consumption on the BMI of teens, you would first want to notify the reader of the relationship being examined:

> This study explores the influence fast-food consumption has on the BMI of a sample of youth between the ages of 13 and 17.

You could then tell the reader what you expect to find.

> This project posits that increased levels of fast-food consumption will be positively correlated to higher BMIs among teens.

Some authors include in the introduction whether or not their hypothesis was supported by the research, while others wait until later in the paper to inform the readers of this. Don't worry about spoiling the surprise, as the reader already knows what you will find—you already identified your findings in your abstract (discussed later in this chapter).

You could also begin with a question and answer the question in your paper. For example:

> How does fast-food consumption influence the BMI of a sample of youth between the ages of 13 and 17?

Then inform your readers that your paper will explore the response to the proposed question.

Again, these are basic ideas about writing the introductory section of your paper. You could also seek out examples of article introductions you like (it would be best to look for articles in the journal in which you hope to publish) for ideas on how to organize and structure your introduction. It's important to remember, your introduction does not need to be too detailed, as you will explain your literature, methodology, findings, and analysis in the body of the paper.

LITERATURE REVIEW

Although literature reviews were discussed in great detail in Chapter 4, and briefly in Chapter 6, we will review them again here and focus on how they are often written as part of a research paper. Scholarly journals that publish empirical research typically require that your manuscript contain a review of the literature on your topic. Not all social science journals have a separate section called "literature review." Some label this section "background," as it reviews the background literature on your topic of interest. The literature review can also be included in the introduction of the article or within a background or context section. A background or context section is a brief section often found within the introduction that provides the historical framework for the study. Either way, you need to show that you reviewed the relevant literature on your topic.

The purpose of this section of your manuscript is to discuss what previous research has said about your research topic. It also describes the literature used to develop your research hypothesis or questions. The literature review explains to the reader what literature informed your argument. Most research tests hypotheses, and, as a result, literature reviews are usually found in the beginning of the paper. However, for projects that utilize a grounded approach, as explained earlier in this chapter, literature reviews generally follow the methodology section.

Your review of the literature should be written as an essay, with an introduction, body, and conclusion. The literature you present in your manuscript should be the most pertinent literature on your research topic, and it should help you organize and justify your research project. Even though a literature review for a manuscript for a scholarly journal is much shorter than one written for something like a dissertation, it will still need to be very well organized and structured. We suggest creating an outline for your literature review based on your annotated bibliography. This will help you see how best to organize and structure your review.

A majority of research manuscripts utilize thematic literature reviews. In this case, you will organize your literature review section by themes found in the literature. Each theme should be discussed separately, with effective transitioning sentences or subheadings separating each theme. Most literature reviews cover several different themes found within the literature. Remember not to go article by article but, rather, theme by theme, and focus on the links found between the books and articles. Since the literature review for a journal manuscript is relatively short—as manuscripts, on average, tend to be around 20 pages long—the literature review should be focused and straight to the point.

As we mentioned before, the nature of your manuscript and the methodology employed may determine the structure and placement of your literature review. Grounded theorists collect and analyze their data before the literature is examined and look for the theory to emerge from the data. The idea is that this reduces researcher bias when it comes to data analysis. The researcher lets the data speak to her before consulting the literature to explain the observed behavior. If you are taking a grounded approach in your study, you should look for themes to emerge from your data in a similar fashion as you would in looking for subtopics in your review of the literature. Once you have identified these themes in your data, conduct a review of the literature to see how previous research has addressed what you observed in your findings. The more literature you examine, the easier it will be for you to present your explanation and theoretical analysis, which should be incorporated within your literature review.

Your literature review will likely be organized by subtopics, which can address a particular theme, methodology, theory, or finding. The number of subtopics you will have or address in your literature review will depend on your topic and your research project. You may address only two or three subtopics, or you may have more. Again, all the research emphasized should directly relate to your project. See the sample breakdown below of the organization of a literature review on the involvement of college students.

I. Subtopic 1 (Student Community Involvement)

- Article 1
- Article 2
- Article 3
- Article 4
- Article 5

II. Subtopic 2 (College Student On-Campus Involvement)

- Article 1
- Article 2
- Article 3
- Article 4
- Article 5

III. Subtopic 3 (College Student Off-Campus Involvement)

- Article 1
- Article 2

- Article 3
- Article 4
- Article 5

Remember that these are not summaries of the different articles but references to the ways the articles connect to each other and the subtopic. Incorporating theory is also an important part of the literature review, as it explains to the reader how you developed the theoretical framework for your study. In incorporating other theoretical perspectives, you want to make certain that you not only understand the theory but also can explain how it relates your research.

You will then be able to develop the theoretical framework you will use to test your hypothesis based on other research and theories presented in the literature. This framework can either be incorporated into the literature review or can be a separate section presented after the literature review. However, the purpose of this framework is to explain how you came about the theory used to dictate your project.

Pay special attention to the following:

Be selective. You should be as thorough and exhaustive as possible in your initial review of the literature. However, when you write your manuscript, you should include only the literature that informed your project.

Focus on scholarly journal articles and books. Scholarly journal articles and books offer the best resources to help you develop your hypothesis, as they have been reviewed by other scholars in the field and have been deemed an important contribution to the field. Also, if you do not use scholarly articles and books, your reviewers may think you did not perform a proper review of the literature, and this may reflect negatively on their acceptance decision. We advise against including too many references to webpages, magazines, newspapers, and encyclopedia entries, but if you do include these sources, use them with caution.

Check literature review placement. If you are writing your literature review for publication, be certain that your placement of the literature review is in compliance with the other articles published in the journal or with the journal's specifications. Again, the literature review may be incorporated into the introduction of the article or could be labeled as "background" or "context."

Don't go article by article; go subtopic by subtopic. Your literature review should be written as an essay. Do not move from one article to another, evaluating each one. Instead, present the literature based on the subtopics and analyze the articles found within those subtopics.

Focus on recent literature. While you may have begun the research project with a collection of resources, we suggest that you continue to look through research during the entire research and writing process. In fact, you should keep looking until you submit the article for review. You will also need to show reviewers (and your overall audience) that your paper is timely and fits within the current dialogue on the topic. Leaving out an important study that relates to your topic could make evaluators think you did not perform a thorough literature review, possibly resulting in them questioning the quality of your work. Don't forget, new papers are published every day.

Focus on the top articles in the field. Within each area of sociology, there are key studies or research that most scholars in your field will have read or are familiar with—and that includes reviewers. Were the studies you chose to include written by the top scholars in the field?

Don't quote too much. Try to use your own words in defining something or providing a description. Researchers want to read your voice and your interpretation of the readings. You will provide a list of all the books and articles you used for your project in your reference section, so if readers want to know exactly what other authors said about a topic, they can find that particular article. Keep in mind that if a researcher quotes too often throughout his literature review, it is often a signal that he didn't understand the material well enough to put it into his own words.

Do not cite citations. Use primary literature. If you find an article or book that directly quotes or cites another source—a source that defines a particular sociological term, for example—and you want to incorporate that term or definition into your paper, manuscript, or thesis, do not cite another researcher's citation. Instead, seek out the original article and cite that instead.

Make sure you cite the proper article. Keep track of the different articles and books you use throughout your review of the literature. Be organized so you don't mix up research, forget to attribute a theory to the correct person, or mistakenly leave out a citation.

METHODOLOGY

Now that you have introduced the reader to your topic and project, reviewed the literature, and explained your hypothesis, you must inform your readers how you went about proving or disproving your hypothesis or answering your research questions. In the previous chapter, we discussed the writing within various research methodologies and provided an overview of several of them; in this chapter, we will explain how research methods are most frequently described in research papers. The methods section explains the *what, who, why, when, where,* and *how* of your data collection process.

- *What* methodologies were used to collect the data?
- *Who* is included in the data? Who was spoken to? Observed? Surveyed?
- *Why* were these data used or these respondents chosen?
- *When* were the data collected?
- *Where* were the data collected?
- *How* were the data collected?

The purpose of the methods section is to describe to your reader the methods used to address your research question and, importantly, to justify your methodology. The methods section also usually explains how data were analyzed. However, some writers opt to include this in the results section of the paper instead. Again, your methods section should provide enough information that another social scientist following your methodology would find similar results (reliability, as discussed in Chapter 7). This makes your research stand up to scientific inquiry.

The structure of your methods section will be determined by the project itself. The methods section describes your research plan as well as your data, including the data collection process and analysis. There is usually a difference in how qualitative and quantitative researchers present their methodology. However, the write-up of both methodologies describes the research plan and the study participants/materials used as data. Either way, you will need to present your methodology in a clear and organized manner.

Research Process

Describe the data and briefly discuss your research plan or the process by which you identified and gathered the data. What specific methodology did you employ to gather your data? Did you conduct a content analysis, ethnography, or interviews? Did you distribute surveys or questionnaires? Here you will describe your unit of analysis (what you are actually studying) and identify the study variables and how they were measured. You will also want to explain to your readers what your research design is and, importantly, *why* this methodology was chosen.

Sample

Describe your data and your reason for selecting these particular subjects or materials to obtain your data.

Study Participants

Explain who your study participants are, why they were selected, and how you were able to access them. Essentially, what criteria were used to select your study participants? How are these participants representative of the issue you want to examine? How many participants do you have? Some authors opt to include demographic information, such as race, gender, age, sexual orientation, religion, etc., of the subject in the methods section of the paper. Other writers opt to include this in the results section, as any findings concerning demographic information are a result of data analysis, which is usually discussed in the results section.

There are a few different ways to discuss demographic information. For example, research that explores student cohesion may indicate that race plays a role in this perception. In fact, this may be an important variable in your analysis. Therefore, it would be important to provide this demographic information about your study participants to the readers. However, you need to provide only the information that is necessary to explain your hypothesis. Typically, in qualitative projects, the researcher will provide a lot of demographic information about the subject, as qualitative work is often more descriptive in nature. As such, race, class, gender, etc. are often used to describe the subjects. On the other hand, in quantitative projects, these variables are typically used as a unit of analysis.

Race/Ethnicity

Describing the race/ethnicity of the study participants is common among articles based on empirical studies. You should pay attention to whether this is done in the journal you are interested in publishing in, as well as how it is done. For instance, if articles in the journal refer to Caucasians as White, you may want to consider doing this. However, it may make more sense to use the same terms you used in your interviews or survey to describe your subjects' race/ethnicity. If your survey asks the respondents to select from a list of racial/ethnic groups that you provided in the demographic section of a survey, you should refer to those terms in the same way throughout your manuscript. For example, suppose your survey states the following:

Please select the racial/ethnic group with which you most closely identify:

- Black
- Latino
- White
- Asian American

You should refer to your subjects the same way in your manuscript.

- **Correct:** A majority (N [N is shorthand for "number of respondents"] = 139) of the respondents identified as **Asian American.**
- **Incorrect:** A majority (N = 139) of respondents identified as **Asian-Americans.**
- **Incorrect:** A majority (N = 139) of respondents identified as **Asians.**
- **Incorrect:** A majority (N = 139) of the respondents identified as **Korean.**

Maintain consistency in the use of terms throughout your text, for demographic variables as well as for others. This is done for a couple of reasons. The first is not to confuse your readers, as the different terms used to describe particular racial/ethnic groups may mean different things. For example, there is a big difference between an Asian person and an Asian American person. Someone who is Asian is not necessarily Asian American. Likewise, someone who is Asian American isn't necessarily Korean, specifically. The second reason to be precise is to show respect to your study participants. The participants have identified themselves as Asian American, and it is not up to you to use another term to describe them. Researchers also often include "other" as an option on surveys and allow for the respondents to write in an additional race/ethnicity with which they identify.

Age

You can describe the age range of your study participants in a variety of ways. Again, depending on the nature of your project, you may find it necessary to be more or less specific concerning the ages of participants. If you are describing a group of people who would commonly be in the same age demographic, such as college students, you might provide an age range:

The participants ranged in age from 18 to 25.

If you are comparing individuals at retirement age with those a year before, however, specific ages may be important. You can also provide the mean, median, or mode age of the study participants. As you may remember from your research methods class, mean is the arithmetic average, median is the middle item in an ordered list, and mode is the item appearing most frequently in a list. In the description of the ages of respondents, an age range or the mean age of the respondents will typically suffice, although a mode could be informative in certain situations.

Gender

If it is necessary to describe the gender of your subjects, then you should do so. Most studies allow for respondents to choose between only female and male. As there are often only two options, it is not usually necessary to list the number of both female and male subjects. You would simply write:

There were 52 respondents in total. A majority of the respondents, 42, identified as female.

Here you would not need to describe how many men have participated in the study, as it would logically be 10 men. However, if you do choose to include a more open-ended gender option, you may need to include counts for other categories. For example, this may be the case if study participants may be transgendered or intersexed. You may ask them to which gender they most closely relate.

Unless your research consists of subjects who are all one gender, be sure to use gender-neutral language in not only your description of your subjects but throughout your manuscript. For example:

Use

Five of our subjects are postal carriers

rather than

Five of our subjects are mailmen.

Other demographic items you also may want to discuss, if they pertain to your research questions, include class, religion, nation of origin, education level, etc.

Materials

Explain what materials (such as books, newspapers, magazines, films, diaries/journals, pictures, artwork, etc.) were used, how they were selected, and how you were able to access them. List and describe the materials you used. If you performed a content analysis of Western films of the 1950s, you will need to list each film and explain why these films were selected. You may also want to provide more information about these movies, for example, in the endnotes or appendix of the manuscript (we provide a more detailed discussion of the appendices and endnotes at the end of this chapter). If you analyzed brochures, you will need to let the audience know what you looked for and how this will help you explore your hypothesis.

Do your data consist of an analysis of the transcripts collected in a focus group? Do they consist of a historical narrative? Whether you used secondary data (data collected by someone else) or have collected your own data, you will need to describe your data in detail to your readers. Did you conduct interviews? What were the interview questions? How long were the interviews? Consider providing sample interview questions in the text of the manuscript or even providing the whole instrument in the appendix of the paper.

Data Collection

Once you have described your sample, you will need to describe your process of obtaining the data from the study participants or materials. You will not just describe how you collected data but the specific procedures for data collection.

Location

Describe your research site. Where did you go to find your study participants and collect your data? Did you conduct an ethnography? Depending on the nature of your project, you may want to provide a description of the neighborhood or community in which your study participants reside. Did you conduct phone interviews? Did you interview people in your office? Did you interview them in their homes, churches, or places of employment? You have to describe where your study participants came from.

Time Frame

Identify the time frame for data collection. Identify the number of months or years it took you to gather the data. You may also want to explain how long it took for your participants to complete the surveys or interviews. If you conducted an ethnography, how long were you in the field?

Response Rate

The response rate is the percentage of people who actually responded to the request to participate in the study. Discuss how many people were initially approached, how many agreed to participate, how many people were actually interviewed, surveyed, etc. Response rate is very important to a research study. Let's say you read an article that says 129 people participated in the study. Would you change your opinion about the research, recruitment methods, or even study participants if you knew that the researcher had initially approached more than 4,000 people to participate in the study and only 129 chose to participate, as opposed to a project where only 140 were approached and 129 chose to participate?

You may also want to note if your respondents were compensated for the time it took them to participate in your study, as this may have influenced your findings or the number of people who participated in your study.

Analysis

The discussion of your data analysis can appear either in the methods section or the results section. However, it is typically found in the methods section of your paper, as data analysis is part of your research methods. What method did you employ to analyze the relationship between the variables? Explain how you will analyze your data. Was your project quantitative? Which statistical software package (e.g., SPSS, SAS) did you use to analyze your surveys? What statistical tests did you use? Did you perform a simple bivariate analysis or a multivariate analysis? Was your project qualitative? Which qualitative software package (e.g., ATLAS.ti, NVivo) was used to analyze your interview data? Did you analyze your qualitative data by hand?

It is also appropriate here to tell the reader what the unit of analysis is. What were you looking for? Did you explore certain themes or concepts? Let the reader know what these are so they know what to expect when you present your findings and your analysis of the findings. Keep in mind that you are writing about how you conducted your analysis here, not what you found after conducting it.

For longer research reports, such as book manuscripts or dissertations, you may want to include a brief review of the literature that justifies (or refutes) your methodology. This could also be useful if you are using a methodology not frequently used to study a topic such as yours. The literature can support your use of a particular methodology.

RESULTS

This section, also often labeled "Findings," explains the results of your study that are relevant to your research hypothesis and questions. This section should be written in a straightforward manner. To start off this section of your paper, you will want to restate your hypothesis to remind the audience what you planned to look for and what you expected to find. You will then proceed to discuss your findings. It is important to emphasize that this section is where you present your findings to your audience, not where you interpret or discuss your findings. Save that for the discussion section of your paper. You will, however, report your results and explain whether or not your hypothesis was supported. Here you will also describe how the demographic variables, such as race, age, gender, etc., influence your findings. You should present your findings organized around the various codes or themes you used to analyze data, keeping all like information together. As it is possible that your research might reveal an unexpected but important relationship, you can also include that here. You could also provide separate subheadings for each section.

It is important to present your work in a clear and organized manner. If you used a mixed-methods approach (both quantitative and qualitative) in the data collection, you should try to keep your discussion of the results of different methods separate. Present the results yielded from your qualitative analysis in a different section from the results yielded from your quantitative research. Scholars typically write and present the results of their quantitative and qualitative research differently. However, the incorporation of quantitative and qualitative research will vary depending on the nature of your project and the journal to which you would like to submit your paper.

Quantitative Research

For quantitative researchers, it is very important that the results section be written in a way that clearly explains the statistical procedures and measures conducted. Depending on the journal, you may want to avoid numbers and statistical formulas and think of this section as a translation of the statistics performed and founded for the audience. You would, therefore, want to approach your writing of this section as if your average reader has very little experience in statistical procedures. However, for some journals, a more complex mathematical presentation of the results is expected. Be aware of the type of journal you are submitting to so you can make sure your paper fits that journal's audience. In both situations, you will want to remind the audience of the statistical tests you performed and report the results. Explain the direction of the results and/or levels of significance. You may also need to explain the critical values and degrees of freedom. The purpose of conducting a statistical analysis is to ascertain the probability that the variance between the items in your data is a result of actual differences between people, rather than errors in your findings.

In your description of your statistical procedure and results, it is important to word your findings properly. Present the results of your test in sentence format. Explain in words what is being evaluated and what kind of effect those factors have. What was the significance level of the interaction? If an item is statistically significant, it means there is a higher probability that your findings are the result of the independent variable rather than random error. You should also inform your audience of the alpha level at which your data were statistically significant. For example:

Data were statistically significant at the alpha level of .001.

As you may remember from your research methods class, the lower the alpha level in your results, the less likely that some random error caused the findings. To illustrate:

Gender was statistically significant at the .05 level in predicting one's perception of household chores.

This example would demonstrate that the relationship between gender and household chores was likely not a result of an error in the data but that women and men actually perceive chores differently. Make sure to include your major findings in the results section. Include any descriptive and/or inferential statistics you may have found. How did the respondents' demographic characteristics influence the relationship between the dependent variable and the independent variable? If it is important to your research, you will want to explain this in detail.

Qualitative Research

Papers based on data gathered by qualitative research methods (e.g., focus groups, interviews) tend to allow for a bit more freedom in how work can be presented compared with the way quantitative researchers write their reports. Qualitative papers often blend the methods and results sections, as often the way researchers gather data *is* the data.

Another major difference between presenting qualitative vs. quantitative research is the rich description often used in explaining research settings or sites. Data collected through qualitative research methods, such as interviews and focus groups, tend to describe the subjects individually and in much more detail. This is done in part because qualitative researchers may not have as many respondents as quantitative researchers do. More respondents decrease the probability that the findings were influenced by error alone.

Qualitative research is more exploratory and, as such, provides the audience with a more in-depth understanding of the experiences of the study participants. Here, description is critical. You should include demographic information about the respondents, such as their age, race, and gender. You may want to describe what your study participants were wearing, the settings in which you interviewed them, their professions, etc. This is especially helpful the first time you introduce a respondent to the reader. Knowing more information about study participants may provide some context for their responses to your questions or for your analysis of the social issue being examined. The following is a quote one might find in a qualitative paper on the influence of small classroom size on student learning:

One respondent, Ms. Simmons, stated: "The more time I spent with students, the better they read!"

This example provides a deeper description of the participant:

Ms. Simmons, a second-grade teacher who has been teaching in the Los Angeles Unified School District for more than 45 years, believed that spending one-on-one time with students helped improve their reading skills. After one particularly busy class, Ms. Simmons exclaimed: "The more time I spent with students, the better they read!"

This description helps put the quote in context. The fact that Ms. Simmons has been teaching for 45 years may add some authority to what she said. Would you think differently of her quote if she had taught for 2 years? Providing more of a description of the participant helps provide legitimacy to both the participant's quote and your analysis of it.

In qualitative projects, interview quotes or descriptions of the data (for content analysis, for example) should be presented as data. Taking the above example, you could write:

A majority of the respondents in my sample indicated that the more time teachers and staff spent with students, the better they did in school.

Ms. Simmons, a second-grade teacher who has been teaching in the Los Angeles Unified School District for more than 45 years, believed that spending one-on-one time with students helped improve their reading skills. After one particularly busy class, Ms. Simmons stated: "The more time I spent with students, the better they read!"

The quote simply provides an example of what other study participants have indicated. As qualitative researchers typically analyze written documents, such as fieldnotes, diaries, journals, etc., as data, incorporating the text into the results section is customary. It is common to see passages from a researcher's fieldnotes used as data to describe a location or respondent. This helps add depth and give the reader a better understanding of the data.

Tables, Diagrams, Graphs, and Charts

Tables, diagrams, graphs, and charts that can better illustrate your findings are typically included in the methods or results section. Including these graphics allows others to visualize the relationships between the variables. A variety of charts and tables can be created, and the type of visual you create, as well as the format, will vary depending on the research method performed, type of analysis, software program, journal you are submitting to, etc. The visual most frequently used within research manuscripts is tables. As such, we will focus here on how to incorporate the discussion of tables into your writing. For advice on how to create charts, tables, graphs, and diagrams, and what types and forms are appropriate for the specific journal, you should examine how others have formatted and structured them within articles published in that journal.

Tables and graphs are most frequently found in papers that utilize quantitative methods and are used to provide a visual of the statistical information and findings. Tables are often used to chart information such as independent and dependent variables, demographic information, percentages, mean, standard deviation, significance tests, alpha, and regression coefficients. A well-constructed table allows for the reader to visualize information easily in a compact presentation. Tables can be constructed from the output of statistical software packages such as SPSS or manually created in programs such as Microsoft Office. As mentioned above, the structure and format of the table vary depending on the nature of the project and what you are trying to convey through the table. The sample table below illustrates statistical findings explaining on- and off-campus community involvement among a sample of college students.

When you submit your manuscript, it is customary to include the table or chart in the appendix and indicate in the text where you would like the journal editor to include it. Do not refer to the table's location in your text. Avoid the example below:

As illustrated in the table above, the rates of obesity have declined among . . .

The decision of where the table should be included ultimately is left up to the editor. Instead, say:

As illustrated in Table 1, the rates of obesity have declined among . . .

Table 1 can be located anywhere; just be sure to label the chart appropriately so it corresponds to how you refer to it in the text. You can provide a guide as to where you would like to see it placed in your manuscript. For example:

Table 1 Unstandardized Regression Coefficients for On- and Off-Campus Community Involvement Among College Students

	Dependent Variables On-Campus Community Involvement ($N = 453$)		Dependent Variables Off-Campus Community Involvement ($N = 453$)	
	Model I	Model II	Model III	Model IV
Independent Variables Community				
Connected college campus	.284*** (.335)	.278*** (.328)	.230*** (.252)	.225*** (.246)
Connected to off-campus community	.130*** (.037)	.123*** (.131)	.072† (.071)	.073† (.072)
University faculty/ staff support	.006 (.009)	.009 (.013)	.038 (.053)	.026 (.902)
Comfort in campus communities		.112*** (−.024)		−124*** (−.164)
Comfort in off-campus communities		.017 (.025)		.078* (.107)
Constant	1.285***	1.273***	1.536***	1.460***
Adjusted R	.160	.158	.088	.091

Notes: † $p \leq .10$ * $p \leq .05$ ** $p \leq .01$ *** $p \leq .001$; (*betas* in parentheses)

The chart or table itself may appear in the appendix, or the journal editor will do her best to place it near the location you indicated. The journal will include in its directions where you should include the chart or table when you submit the article. It may be in the appendix or in a separate file. You should check the journal to which you are interested in submitting your paper to be certain it includes tables in its articles and to find out what format it uses.

Wording of Findings

Be sure to word your findings properly. Your findings are based on a sample of people, books, films, etc.—samples you hope are representative of the general population with those same characteristics. As such, you cannot use sweeping generalizations to describe your participants or results. For example, in reporting your survey findings on perceptions of race in the United States, you cannot say:

> Despite Barack Obama's presidential victory, Blacks believe they are still oppressed in the United States.

Although all the Blacks in your sample may have reported that, it is important to clarify that you are referring only to the Blacks in your survey, not to all Blacks. If you are not precise in your language, it reads as though all Blacks believe this, which is clearly not the case, as you did not survey all Blacks in the United States. This could be rewritten more accurately:

> Despite Barack Obama's presidential victory, the Blacks in this survey believed that they are still oppressed in the United States.

Thus far, we have written up the important literature on the topic and the research hypothesis. We have discussed how you need to explain to your audience the methods you used to prove or disprove your hypothesis. You learned how to present your results and inform your audience whether or not your hypothesis was supported. Now it is time to talk about the analysis and interpretation of your results, and this leads us to the discussion section.

DISCUSSION

After you present your findings and explain to your audience whether your hypothesis was supported or not, you will want to analyze your findings. You will need to support your summation based not only on data but also on where the data are positioned in the larger literature. The discussion section is the most important section of your paper. We stated in the beginning of this chapter that your research paper is not just your way of entering into the "conversation" (albeit a written conversation via a journal) about a particular topic; it is also your contribution to this topic. The discussion section is just that—where the discussion of your research topic takes place, where you enter the conversation. As we mentioned above, the focus in your results section is on presenting your results to the reader, without interpreting their meanings. The discussion section is where that interpretation occurs. There are a few key parts of discussion sections, regardless of the methodology used to gather the data, that you may want to include.

Restate Hypothesis

To begin, restate your hypothesis and what you expected to find as a result of your project. It may feel as though you keep repeating your hypothesis, but it is important to remind your reader of your hypothesis, and the repetition also helps keep you on track and focuses your paper. If your hypothesis was supported by your research, explain how it was supported and what factors you think influenced this. Similarly, be sure to explain why and how you think you obtained these results if your hypothesis was not supported. Inform your reader of what these results mean and what the larger implications may be, not just for your research but also for the field of sociology. Again, the purpose of your research is to contribute to a particular area of study, so you want to clearly explain *how* it contributes to the field.

Connect to the Literature

After you discuss your hypothesis, you should then discuss the important results of your project. Inform the reader of what these results mean and the implications for your research. The same way you broke down various topics, subtopics, and library findings in the literature review may be helpful here. You can provide subheadings to keep yourself organized so you go topic by topic. It is also important here to tie your findings back to the literature and the theories you discussed in your literature review. Was the literature supported, or did your findings refute a previous study? Here you will have a dialogue with the literature and explain how your findings/research contribute to the field.

Larger Implications

As sociologists, much of our research addresses some kind of social problem or ill. Many of us write with the intent of influencing public policy or the community in which we study. For instance, our findings can be used to reduce health disparities or increase the quality of education, not only for our respondents but also for others in need. In your discussion section, you should explain what public policy and even practical implications your research has. Explain why people should care about your findings.

Areas for Improvement: Flaws and Future Research

No research project is perfect. Just as you feel you can improve on other people's research—and may even believe your project is an improvement on another project—it's important to realize that your research could be improved on as well. How would you improve your study? Many researchers choose to include a description of the "flaws" in their research and even label them as such. We, on the other hand, encourage you to think of them as areas of future research, which will be discussed further below. View any "flaws" you may find in your research design or methodologies as an opportunity for you or someone else to replicate the study. If your project explores the relationship between fathers and their children and you obtained your sample of 500 fathers from a list of fathers active in the Boy Scouts, this could be problematic. Even though you may think you have a really good sample based on race, class, education level, etc., your project is still biased. Who is to say that the opinions and behaviors of the 500 men are really representative of the typical father? Does the typical father participate in the Boy Scouts?

While there will always be sampling bias with most forms of data collection, it is important to realize what these biases are and honestly report them to your readers. Overlooking the ways your research can be improved, especially if you have an obvious flaw in your project, is ill advised. This will present negatively to reviewers and may also lead your audience to doubt your findings. By indicating where your flaws are and where your research could be improved, you are not only preparing yourself to continue your research but may also inspire another researcher to answer your question or address your flaws. While addressing flaws may seem discouraging, this is how we keep conversations going within our field.

Now that you have analyzed your findings, you can use this section to think about what your future research will entail. With the old saying in academia, "publish or perish," thinking about future research is always good. We know it may be early to think about a career in academia, but writing and keeping up with the conversation in your area of interest is always important.

CONCLUSION

As with the literature review and the introduction, researchers often combine the discussion and conclusion sections of a paper. Much of the information you can include in the conclusion of your paper you could also include in the discussion section, yet for the purposes of clarity, we will examine the conclusion separately.

Your conclusion is where you do just that, conclude the paper. Just as you introduced your research to your audience in the introduction, you will conclude the discussion on your research in this section. Start off by restating your main point and the overall purpose of your paper. Was your hypothesis supported? If so, briefly explain why and how. Remind your reader why your project is important. Additionally, some researchers opt to include policy implications and areas for future research here, instead of in the discussion section. Some journal editors may specify where your discussion of these topics should be placed. However, it is always advised to end your paper by answering the question, "So what?" This question explains why our research was important and the contributions it can make, not only to our field of study but to the larger social picture.

ADDITIONAL MANUSCRIPT SECTIONS

Abstracts

Abstracts are short, one-paragraph (or so) summaries of the various sections of your paper. Abstracts are typically 100 to 300 words in length, but journals are often very specific about the required length of submitted abstracts. Most research papers within the social sciences contain the following summarized information in their abstracts: the research question/problem, the methods used, the results, and a sentence or so explaining the study's larger implications. In writing the abstract, be sure to provide the reader with a thorough summation of your important findings and conclusions. Remember, a well-written abstract is often what gets the readers' attention and encourages them to read your paper. Think of the abstract as a brief synopsis of your paper.

Titles and Subtitles

Titles were addressed in Chapter 4, but we will briefly discuss them here as well. Ideally, your title will accurately represent your project and jump out at the reader. Be creative. Your title can be a play on words, a famous saying, or even a quote from a subject. It is customary for social scientists to create subtitles as well. A subtitle is often used to describe the actual issue being addressed in the text. Providing a subtitle that clearly explains the project to the reader can be especially helpful if the main title is catchy but vague. This can also be reversed, where the subtitle is catchy and the title explains the topic. Examples of titles and subtitles from some well-known sociological texts include the following:

- "There She Is, Miss America:" The Politics of Sex, Beauty, and Race in America's Most Famous Pageant
- Black Picket Fences: Privilege and Peril Among the Black Middle Class
- Stigma: Notes on the Management of Spoiled Identity

Keywords

Keywords are terms that describe the main themes and topics found in your paper. These are helpful because they help researchers find your article. As explained in our discussion on keywords in Chapter 3, these are three or four words that can be put into a library database to find appropriate readings that will inform your project. Thinking of the words you put into databases to find the articles you included in your literature review may help you discern what your keywords should be. If someone asked you to describe your research in three or four words, which words would you choose? Examples of keywords include *race, class, homophobia, gender discrimination, education,* etc.

References

Your reference section is based on the literature you actually referenced throughout your paper. This section comes at the end of your paper. Be sure to check the formatting guidelines dictating the proper citation style. As previously mentioned, most social science journals require references in ASA or APA format. The citations should be listed in alphabetical order by the first author's last name. Be sure not to change the order of the names for each article or book. The names should be listed in the exact order they were presented in the original work, as they are either in alphabetical order, as in this text, or positioned to indicate who did a majority of the work on the project or who the primary investigator is. As a result, they get first billing.

The reference section should include only the literature you referenced in your paper. It is important to remember that a lot of editors include the reference section in the total word count for the paper, so be sure to consider it in your total word count. See Chapter 3 for more information on formatting the reference section appropriately.

Appendices

The appendix is where you will include additional information that may help illustrate an example. Often, authors include the actual survey, consent form, and other materials used to gather data. Label the documents you include in the appendix and refer to these labels in the text. If you refer to a survey question that is not included in the main body of the text, you might say, "See Appendix for example."

Footnotes/Endnotes

Footnotes and endnotes are also used to cite information or to include a little note or background information on a topic that, although it relates to the issue, does not fit in the main text. The primary difference between endnotes and footnotes is their placement within the text. Footnotes are found at the end of the page on which the related citations appear. Endnotes, more frequently found within journals and books, are placed at the end of the article, chapter (in an anthology), or book. Endnotes are used as the citation style for writing in Chicago format.

Use footnotes/endnotes sparingly, as you should try to include only pertinent information on your topic in your manuscript. Footnotes and endnotes should be used only if you think they will provide context or additional information for some readers that does not necessarily fit within the actual text.

REVIEW YOUR WORK

There are a few steps you want to take before you submit your manuscript. Remember, presentation is everything! When you review your work, do not look only for grammatical errors (although you do want to check for those) but also check for the soundness of your argument. As usual, thoroughly review and revise (see Chapter 9) before submitting anything to a journal. Ideally, your work should be extensively reviewed by at least two other people. Review the following aspects of your manuscript in particular.

Argument. You should be able to identify your thesis quickly. Is your argument sound? Do you support your thesis with adequate evidence from your data? Do you provide a clear and logical argument concerning your analysis of your findings? Make sure your paper is focused and that you stick to the subject and examine only what is relevant to your thesis.

Terminology. Be certain your wording and use of terminology is correct. If you are not submitting your work to a sociological journal, you may want to avoid using too much jargon or terminology that those who are not sociologists might find confusing.

Transitions. Make sure the paragraphs flow together and that you have proper transition sentences or subheadings in your text.

Grammar/spelling. Check for errors in sentence structure, punctuation, spelling, passive voice, and citations. For journals, you should avoid contractions when using your own words and are not quoting someone who used contractions in his work.

Format. Check for margins, font size and style, spacing, indents, structure, charts, citation style, in-text citations, and end-text citations.

Word count. Be sure to stick to the word count. Journals usually provide a word-count range for manuscript submissions. If you feel as though your article will go over this range, contact the editor and ask if it will be acceptable. Sometimes journals will allow you to submit a longer piece. Again, the reference section is often included in the final word count.

Tense. Methods sections are typically written in the past tense; however, fieldnotes are written in the present tense. Literature reviews can be written in both past and present tense, but much of that depends on the literature you are describing. The discussion section is typically written in the present tense. The conclusion section can be written in the past or present tense.

First person. As described in Chapter 2, debate exists concerning how much professional distance should be maintained in your work. Some writers argue that writing in the first person is unprofessional and that you should maintain a professional distance from your research. Others argue that placing the researcher into the work grounds the project and allows for the researcher's perspective to come through in the writing. Typically, qualitative researchers write in the first person (*I*, *me*, and *we*) and quantitative researchers write in the third person (*he*, *she*, and *it*). In qualitative research, particularly ethnographic work, the researcher is often an active participant in the data collection process. As such, it makes sense that she writes in the first person.

SUBMISSION AND REVIEW

After you have spent considerable time going through your manuscript to make sure you have followed all the instructions and will be submitting a clear and coherent piece of research, you are ready to submit! (If more than one author writes the manuscript, the first, or lead, author is the one responsible for sending the manuscript and keeping in contact with the journal's editor.) Currently, most manuscript submissions are done electronically. You will have to go to the journal's website and follow submission instructions, which will typically include uploading the article, abstract, and title page separately from the submission or cover letter (see Chapter 2 for more information on writing letters). The letter is typically written by the first author and includes the contact information for the authors as well as a brief summary of the project. Most journals will require you to keep your name and all contact information separate from the paper itself, which is why you generally upload the letter and abstract/title page separately. This is to help ensure that your paper receives an unbiased review. Even if a submission doesn't ask for a cover letter, many writers submit one so the journal editors can gain some level of understanding of what the article is about and who wrote it before taking the time to read it in detail.

Review Process

The review process tends to take quite a while, and receiving a decision on your paper may take 6 months or even a year (depending on the journal). Once the author submits her manuscript to a journal editor (either electronically or through standard mail), the manuscript is officially "under review," and the editor will perform an initial review of the manuscript to ensure that the paper fits the journal's criteria. Editors focus on format (e.g., ASA, APA) and the research's potential contribution to the field. However, they are also interested in how the topic and overall structure of the manuscript fit their particular journal.

Once the editor has conducted an initial review of your work, she can make one of two decisions: send the paper off for further review or reject it. If you have received a rejection, the editor will tell you why the paper is being rejected. The material in the paper may not fit within the journal's criteria, the paper could have been poorly written, or the editor might not see the paper as a contribution to the field. You will usually be notified within a month or two if this is the case.

In academia and in research, the review process legitimizes one's research project or proposal, as reviewers typically consist of authorities in the field of study who are able to offer their expert opinions on the value of the paper and its contributions. When a paper is sent out for review, it typically goes through a double-blind review process. In blind reviews, the name and easily identifiable information of the author are removed and often a number is assigned to the paper. In double-blind reviews, both the author's name and contact information are removed and the reviewer's identity is also kept confidential. This allows for less bias in the evaluation of the paper. The world of sociology is surprisingly small, so the chances of a reviewer being aware of the author's previous work or even knowing the author herself are quite high. This could result in the evaluator not effectively evaluating the paper you submitted because he is influenced by your previous work. This would not be fair to you or your research. An important added benefit of the blind review process, as previously mentioned, is that a researcher can have her paper published regardless of whether or not she has obtained a degree, graduate or otherwise.

The editors will typically send manuscripts to at least two scholars who conduct research and have published work similar to the research presented in the manuscript. Once the reviewers completely read and evaluate the manuscript's potential contribution to the field as well as providing an overall review of the work, they will make one of three recommendations: rejection, acceptance, or revision and resubmission.

Rejection

There are a number of reasons why reviewers might recommend that the editor reject an article. These decisions are usually not taken lightly, and the reviewers must explain to the editors why they do not recommend the paper for publication. If the editor agrees with the reviewers' comments, then the paper is rejected. The author will be notified of the rejection and will often receive the reviewers' comments along with the editor's comments.

Acceptance

Reviewers can recommend that an article be accepted and published by the journal without any revisions. This is quite rare, and you shouldn't expect this to happen. Most often, acceptance occurs only after the article has been revised and resubmitted.

Revision and Resubmission

"Revise and resubmit" is a common response and indicates that the reviewers and the editor like your work or think your work would make a valuable contribution to the journal and the field of study but needs to be revised before it can be published in the journal.

The editor will inform you of the publication decision concerning your manuscript, either via e-mail, a letter sent by standard mail, or, in some cases, fax. The reviewers' comments and suggestions will typically be included with the editor's letter. If your paper has been accepted, you simply need to read through the e-mail and see what needs to be done next. If it has been rejected, take a deep breath and a few days off. Then revisit the editor's letter and comments to see why exactly it was rejected. It could be because the manuscript was deemed inappropriate, possibly in terms of topic or methodology, for the journal. There could also be a specific problem in the content of the manuscript. Although discouraging, these comments could provide useful advice for revisions or possibly for submitting your work to another journal.

If you have received a revise-and-resubmit recommendation, read through the letter and comments to see what changes need to be made. You should always take a few days away from the project after reading the revision suggestions. The suggestions of the reviewers may appear confusing, contradictory, and overwhelming, but at least your work has been positively reviewed, for the most part, and may end up being published. Once you have taken a few days to review all comments and suggestions thoroughly, make a decision on which ones you agree with, which you don't, why, whether or not you plan on revising the work or submitting the piece to another journal, and, if you plan on going forward with the revision, how the manuscript will be revised. Since a revise-and-resubmit decision is a sign that the editor and reviewers are interested your work and feel there is a place for your paper in their journal, we would generally suggest attempting to revise the work.

Before you actually set out to revise your paper, make sure to respond to the editor with your decision about whether or not you plan to move forward with the revision. This letter should thank the editor for the time invested in reviewing your work. Go through all the reviewer comments and explain, in detail, how you will incorporate them into your resubmission.

Before beginning to edit your manuscript, you should wait to hear back from the editor to make sure you both are on the same page concerning your potential changes. Also, be sure to come up with a time frame for your resubmission. Make sure to give yourself enough time to address all the comments and to submit a well-written and revised draft. However, you also don't want to take too long to resubmit your work. It is typical to resubmit within 6 weeks, but be sure to ask for or inform the editor of your resubmission time frame. Once your intended revisions and time frame are approved, it is time to begin the revision process. We discuss revising drafts in the following chapter, so we won't go into too much detail on revision here, but you should be certain to address all the reviewers' comments and suggestions. If you don't agree with some of the reviewers' suggestions, be sure to inform the editor why you did not follow those suggestions.

Once you have completed your revision—which, depending on the types of comments you have received on your first draft, could take anywhere from a few days to several weeks—it is time to write a detailed note in response to each reviewer's comments as well as how you addressed it. You will compose a letter to the editor explaining these changes (see Chapter 2). The letter and the new draft should be submitted to the editor within the deadline you both agreed on.

Based on this revision, a decision will be made by the editor either to accept your paper and publish it or not. You may receive additional suggestions and comments from all the reviewers. Again, if you do not agree with the suggestions and comments, you are free to pursue publishing your work with another journal. However, since you have made it this far, it is probably worthwhile to revise your work and resubmit it.

Most journals allow authors to submit their papers to only one journal at a time. This is done because editors and reviewers spend a lot of time and energy reviewing your work and they do not want to put in that effort only to have you publish with another journal. Unless a journal has indicated that simultaneous submissions are okay, you should try working on something else while waiting to hear back from a journal.

As previously mentioned, the review process can take several months, depending on the journal. Different journals, especially top journals within the field such as *American Sociological Review* and *American Journal of Sociologists*, receive hundreds of papers a year to review. It takes a lot of time and resources to look through all those papers and decide which will be sent out for review and which will be rejected. If you feel as though the journal editor is taking too long to get to your paper, you can opt to pull your paper and submit it to a different journal. However, you should always give the editor adequate time and remember that if you move your work to another journal, you will have to start the review process all over again.

SUMMARY

The focus of this chapter is on writing papers based on empirical studies for scholarly journals. We considered selecting the right journal as well as the structure of the typical sociology paper based on empirical research. In particular, we discussed the following areas:

- The introduction to the paper
- The literature review
- The methodology section and description of the research and data collection process
- How to discuss the results or study's findings based on qualitative and quantitative research
- The discussion section, which restates the hypothesis and connects it back to the literature
- How to conclude the paper
- The additional manuscript sections, such as the abstract, keywords, and references
- The steps necessary to submit the manuscript
- The peer-review process

This "Writing in Practice" essay was written by Dr. Colin Jerolmack, assistant professor of sociology and environmental studies at New York University. Dr. Jerolmack describes his experiences submitting articles for publication in scholarly journals and offers advice for publication.

WRITING IN PRACTICE

by Colin Jerolmack

Of my seven peer-reviewed articles in print, the most recent is actually the first paper I tried to publish as a graduate student. Before finding a home in the journal *Sociological Theory*, it was rejected by two other journals. The path to publication took 4 years and included well over a dozen major rewrites. Though I am the only author listed on the final product, my article was, in fact, a collective effort. It was through feedback from and conversations with my professors, colleagues, peer reviewers, and editors that I discovered what my paper was really about and what my unique contribution to the field was. Writing for publication is never an individual project, and great ideas seldom come from personal meditation. The next time you glance at a journal article, be sure to scrutinize the acknowledgments. Each person thanked by the author has likely read multiple drafts and contributed important insights to the manuscript. Also, the article's long path from first draft to publication likely included at least one rejection.

To demystify the process of writing peer-reviewed articles, allow me to tell you a story about one of my own. I once wrote a paper in graduate school, based on ethnographic research, about a group of male Turkish immigrants in Berlin who kept domesticated pigeons. These homesick men had cared for pigeons in Turkey, and I discovered that continuing this practice in Berlin enabled them to feel a tangible connection to their culture and homeland. While this seemed like an interesting finding to me, I did not know enough about sociological studies of ethnicity and immigration to know how my study could contribute to that literature. The first thing I did was draft a 20-page paper that simply described the men's relationships with their pigeons, the meanings they ascribed to them, and some of the recurrent themes. The paper contained few references and lacked a theoretical frame.

Though I knew the paper was raw and unfinished, I showed it to my advisor. He helped me clarify my thesis, pointed out flaws in my argument, and highlighted sections of the paper where I did not provide sufficient evidence for my claims. Perhaps most important, he suggested that I show the next draft to professors who were experts on ethnicity and immigration. This is what took my work in progress to the next level. These professors helped me create a reading list, map out a literature review, and identify which aspects of my findings were unique. After an extensive reading period,

(Continued)

(Continued)

I drafted a literature review and a tentative discussion section. In addition to returning to my professors for further guidance, I turned to my graduate-student peers to act as a sounding board. Did the topic seem relevant? Was the writing clear and logical?

Now I was getting somewhere. The feedback I received from my professors and student colleagues enabled me to craft a 35-page paper that contained all the major components of an article. I also used published articles as models for how to structure my paper. I was starting to gain some confidence that I had something important to say. After showing a revised draft to my advisor again, I made some changes, shipped it off to *American Sociological Review*, and hoped for the best. After 3 months, I received a letter from the editor and three anonymous reviewers. The editor rejected the article but invited me to resubmit a new draft that addressed the criticisms of the reviewers. It was apparent that each reviewer carefully read and thought about my paper, and they offered specific suggestions on how to make the paper publishable. Further, the editor offered his own advice on how best to move forward. I was hopeful. I had been given my marching orders, and I felt as though I could see a clear path to publication.

The revisions were difficult, requiring me to read more literature, tweak my theoretical frame, provide more data, and expand my discussion and conclusion. But I was once again able to turn to my professors and student peers to help me. After 2 months of revisions, I was ready to send my paper back to the journal. The effort paid off—within a week, I received a letter saying that my paper had been accepted! At the editor's request, I made some additional minor changes; afterward, the journal copyedited the document to prepare it for publication. A few months later, I eagerly opened the latest issue of *American Sociological Review* and flipped to my article. I marveled at how far the paper had come from that first 20-page draft, and I thought about the numerous unsung heroes who helped me out every step of the way. In the beginning, I was not even sure if I had anything important to say, and now I had published an article in sociology's best journal.

To publish an article, you have to be ready to swallow your pride and face rejection. That's the discomforting part. But the comforting part is that you do not have to figure out how to do it all by yourself. A publishable paper arises out of the writer's active engagement with a community of scholars. Even though I now advise students on how to publish *their* work and regularly serve as an anonymous peer reviewer for journals, I still rely on feedback from my colleagues just as much as I did with my first article. I still have to write multiple drafts. It is still often the case that I don't realize what I truly want to say until my article is near completion. And my articles still get rejected half the time. But criticism and rejection no longer bother me, because I recognize that they are necessary steps on the path toward making my work better and seeing my ideas in print.

—Dr. Colin Jerolmack, PhD, assistant professor of sociology and environmental studies at New York University.

NOTES

1. Dickens, Charles. 2010 (1859). *A Tale of Two Cities*. Alberta, Canada: Qualitas Publishing.

2. Austen, Jane. 2002 (1813). *Pride and Prejudice*. New York: Penguin Books.

3. Orwell, George. 2003 (1949). *1984*. New York: Plume.

4. Ellison, Ralph. 1995 (1952). *Invisible Man*. New York: Random House.

5. Centers for Disease Control and Prevention. 2011. "National Diabetes Fact Sheet: National Estimates and General Information on Diabetes and Prediabetes in the United States, 2011." Atlanta, GA: U.S. Department of Health and Human Services, Centers for Disease Control and Prevention.

6. Mills, C. Wright. 1959. *Sociological Imagination*. Oxford, UK: Oxford University Press.

CHAPTER 9

EDITING AND REVISING

Revision is one of the most important parts of the writing process. This is a point in writing that can be both the easiest and the most difficult to overcome, as well as a part that is often forgotten or not given the proper amount of attention. Revision is included in this book because we want to make sure it is not forgotten. This chapter is placed near the end because that is often where we place revision within our writing process. But that does not need to be where it stays.

Revision is an iterative process that is constantly occurring and ultimately changes your final product. You may go over a paper numerous times, changing something during each iteration. Sometimes you revise while you are writing, and other times you wait until you have completed something before revising and rewriting and revising again. It is important to remember that revision is not just something you do when you have the time; revision is something you are always doing. We hope this chapter will improve on your ability to revise and make the process the second nature it should be.

FIRST DRAFT

Writing always begins with a first draft. For students, procrastination can prevent moving forward in the drafting process. In many cases, the first draft becomes the only draft, as we run out of time to make revisions, decide it is not important, or lose interest once a version has been written. There is no particular attribute that makes a draft a first, second, or final draft. There is not a specific structure for a first draft.

For some, a first draft is little more than a fleshed-out outline. It can include the vague headings and subheadings you created to organize your research, along with notes to expand on each of your headings. It can be a new organization of your annotated bibliography (see Chapter 3). For others, a first draft can be more like a stream of consciousness. In this context, a stream of consciousness is a written illustration of your thought process. Rather than worrying about creating grammatically correct sentences, full paragraphs, or a coherent argument, you follow your ideas where they take you. Often, this includes questions you may have for yourself, places where you would like to follow up with more research, or even notes to remind yourself to speak to people who may have relevant information. Your first-draft stream of consciousness becomes a display of every thought you have about, around, or concerning the topic. Yet, there are others who feel that a paper needs to be complete in structure before it can be considered an actual draft. Again, there is no standard for a first draft.

What is most important about this step is that you get something down on paper. You cannot write until you have written. If that first step is difficult for you, you might want to try free-writing or stream-of-consciousness methods to start. Consider these questions: What do you know about your topic? What questions still remain on your topic? What brought you to this topic? What did you learn that you didn't know before? You can write this as a letter to yourself, a journal entry, or a series of notes. Write it in a way that is comfortable for you, and don't worry about structure or spelling or grammar. Just write. Once you have collected and organized your thoughts on paper, you will have a better idea of what you know and what you need to know. This may also help you think about how you have organized your research in your head.

For those who write with a little more structure, an outline (see Chapter 3) is an important foundation on which to build. Your first-draft process can begin with an outline as your basic structure. You create your draft by slowly filling in the meat on top of the outline's bones. Even if you simply have an outline with some notes, quotes, or places to look for notes, you can still consider this to be a first draft.

FIRST REVISION

Depending on the level of completeness of your first draft, you may or may not want to share it with others. Writers tend to be protective of early drafts, and the point at which you allow them to leave your hands is a matter of personal choice. As a graduate student, you might have a writing group to look at drafts of major writing projects, as there will be many of them, but as an undergraduate, you probably do not. However, being able to at least bounce ideas off of or read a draft to someone is important to your writing process. It allows you to see how other people understand your work and provides you with feedback on what you have written so far.

If you do have a writing group, guidelines may be set as to what constitutes a first draft. An outline may be sufficient for your group to read, as may be a stream of consciousness. In other situations, you may have a group where documents closer to completion are more appropriate, and, in that case, you may want to go through a revision or two on your own before you share with your group.

Some students may be worried about sharing their writing because of the unlikely possibility of someone taking their ideas. If you are at the graduate level, or you have someone at a professional level who works with you on your writing (such as a professor), you can make sure you have created at least two drafts of any major writing project before giving it to them. We don't expect your professor or colleagues to take your ideas, but multiple drafts may make you feel safer.

Once you have written your first draft, it is important to take a break from it. If you're writing a paper to submit to a scholarly journal or a grant proposal, that break can be a few days, a week, or more. If you're writing for a homework assignment, you might be able to take at least a couple of hours to distance yourself from your work. You will find that the quality of your work will go up as a result of taking the time to do a second read-through with a clear mind.

QUICK EDIT

Even a quick read-through can catch some common problems and produce a second draft; so many of the strategies included in this chapter can be modified for when you have little time. However, the guidelines in this section are specifically for when you have only a few moments to revise your work. It is better to edit quickly than not to edit at all. Make sure to pay close attention to the following areas:

Check Punctuation, Spelling, and Grammar

If nothing else, your readers appreciate a paper free of spelling, punctuation, and grammatical errors. Too many people present themselves as significantly worse writers than they actually are because they do not take enough time to catch the little mistakes they made. Read through your entire document, out loud, with a pen (or a mouse, touchpad, or touchscreen) in your hand. Where you pause, add a comma; where you stop, add a period. If a word looks odd to you, put it in a spell check, search engine, or dictionary and find out if it's right. Most word processors also have incorporated spell and grammar checks. If they do not automatically indicate to you misspellings and grammar errors, you should, at the very least, run these checks to ensure that such problems are handled. However, keep in mind that spelling and grammar checks are not perfect. They will not always catch a word you missed or used in the wrong context. Make sure this is not your sole method of editing.

Main Point

Be sure that the paper addresses what it needs to address. If you were told to answer a question, make sure what you have written provides an answer. If there are multiple points or questions, they should all be addressed in your writing assignment.

Supporting Evidence

You should be able to draw a web through your paper, connecting each thing you write back to the main point. The more secondary points you have to draw your line through—because a particular point supports a secondary point rather than a main one—to reach your main point, the more complicated your piece is and the higher the potential for confusion. Your reader should not have to go back several pages to figure out how to connect, for instance, promotion opportunities in the workplace with the lines at women's bathrooms. Even if you are writing an elaboration paragraph (see Chapter 2), the reader should be able to trace a direct link to a secondary point, which would then lead them back to the main point.

General Structure

Not all assignments call for an introduction and a conclusion, but unless you are simply answering a question posed to you, it doesn't hurt to include them. You can see Chapters 2 and 8 for instructions on the general structure of a paper and writing introductions and conclusions, but even a simple sentence that describes the route you will be taking with readers and another that tells them where they have just been provide useful bookends or a road map for the body of the paper and raise its quality level.

EXTENSIVE FIRST EDIT

Depending on the state of your first draft, it may need more than a quick glance to become a document you can share with others. If your first draft was only a meaty outline or a stream of consciousness, your first edit will have to turn that into a formal paper. While everyone has her own writing process, the first step in forming a second draft from a minimalist first draft is to find out what you have and what you still need to add to your document. Outlining, or re-outlining, is a good way to do that. In your outline, you should make sure every paragraph of your paper is accounted for. If you have used subheadings, you can use the same ones in your outline, and within those, your subsections can represent each paragraph. In a smaller paper, you might give titles to each paragraph and use these as the outline subheadings.

In creating your new outline, review the points you need to make and the evidence needed to support those points. Even if not included in your first draft, be sure there is a place in your outline for each part you intend to write and the evidence needed to support it. This way, you have a clear record of what you have done and what has yet to be completed. Once you have combined your outline with your stream of consciousness/free write, you can follow a lot of the same guidelines for other editing.

GENERAL REVISION

Ideally, revision should happen over several readings. You are examining a few different aspects when you revise, and it is difficult to do them all in one read-through. The more revising you do, the more likely you are to find you have a personal preference in terms of what kinds of revisions you do and when you choose to do them.

However, much of what you will read on revising will divide the work into content and form. Some people will prioritize one over the other and say that you cannot properly address one until the other has been perfected. Yet, consider a paper that is filled with evidence but consists of sentences that do not follow each other logically, or a perfect five-paragraph essay in which each paragraph covers a different topic. Content and form work hand in hand, and in editing, it's important that both get the appropriate amount of attention.

Generally, revision is a spiraling process that can be never-ending if you allow it to be. You can ask almost any writer about a work he "completed" and he will tell you about a mistake he made, something he wished he had done differently, or edits he made too late. Some academics hate to read their past writing because they know they are going to find those mistakes they missed. Others look back on their previous work as an opportunity to learn from their missteps. Revision is really never complete, but once you are comfortable with your writing, you can make a decision on when to stop.

Regardless of when it ends, revision always begins with a read-through. As mentioned above, this is best done after you have put the piece aside for a period of time. A week or more is ideal, but if this is impossible, a few days works well or, at the very least, an hour or two. Without that time to give your mind a break from your work, you are very likely to miss errors, and you lose the ability to recognize what you have excluded because it may still be present in your mind even if it isn't in your paper.

As you read through your work, be prepared either to edit or to make note of where to edit. For some of us, especially those who did not grow up completely immersed in a digital culture, editing is easier by hand. Without the same level of editing software on tablets or smartphones, a pen or pencil and a hard copy allow for mobility that a computer or laptop may not.

Word-processing programs are equipped with different supports to assist in your editing process. For some, especially those who edit others' work or have others edit their work, add-ons such as Microsoft Word's "track changes" feature are invaluable. Track changes allows you to insert or delete pieces of text without losing them completely. Depending on your settings, track changes will either strike out deleted text or place it in a bubble alongside your text. This allows your changes to be temporary until you have accepted or rejected them. Track changes will also keep track of who has added which edits and when. While Google Documents does not keep a record of changes in as visual a way as Word's track changes does, it also has the option to see what changes you or others have made to your document. Additionally, one of the important aspects of something such as a wiki (interlinked and connected webpages) is the ability to collaborate and see what each person has done.

For those who choose to edit by hand, copyeditor symbols are often used to note changes to be made to the structure of the document.

As we move into the further digitized nature of the written word, mobile devices become another possibility for editing. This is not yet a norm, but as more people use e-readers, tablets, and phones to read their documents, especially longer ones, they will also use them more for revision. While much of the technology currently available does not allow for complex editing, such as that available on a computer, you can always take notes on what to enter into a document later or simply change the document, if that option is available. Tablets and smartphones can connect the digital age with the editing we do by hand, and you may also be able to find word-processing–based applications to assist in the process.

Figure 9.1

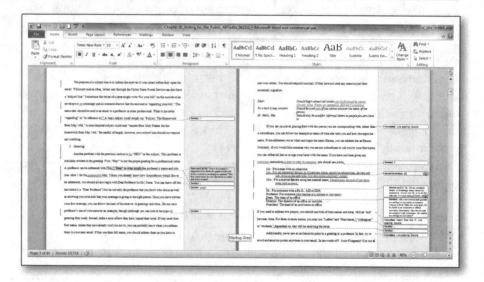

Figure 9.2

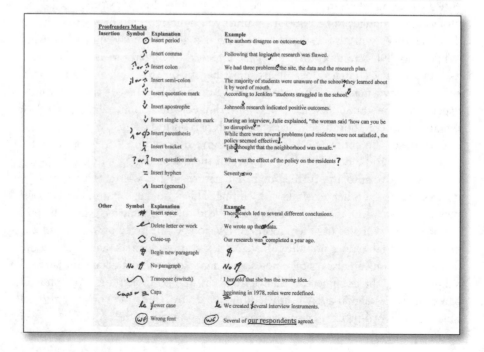

When revising, remember that you are trying to make the document into something another reader can understand without you having to hold her hand. The reader will not know what you meant by something unless you explain it. She will not know what your voice sounds like or how you meant to set up your argument unless you do it. For this reason, having someone else (or yourself after some time away) read your document can be very informative.

Revision works best when you recognize all the pieces of your document and how they work together to support the whole. This is likely easiest when you start with the larger pieces and work your way down to the smaller elements.

FULL DOCUMENT

When considering the paper as a whole, ask yourself whether it serves the larger goals of your assignment, research question, or hypothesis. The most important question for each section of the paper is, "Does this answer the question?" You want to be sure that by the time someone has completed your piece, he has the answer to the question you posed or has received an adequate reason for why the question cannot be answered and/or how it might be answered in the future.

As sociologists, the questions we research cannot be answered with simply a yes or no; they are questions that explore how and why things happen and the relationships between various elements. So, when considering whether your question has been answered, you need to consider not just the simple yes or no but the explanation of the relationship—not only the who, what, where, and when but also the why and how—and recall that the last two are generally the most important to sociologists.

If the question has not been answered, what is unclear or missing from your work? What would answer the question? This may be the most difficult thing to judge if you are editing your own work, as the answer to the main question may seem clearer to you than it would to your reader. Once you can say that your question has been answered, you can go on to the next section. Keep in mind that you may need to come back to this question after you've gone through the rest of your revisions to ensure that your paper still fulfills its purpose.

SUBSECTIONS/SUBHEADINGS

We have examined, in their respective chapters, the types of sections, headings, and subheadings you might need for your paper. These depend on what you are writing, as each section exists to support the overall purpose of the document. The sections should serve as landmarks or signposts leading the reader through the map of your document. In fact, you should be able to take only the introductory and concluding paragraphs of each section and know exactly where you are going, where you've been, and why. Each section should begin with a paragraph that explains where you are taking the reader, why you are taking her there (what does this have to do with the main purpose of the document?), and where you are taking her next. A good exercise during revision is to create an actual document map, which includes each introductory and concluding paragraph. If you can follow the path of your paper through those paragraphs, it likely holds together well. If you find that once you don't have access to the meat of your subsections, you can no longer follow your argument, you will need to clarify the confusing paragraphs.

While headings and subheadings are intended to provide directional arrows for an individual working his way through your work, they are not an excuse for ignoring transitions between paragraphs. You should avoid, or edit out, all unnecessary turns into a new topic (or a new take on an old topic) without some kind of proper indication of what is happening. Transitions between paragraphs are built on transitory terms. Are you building on your previous point (*additionally, secondarily, next, finally*)? Are you presenting an opposing viewpoint (*alternately, however*)? Are you providing a conclusion or evidence for the point you just made (*therefore, it follows*)? These particular words do not need to be present every time you make a transition, but the idea behind them should be, and some type of indicator needs to be used to tell your reader where to go.

Introductions and conclusions are specific types of subsections. Although the body of your work will change depending on the type of writing you are doing, these sections will be present in every academic piece you write. For many writers, the introduction and conclusion are the hardest pieces of the writing process. Introductions and conclusions ask you to take the bulk of your work and turn it into something more manageable. They also force you to take yourself outside of the specifics of your work and connect it to something larger in your field, in academia in general, or the world at large. Often, it is during the revision process that these pieces get the fair treatment they need.

You want to think of your introduction and conclusion as an hourglass. You begin your introduction broadly, bringing the reader in by making a connection to a larger issue or problem. Then you become narrower as you approach your hypothesis, thesis, or research question. Following the explanation of your topic in the body of the text, the conclusion brings your work back to your research question or thesis to ensure you have addressed it and then broadens again to a larger issue or the application of your work. Chapter 8 goes into further detail on the composition of an introduction and conclusion.

Once you have completed the paper, you should always return to the introduction and conclusion. You want to ask yourself, What are the larger issues this research addresses or could be applied to? Did I mention them in the introduction? Did I explain how I addressed them in my conclusion? Ask someone to read your introduction and conclusion. Can she tell what the rest of the paper is about? You may need to completely rewrite your introduction and conclusion once you've written your paper, as a paper can sometimes go in unexpected directions, but don't be afraid of that process. It is better to rewrite than to keep an old introduction to a paper that turned out completely different than you originally intended.

From the introduction and conclusion, we can move into even smaller subsections. Each paragraph is used to build your piece, and the paragraphs themselves are built by words and sentences. In an ideal editing situation, you should go through your piece to ensure that every part is necessary. Does each word support each sentence? Could this be accomplished in a better way? Does every sentence support the paragraph? Could this be done better? Does every paragraph support the subsection or document as a whole?

Recall that each paragraph should be a mini paper within itself. Each should have at least one introductory sentence, and the body of the paragraph should end with concluding sentences that transition into the next paragraph. While you may not have accomplished this during the original writing, you have an opportunity during revision to address these areas to create a better flow in your document.

If you have made any major revisions, you should return to your larger questions. Is your piece still on topic? Does it still serve the purpose you had intended? If not, make sure to review the changes you made to maintain the overall meaning.

DETAIL WORK

Finally, people often face common problems in writing academically. You should take special note of these items to be sure you do not overlook them in your own writing.

Voice

For most of the writing in this book, you are attempting to write in an academic and formal voice. Producing this means reading a lot of the type of writing you are trying to create and comparing your work with that of others. If you are writing for a particular journal, do not just read a handful of articles from a variety of different journals. Find articles from the journal you want to publish in and read those. If you are working on a grant, try to get access to other grants to give you a structure within which to place your piece.

Changing voice may include removing informal words and replacing them with more formal ones. This could also include varying sentence length by shortening some and lengthening others. You should rely on the ear you have developed from reading similar writing to find the appropriate balance between long and short sentences. Another revision that can help with voice is structuring active sentences. Passive sentences often sound more academic; however, a captivating voice includes an active presentation.

Structure

While the structure will vary depending on what you're writing (see Chapter 8 for more information), you should be sure to be consistent once you have chosen your structure. If you are supposed to go from an introduction to a literature review, methods, results, discussion, and conclusion, you should make sure to do that properly and smoothly. You should also make sure that each section includes the appropriate type of information (see Chapter 8 for more on this). Your subheadings should make sense as the name of a section and as a stop on the path through your paper. Some people advise that section titles should not simply be a suggestion but, rather, should be clear and directly referred to in the context of the surrounding section— the more creative a subheading, the less of an academic impression your paper will leave. Subheadings should work together with the content to hold the entire piece together.

Specificity

Check your paper for places where you have used general words such as *them*, *they*, *we*, or *us*. Even words such as *researchers* or *academics* could be more specific. Who, in particular, are you referring to? If you do not change the word to someone (or several someones) in particular, the sentences either before or after should give a specific example of who the people are to whom you are referring. Time periods should also be specified. If you do not know the exact time period, and cannot find it, you should be as specific as you can. This will at least provide your readers with some context.

Quotes

Quotes are the evidence that supports your points. Generally, you want a paper to be no more than 10 percent direct quotes from other sources (this does not include quotes from qualitative research you have conducted). You should be careful not to overburden your writing with direct quotes from other people, but you also must take care to provide enough evidence to support your arguments.

You should also be sure that the quotes you have used are well explained (a sentence before or afterward will usually accomplish that) and are the best possible quotes to make your point. If you remove the quote, can a reader still make a connection between the point you are making and your explanation of the evidence? If not, change the quote or rethink the connection. This is something you may have to check and recheck several times. Do not forget to reread your quotes as you revise your piece. While the quote will not change, the context that follows it might. You may have removed the point you made but forgot to remove the quote supporting it.

Each quote should be properly referenced in American Sociological Association, American Psychological Association, or some other formatting style, and every paraphrase should be indicated with the proper citation (see Chapter 3 for information on referencing). Any time you do not do this, you are plagiarizing (see Chapter 3). Additionally, without some indication, switching from your voice to the voice of whoever wrote the piece you are quoting breaks the flow of your work.

Don't forget to circle back through the paper if you have made any major changes to your work. Few things are more frustrating than putting a lot of work into writing and revising a piece and then ruining the flow or the structure because you didn't have the time to look it over again.

The revision process can take a long time if done well. We have given you some suggestions for shortening the process, but if you have the time, you should take it. It is certainly worth it. A detailed revision process can help turn a good paper into a great one.

SUMMARY

This chapter focuses on the process of editing and revising. It covers important topics for writing at all levels:

- First drafts and first revisions
- Quick to extensive revisions

- Revising at the level of the complete document, the subsections/subheadings, and detail work

While this "Writing in Practice" piece covers more advanced writing, the advice is applicable to all writers. We all go through the process of getting feedback and feeling discouraged about it and/or not knowing how to respond. Dr. Holstein's advice is as useful to those writing first drafts of papers for their undergraduate courses as for those who have received a "revise and resubmit" recommendation on an article.

WRITING IN PRACTICE

by James A. Holstein

Most sociological publications go through multiple revisions before appearing in print. There isn't a publishing sociologist around who hasn't submitted a paper (seemingly honed to perfection) and subsequently been asked to "revise and resubmit" the paper for further review. It's vital that authors don't take this as rejection but, rather, as an opportunity to enhance, enrich, and otherwise upgrade the manuscript—to make it really good.

Over the years, I've submitted dozens of journal articles, but only a couple of these manuscripts were accepted without substantial revision. I've also served as editor of a major sociological journal that considered hundreds of submissions annually. As editor, I never accepted a paper without requiring some form of revision. Most articles go through at least two or three new drafts before publication. Thus, revising a paper—sometimes dramatically—is par for the course, even for the most successful authors. It's an integral part of the writing and publishing process. Journals are typically peer reviewed—that is, critiqued by a number of experts in the field—and, like your professor, the reviewers' job is to offer *constructive* criticism. Responding to conscientious professional reviews is an opportunity to improve your paper. To that end, I'll offer some suggestions about approaching the revision process from a positive perspective.

Don't (Over) React Immediately or Defensively

If asked to revise a paper, don't be disheartened. Resist the initial impulse to throw the request in the trash. Read the explanation and/or reviewers' comments, but don't dwell on them. Set the comments aside and let your thoughts "mellow" for a day or two. As emotions subside, read the comments again, carefully assessing what they say.

Take Stock

Make a careful, comprehensive outline of things you need to address. Don't omit issues from your list just because you disagree with whoever has reviewed your paper. The critiques are there; don't kid yourself about being able to ignore or finesse them. If a professor or set of reviewers identifies concerns, you need to deal with them.

Ask the Editor or Professor

Perhaps the most daunting aspect of revising is dealing with countervailing or contradictory suggestions. Nothing is more vexing than for one reviewer to suggest "X" while a second reviewer suggests "not X" and still another thinks the issue is really about "Y." One way to deal with the quandary is to seek the professor's or journal editor's guidance. The editor may have already offered suggestions in her or his appraisal of the paper (if so, take this to heart), but a straightforward request for advice and direction, either in a phone call or e-mail, is perfectly appropriate. Remember that the editor has a vested interest in seeing your paper published, too, so she or he is highly motivated to help with a successful revision.

Create a Strategy

There are many ways to address criticism, but you need to be clearly responsive to the reviews. Frequently, you can address reviewers' comments straightforwardly, as matters of clarification. Setting emotion and ego aside, develop a list of changes that can easily be made. More problematic issues will require additional consideration. Here are three common approaches that writers take to dealing with major criticisms, with some thoughts about their appropriateness:

- **"I didn't say that!"** (Or, alternatively, **"That's what I said!"**) If you didn't say what a reviewer claims you did, or if you think you said precisely what a reviewer said you ignored, look carefully at your manuscript to determine why the reader misunderstood you. Ask how *you* might have caused the confusion. Was the writing unclear or the logic faulty? Did you assume too much about what readers would or would not know? Clean up your argument and be very explicit about what you mean to say.
- **"I don't want to say/do that!"** After carefully considering reviewers' comments, you may disagree with some suggestions or criticisms. Rather than ignoring those comments, anticipate them in your text. Engage alternate arguments and potential criticisms, briefly outlining those lines of thought and explaining why

(Continued)

(Continued)

your approach is more appropriate. You don't have to agree with a critic to engage the critic's argument and state your case.

- **"I never thought of that!"** When reviewers' comments "make sense," take advantage by exploring the possibilities you may have previously overlooked. Don't be stubborn when new opportunities arise.

Pay Close Attention to the Writing: Make It Crystal Clear!

- *Read your manuscript aloud.* This helps identify unclear writing.
- *Don't assume anything is self-evident.* Make your arguments clear and explicit.
- *Explain your analytic vocabulary.* Eliminate gratuitous jargon while making sure the reader knows exactly what you mean by the specialized terminology you use.
- *Don't skimp on the methods section.* This is where you demonstrate that your arguments have empirical merit. It's where you convince readers to believe what you say.
- *Streamline!* Make arguments and prose simple, direct, and parsimonious. Write in an active voice. Avoid redundancy. You can usually reduce wordiness without sacrificing anything but length. "He said X" is three words. "X was made evident in conversation by him" is seven. Do the math!

Dealing With Advice That Seems Conflicting

Here's a common challenge that makes authors cringe: "Say more about several issues, but cut the paper by 2,000 words." The reviser's dilemma: How do you say more with less? First, decide what is absolutely essential to the paper. Then ask the editor for advice on what you might reasonably cut. Do the best you can to address problematic issues while continuing to streamline.

Write a Succinct, Comprehensive Memo Explaining Your Revisions

If you are submitting to a journal, editors often ask authors to submit memos of explanation or letters to the editor along with their revised manuscripts. Invited or not, this is an excellent opportunity (1) to indicate how you've taken reviewers' comments to heart and (2) to explain why particular comments haven't been incorporated into the revision. This memo helps reviewers discern how you've addressed criticisms, and, at the very least, shows the editor and reviewers that you didn't simply ignore or dismiss them.

—Dr. James A. Holstein, PhD, is a professor of sociology
in the Department of Social and Cultural Sciences
at Marquette University.

CHAPTER 10

WRITING FOR THE PUBLIC

As sociologists, we are often called on to share our knowledge. Sociology professors, consultants, and even students can be asked to examine aspects of society or social interactions, analyze them, and interpret the analysis for those who did not conduct the research. In the case of most of the writing we have described in this volume, the other individuals are sociologists, academics, or professionals in other fields. However, there are times when our expertise is needed to help those who haven't studied sociology as we have and do not see the world from our perspective.

When Michael Burawoy was the president of the American Sociological Association, his 2004 Presidential Address, "For Public Sociology," focused on the theme of that year's conference. This sparked a debate about what it means to be a public sociologist and whether public sociology should be embraced by the academic and professional discipline. While the details of this debate are outside the scope of this book, it's important to note that some debate does remain about whether it is the responsibility of sociologists to create this bridge between academia and those outside of it. We include this chapter, "Writing for the Public," because we believe it is an important but underemphasized aspect of the career of a sociologist. As such, this chapter will examine some of the ways sociologists communicate with the public, including through blogs, newspaper and magazine articles, policy documents, and talking points.

BLOGS

Despite the fact that the term *blog* was created in the mid-1990s—as a joining of the words *web* and *log*—blogs are still fairly new for academics. There are several reasons for this. Blogs are most often associated with members of the information age, and the majority of those currently in the academic field fall outside of that generation. As anyone can create a blog, many of them also contain writing that falls below the standards of academic writing, and this can both show a lack of professionalism and shrink the distance between the sociologist and the public. Each of these results, for some academics, can be problematic.

For other academics, however, the lessening of the distance to the public is the most important aspect of a blog. The ability to take your knowledge from the academy—the ivory tower—and share it with those who may not regularly have access to it makes blogs a unique form of communication. Although people who regularly write blogs, or bloggers, are often criticized for their lack of credentials and sometimes questionable sources, blogs have recently gained some legitimacy. Now, not only do some blogs break news before other news organizations, but well-known companies, agencies, organizations, and individuals now have their own blogs to reach a larger audience and to reach them more quickly.

Another important aspect of blogs is the opportunity for immediate feedback. An academic can post an idea, theory, or opinion and can immediately hear what others think about it. For some, this can be quite daunting, but for those prepared for the immediacy, anonymity, and, often, idiocy that comes from the participants in the blogosphere, it can be helpful to quickly receive feedback on their work and have the option to make connections, debate issues, and share information with people from all over the world.

For academics, a blog can be like a short, interactive paper. While text is often the main aspect of a blog, they also include links to other sites, images, and videos. Unlike most of the writing we have discussed in other chapters, individual blog entries can be short, and the blog as a whole changes regularly as new entries are posted over time. How often you contribute to your blog will vary, but the more often you post, the more likely you are to gain and hold on to an audience.

Audience

The composition of your audience is another unique aspect of a blog. The audience is both extremely general and very specific. As an academic blogger, you have the opportunity to take the audience potential of "everyone" and select from it an audience with particular tastes and interests. Unlike almost every other type of writing we have included in this book, you are not writing to fit a preset audience but are deciding what kind of audience you want and creating a piece that would suit them.

Involved in this process is making a decision between writing for "people in the know" and "people who want to know." This distinction is important. In writing for people who do not already have knowledge on your topic, you will need to add much more description and be clear with every point you make. Your language will likely need to be simpler, and terms you might not need to explain to other sociologists will have to be broken down in a concise and clear way. If your audience consists of people who are familiar with the topic, certain basics do not need to be explained. All things being equal, unless the blog is for a very specific population who you are certain already knows about your topic, it is better to explain, as the odds are high that someone will approach your blog without a deep knowledge of your topic.

Often, you will go into a blog with an idea of whom you are writing for but will notice that your blog voice changes as you write and you become comfortable with what and how you are writing. The audience you end up serving may not at all resemble your intended audience. At that point, you will either revise your voice or change your expectations. Those who connect to your blog likely enjoy it because it either speaks to them, aligns with their interests, or fills a hole in their knowledge.

This does not mean you should not think about your audience beforehand. While things might change, it is hard to know even where to start without considering your audience. Recognize that you can likely select your audience from a nearly infinite population, but you don't want to be too broad or too specific in thinking about them. A blog audience can be thought of as a business person might think about her market. Who are the people you are trying to serve? Who will be interested in what you have to say? In thinking about your audience, you should consider such characteristics as age, gender, sexual orientation, education level, occupation, political perspectives, and/or personal interests. Keep this in mind when you write. If you think your blog's audience should be factory workers in their 40s (perhaps too specific of an audience), consider that they might not understand terms such as *alienation* or *commodification* and you will have to explain the concept either before or after you name it. While it is not necessary for your readers to be able to access new posts immediately, posting at times when they will be able to read it—for example, on weekends or evenings for an audience you know typically works 9 to 5—shows a real understanding of your audience, which they are likely to appreciate.

Topic

Blogs come in many formats (some are unrecognizable as traditional blogs), but they generally accomplish two tasks: They share an opinion or idea, and/ or they pose a question. The question does not have to be explicit, but the expectation for debate is included in attempting to address many issues. In considering your topic, you should think about what might lead to debate within your topic. The topic should be something that can be broken down into specific subcategories or issues. Each individual post will contain one, several, or part of these subcategories. These varied items of interest are what allow you to find and keep your audience.

Your decision to write a blog may have come with a detailed plan of what you want to say and how you want to say it. But if you knew only that you wanted to communicate with a public audience and had not thought about the details, you want to think about that early in the process. Most bloggers make that decision before considering audience, but it is certainly acceptable to do the process the other way around. You can even go back and reconsider audience or topic after finalizing the other decision.

If you intend for your blog to be read by an audience outside of yourself, you should consider finding a unique space for your work. Once you've decided on a particular topic, read other blogs on similar topics. What can you add to the discussion that is currently missing? What angle can you take that picks up an audience not currently involved in similar blogs? Audience overlap is okay, but you do not want to do the exact same thing someone else is doing. If you read the blogs of others and the comments on them, you can learn a lot about writing style and how it affects the audience. Read the posts and take notes; feel free to become what is often referred to as a "lurker"—someone who reads posts but does not respond—but also consider becoming a part of the audience of the blog and responding to posts.

Regardless, you must decide what you want your blog to do. Is it your intention to inform about a particular topic, raise an issue or question, or begin a debate or movement? If you simply want to inform, you do not need to use a blog platform (such as WordPress or Blogger) that allows for comments. You can also disable your blog comment feature. Although, since part of the purpose of having a blog is the communication between author and audience, keeping the comments active is important. You can also restrict commenting or require approval before a comment is officially posted. Additionally, you can implement various add-ons that can act as protections against spam (unwanted commercial postings).

The topic you select should be interesting. To some extent, this goes without saying, but telling someone to be interesting is like telling someone to be funny. Even if you are a naturally funny person, you can't always do it on command. What are people talking about? What are they responding to? Before writing, you should make sure to recognize what in particular is interesting about what you are about to say. It may be interesting to you, to a specific group, or to a general audience, but you must recognize what the interesting aspects are and make sure to highlight them in your content and in your title.

Once you have at least a preliminary idea of what your content will be, remember that what makes the blog is what is contained within it. This is where you make your point, capture your audience, and gather your feedback. Generally, a blog entry will focus on one or a couple of interrelated points. Your blog as a whole will focus on a particular topic or area, and you can continue to work on it as long as your blog remains active, so there is no need to cram everything into one entry. You will have plenty of time to make other points, and if your intention is to create a dialogue with your readers, additional points may emerge through the comments or your responses to comments.

Make sure that, as in all your academic writing, you are clear in what you're saying. In this case, clear also usually means free of jargon and technical language. If your audience is the general public, you should speak to them as though they do not know anything about your topic or area, and they should not have to read entries between your first and most recent post to understand the context of your entry and contribute to the discussion. If your intention is to address others in sociology or other academics, then a level of basic understanding can be assumed. However, since you are writing because you believe you have something new or different to share, you may have to explain some of the things you discuss even to those within your field.

Structure

The work of a blog does not stop after you have found that interesting aspect. In an academic blog, much of the purpose is to share knowledge, so you should be sure to support your claims with evidence. Unlike an academic paper, all your evidence does not have to be from journals or other strictly academic sources (although the point will be stronger if it is). You can use your opinion or links to the research and opinions of others to support your claims. The entire digital world is open to you to explore or reference as you wish, and you should take advantage of that by finding new and interesting videos, images, people, and stories to which to link.

The general structure of a blog is slightly closer to that of a newspaper article than to that of an academic paper, which is likely another reason why blogs are not fully accepted in academia. The exact structure can change depending on the specific blogging software you use, but some generalities are found across platforms. These same aspects can help you identify something as a blog even if it is not explicitly stated.

A blog entry begins with a headline. If you want to bring people to your blog, a catchy yet informative headline is important. It should be written in simple language, and if it is ambiguous, it should not present any perspective you are not willing to deal with. You can use a play on words or an acronym to keep it short and clear. The purpose of the headline is similar to the title of an article or book, except the emphasis is more equally balanced between being informative and interesting, rather than leaning more in the direction of informative, as for manuscript and essay titles.

From there, the structure differs depending on whether you are going to create a long or short entry. There is no hard-and-fast rule on length, but you should consider your audience in determining length. If your audience is older, they may have more time to read long entries, although many of them may not be as comfortable reading long passages on the computer and would prefer a hard copy. With younger groups, it can take a lot of motivation to get someone to read beyond a few paragraphs. In the beginning of your blog's lifetime, you may want to try to keep your entries short. A few paragraphs is probably enough to make your point, and until you build an audience, your readers should be able to avoid scrolling if they can.

In a shorter blog entry, you need only about a sentence to introduce what you are going to say. You should then get to your point, and if you can close with a question for your audience or a point you'd like them to address, it can be easier for your readers to start commenting. Again, if your entry is long, make sure to remind readers of your point before expecting them to comment on it.

Another point you should remember about blogs is something you should remember for anything you do online. Information has a long lifetime on the web; for some things, it may seem to be near infinite. If you look hard enough, you can probably find unused websites that someone put up 10 years ago and never took down, and your blog may be similarly preserved. Search engines continue to collect and hold information long after you are done with your site, so your entries will still be accessible. It is for these reasons that you want to make sure your online presence is what you want it to be. Try entering your name into a search engine sometime and see what you find.

Considering this digital lifetime, you want to make sure to obey the conventions of language and structure described in this and other chapters. Read over your blog before publishing it. Make sure it is well written. While your language doesn't need to be academic and you can write similar to how you speak, it should be professional. Try not to be vulgar, and be careful what you say; if you believe something you say may be problematic to your future employment or education, try creating a persona and writing your blog anonymously. Remember also to add privacy settings to the ownership of the web address, if you have your own.

A blog can be a great way to communicate with students, academics, or other professionals. It gives you the opportunity to more fully understand a topic by breaking it down in a way the general public can comprehend. It can also provide you with a public profile, which can be useful for your research, employment, or educational opportunities in the future. As long as you always protect and monitor how people perceive you online, a blog can be a useful and informational tool.

NEWSPAPERS/MAGAZINES

For many professionals, the purpose of being a part of academia is to become an expert in your field. You may not necessarily reach the point where you are the first person the state calls in an emergency or the person *The New York Times* contacts to verify a story, but there is still some pride in the push to become known among your colleagues and to those outside of your field.

When you reach this point, or as you are working your way toward it, you may be asked to contribute writing to be distributed to a wider audience than that composed of other professors, students, or academics. Sometimes, this is in the form of an appearance on a television or radio show for which you may want to write talking points. These will be briefly mentioned at the end of this chapter. Other times, you may be invited to write a piece for a nonacademic journal, newspaper, or magazine, or you may take it upon yourself to contribute to one of these media in one of the ways open to the general public. Each of these writing types places you in the public eye in a different way.

Opinions and Editorials

Let's begin with the two ways anyone can contribute to a newspaper—the op-ed and letters to the editor sections. Letters to the editor have been found in newspapers as early as the 1700s and have provided an outlet for many who did not have a voice in the media. Op-eds are newer and were developed out of the poor use, or even lack of use, of the page opposite the editorial pages. These began appearing in newspapers in the mid-1900s.

For those who gather more of their information digitally and may have had more limited exposure to newspapers, letters to the editor and op-eds are a way for those outside of the journalism field to contribute to the news and be read by the millions of people who read the newspaper. Before the advent of e-mail, many of these contributions were mailed and were not included in the paper until days later. Now, an immediate response to almost all news stories and larger social issues is possible. We also now often have the opportunity to respond immediately online through comment sections, blogs, and podcasts.

Letters to the editor and op-eds are different from comment sections on websites, as they often hold a level of legitimacy that can be absent from the universe of online commentators. Anyone can participate in most online comment sections—and the language in these comments demonstrates that professionalism is not always upheld—while letters to the editor and op-eds require approval and editing. For this reason, they are more readily accepted by academics.

Both of these types of writing are generally found in the opinion pages of newspapers and magazines. The editorials, letters to the editor, and op-eds are all grouped together as a representation of writing that does not necessarily represent the perspective of the newspaper and the more neutral stance that most newspapers strive to maintain.

Letters to the Editor

A letter to the editor is just that. It is a letter written by a reader of a newspaper to the editor in chief of a newspaper, journal, or magazine. However, the letter can also be written to a television or radio station. A letter to the editor addresses an article directly, usually including the title and the date of the article early in the letter. Generally, a letter to the editor will support or oppose a viewpoint or story presented in the paper or magazine but can also be used to correct a mistake.

Remember that a letter to the editor is a letter. Therefore, it should be written in letter format (even if it is sent in an e-mail) and should be short and to the point (see Chapter 2 for information on writing a letter). Similar to the letters described in the second chapter, you should include your first and last name, phone number, and address or e-mail address. If the newspaper allows, and you choose to, letters can also be submitted anonymously, but keep in mind that some newspapers will not publish a letter without contact information. If you want anonymity, you should say so explicitly. Below the contact information, be sure to begin your letter with "Dear Editor."

Before you write your letter to the editor, you should read the periodical to which you want to contribute. This is how you find out which kinds of letters to the editor the newspaper is most likely to publish. Do the opinion pages include jokes, or are they more serious? Do they use hard-to-understand words, or are they clear in their language? Are the letters very emotional or a little more muted? How long are they? These are all questions you should consider before writing a letter to the editor. You can also find the answers to these questions in the newspaper's own guidelines.

The issue you choose to write about should be something you feel passionate about in some way. Generally, once you've decided to write, it is because something in an article spoke to you and led you to write a letter. While this emotion may have directed you to the letter, depending on the newspaper you are interested in contributing to, you may have to remove overly emotional words or sections from your letter. A letter should avoid sounding too angry or upset, as that can take away from the message you are trying to send.

Your letter should usually be no longer than three paragraphs. Rather than our usual model of working your way toward your point with a detailed introduction, the beginning paragraph of your letter should get to the point quickly. The article you are responding to should be mentioned within the first couple of sentences—usually by both the title and date. If you do not include both, the editors may add it for you, but they are more likely to include your letter if they can connect it to a particular article. Therefore, your first sentences should refer to the article you are responding to and the point made within that article.

The following sentences should present your opposing, agreeing, or corrective perspective. If you agree with the perspective presented, a newspaper will be interested in your letter only if it provides some information, an example, or an understanding that the newspaper did not include. Oppositional and corrective letters, by definition, include new information. Explain your interest in the topic and any expertise you may have. Describe why the article affected you the way it did.

The next paragraph should include your supporting evidence. Coming from a sociologist, your perspective will likely already have some validity attached, but your evidence can come from observation, research, theories, or conversations. While your opinions are valid and can be included in your letter, any point you make should be supported by something other than your ideas; otherwise, there is little reason to write the letter.

You should end with a summary and, if appropriate, something memorable that will stick with the readers after they have finished your piece. It could be something clever or deep or a suggestion for future articles, policy, or processes. This is what will capture the readers of the paper and the editor who makes the decision to include your letter or not. Finally, make sure you sign your letter.

Keep your letters short, and don't overwhelm them with jargon or confusing language. You are writing for a diverse audience, and the same things that catch the audience's eye are going to capture the editor's. Make sure you do not attack the writer of the article or the newspaper as a whole.

Op-Eds

Also referred to as the "opposite-the-editorial" page or the "opinions and editorials" page, the op-ed section often faces the editorial section of a newspaper. While letters to the editor usually respond to an article written in the paper, an op-ed can address any important issue and uses both opinion and evidence to support that perspective. Op-eds are also much more likely to be written by someone with some expertise in a subject rather than by a general reader. This means that more is often expected of those who choose to write op-eds, and, especially in the more prestigious publications, getting published is not easy.

Newspapers will usually choose to include an op-ed when it deals with an issue of importance to their readers. Therefore, an op-ed can be an opportunity for an individual to express his opinion to a large audience of politicians, policymakers, and other readers. Op-eds have also been known to sway those in power, as they are thought to represent the mind-sets of constituencies.

As you would do if you were writing a letter to the editor, be sure to read the periodical of interest before attempting to submit an op-ed. Take note of the way the op-eds are written, the language used, and the structure of the pieces. Again, you should check the paper's guidelines, but reading other op-eds can add context to the paper's specific rules. You should be sure to notice the length of the op-eds as well. They are usually between 600 and 800 words long. As newspapers often reject op-eds simply for being too long, you should make sure not to go over the paper's word limit.

An op-ed should begin with a title—something that catches both the audience's and the editor's eye, as well as making your point. As described in the section on blogs, an op-ed title should be both interesting and informative. Try to fit as much information as possible into one short sentence. Space is restricted in newspapers, which is why articles often include nicknames, slang, or acronyms. If these methods are necessary to get your point across and will not damage your professional image, you should feel free to use them in a title.

Similar to a letter to the editor (but unlike much of the writing we have spoken about in this book), op-eds include the purpose of the piece very early in the first paragraph. The purpose for writing the op-ed should be immediately clear to the reader. Be sure that your purpose involves selecting one perspective and supporting or refuting it. You should start by informing your readers of the topic and your view on it without being too preachy.

The body of the op-ed should take your chosen perspective and support it with facts, research, or data you have collected yourself or from other experts. As the op-ed is meant to add information to the periodical that is not currently available, your piece should provide new evidence or facts that enhance the reader's understanding of the topic. Editors are particularly impressed with information to which they have not, or cannot, gain access.

You should also make sure to end your op-ed with a short summary of your point. This can include such things as recommendations for policy or a call to action. Repeat again what drew you to write your op-ed and how you have added to the debate or understanding of the issue. Remember to sign your op-ed and/or include any contact information and a title, if applicable.

Your language in writing both of these types of contribution can be personal or conversational or even humorous, but it should still match the level of language used in the rest of the periodical and use previous pieces from that section as models. The words and structure used to write a letter for *The New York Times* are different from what you might use for *USA Today* or the *New York Daily News*. You should feel free to use engaging terms, rather than flowery words or an abundance of adjectives, and do not overwhelm your point with a lot of jargon or clichés. Always remember that this will be placed in a newspaper and read by a variety of individuals. Not all of them will understand sociological language.

Length

Ensure that your submission fits within the suggested or required length. Just because you have more to say does not mean the newspaper has more space. Newspapers and magazines receive hundreds of submissions and will often look for reasons to reject them. The length provides a quick way to place them in the rejection pile. Most newspapers will provide length guidelines in their instructions, but if they do not, try to stay between 200 and 500 words for letters to the editor and 600 to 800 words for op-eds.

Emotion

While the level of emotion found in a newspaper may vary, submissions often get rejected because they include personal attacks, profanity, insulting language, or statements that are not factual. You may find that you have to edit your piece several times to tone down some of those aspects that turn professional writing into an angry tirade.

Oversaturation

It is best to respond to an article or issue as quickly as possible, because many other readers may have the same response you do. If you are not able to get your piece in immediately, you can also attempt to connect your point to a more recent issue to ensure that it remains timely. However, as larger newspapers receive many more letters than do smaller newspapers, you may want to try submitting to a smaller paper instead. There, you will have less competition and a higher possibility of being published.

Editing

An editor has a lot of work to do to put together her periodical. She does not have time to also edit your submission. You should make sure you and at least one other person have read it several times to ensure that your grammar, punctuation, and spelling are correct before submitting it to a periodical.

Submission

Many periodicals now will allow submission through e-mail, which you should use whenever possible. E-mail gets your letter to the editor quickly and allows the editor to cut and paste your letter. You might also consider, where allowed, submitting your letter to multiple sources. However, this is generally not accepted with op-eds.

Articles

As a sociologist, you might also be asked to complete an article for a newspaper or magazine. The structure for such articles often follows what is referred to as an inverted pyramid model. Because readers will judge the entire article by what is read in the first few sentences, it is important to catch the audience's attention early. A news-based article will include a quick summary of all relevant details within the first couple of sentences. This allows readers to get all the necessary information quickly and then make a decision as to whether they would like to learn more about the topic.

A feature or column can take a little more time to reveal the pertinent information but should still include a "hook" to grab the reader's attention. This begins with the headline. Especially now, where people rely on quick glances, reading over a shoulder, or snippets from RSS feeds, the headline of an article is very important. The strategy to writing an effective headline can also be used for the first few sentences of your article. This is what takes those readers who have enjoyed the headline and brings them into the remainder of the article.

Your headline should use active, rather than passive, verbs and be written in present tense. Readers should feel as though there is urgency to reading the article—as though the issue or problem is currently occurring (and in many situations, it is). The headline should also be clear and simple but provide enough information to tell the reader what the article is about. Headlines often include abbreviations, but you should review the other headlines in the newspaper to find out the appropriate format. Make sure you do not misrepresent your article through the headline; it should be honest and straightforward.

There are several ways to begin an article to draw the reader in. One good way is to use a story, either personal or from someone to whom you have spoken. This allows the reader to see the article on an intimate level. Another option is to begin with an interesting or outrageous fact. Finally, an article can start with an illustration that connects the reader, or issues she might face, with what you have written. Rely on your personal experiences and what makes an article interesting to you in figuring out how to write your hook, or lead. You could also consult other experts in the field such as those in journalism or public relations.

The headline is often the last thing you write, as it should be written based on the general theme of the whole article. You may also want to wait until your article is complete to write the first-paragraph hook. While you may begin writing your article knowing exactly what is interesting about your topic, your finished product may look different than you expected. Even if you have already written your headline and/or hook, feel free to go back and edit it once your article is fully formed. You should also keep in mind that the editor of the periodical may choose to change your headline if it isn't suitable, if it doesn't fit the available space, or if she can find a better way to write it. It may be disappointing, but remember that your headline is what initially caught her attention, so it was not written for nothing.

Examples of headlines and hooks:

Headline	Explanation
Help Wanted: Busybodies With Cameras[1]	This headline speaks to people not because of the information it provides but because it piques their interest. They react to the "help wanted" and want to know why busybodies with cameras are getting jobs. Similarly, the headline does not provide you with all the information you need to continue the story but begins to draw you in through the lingering questions. This method is more effective in a news story than in a feature.
We don't want an America 'made in China'[2]	The headline of this column reads like a declaration and draws our interest because we can see the emotion around this issue. While we don't yet know exactly what the article is about, we can connect on a basic level to the American items made in China.
Are unpaid internships office entree or free labor?[3]	This is a question we have all asked ourselves. This is likely most interesting to students or companies that might hire interns. This headline provides some insight into the proposed audience for this article.
Hook	Explanations
When I visited the new Martin Luther King memorial in Washington, I was shocked to learn the 30-foot-tall statue of our leading civil rights icon was by a Chinese sculptor, out of Chinese granite, and carved in China.[4]	When we read this first sentence, we get a better idea than we did from the headline of the particular problem the writer has with items made in China. We also get a personalized entry from the writer that uses the word *shocked* to evoke an emotional response in readers.
Are interns exploited in a rough economy?[5]	This represents another question of interest. The word *exploited* adds the passion and perspective of the author.

Columns

One type of article you might write is called a column. Writing a column is similar to writing a blog or an op-ed. The article is primarily based on the writer's opinion and usually supported by fact. As a column appears regularly in the same newspaper, it is usually assigned to someone who is well known or has many credentials in the field. An individual might be paid for her contribution or may distribute it at no cost to the newspaper. A column may also appear in multiple papers and be in syndication. Historian Manning Marable, for example, published his column, "Along the Color Line," in 400 newspapers around the world.

The topics of columns are varied. Newspapers may run advice columns or columns that deal with finance, food, or lifestyle. Your column could be on sociology in general or the specific area in which you have the most expertise. Writing a column takes more commitment than any of the other types of writing you might do for a magazine or newspaper, as you are expected to do it daily, weekly, or monthly, and you will likely need to prepare your columns several days in advance to make sure they are ready for publication each period.

Similar to the other kinds of opinion writing discussed in this chapter, if opinion is used in your column, you should focus on only one or two opinions and use evidence to support them. In a column, you should argue your point and urge the reader to agree with you. It is okay to be alarmist to some extent, as long as you are able to provide a reason for why a reader should embrace that perspective.

When writing your column, make sure to keep in mind the region the newspaper serves. If you are familiar with the area, drawing from your experience can help you connect with your audience. You may be able to provide your audience interesting information they are not familiar with. You want your audience to want to continue reading. If they believe they can learn something from you or if you have given them something interesting about a topic that they want to explore further, they will appreciate your insight and possibly come back to your column.

If you include yourself in your column, the readers will come to think of you as someone they know, which can also strengthen their attachment to your column. Speak to them about what you are passionate about and encourage them to become passionate too. Explain your issue, comment, concern, or problem, and share with the audience the emotion that drove you to write about it.

Remember that, as a columnist, you are trying to build an audience that may follow you to other mediums. You want to make sure you are speaking from your heart while still using your knowledge and expertise to reach your audience. While the opportunity for dialogue is not present as it is in blogs, your audience may attempt to make contact through letters to the editor or comment sections in online locations. You should be prepared for this possibility. For more information on building and writing for an audience, see our discussion of blogs above.

Finally, as a column is a regular occurrence, you want to make sure your audience wants to return. Connect to your readers so their weekly readings of your column seem like meeting with an old friend. Keep your audience wanting more, and encourage them to take action on issues of importance to you. Make them understand why they should also think these issues are important.

Feature Articles

Features are usually longer than a regular newspaper article and do not necessarily require the immediacy found in other news articles. Features often focus on a bigger issue or topic that is far-reaching enough to remain fresh for quite a few days. The topic may be on a particular person, activity, or event. Features are often used to add a new voice to a periodical, and they can insert humor and a "slice of life" into a newspaper that otherwise might not include such stories. The lack of a time constraint provides the opportunity for further research, interviews, or data gathering. The writer of a feature article is also expected to have some expertise in the area and has likely been selected for that reason.

The headline and introduction should again act as a hook, but you should keep in mind that the intention of the feature is to provide a more in-depth perspective of a particular topic. This should be reflected in your title and/or introductory paragraph. You should let your readers know that they will be taken on a longer journey than they might be with an op-ed, letter to the editor, or other article.

You want to begin your feature by establishing a particular tone, and you may need to include background information in the first paragraph to prepare readers for the direction in which you will point them. As suggested above, you may want to try to capture the readers' attention by saying something unusual, funny, personal, or controversial, or even using a quote related to the article.

The body of the feature can include a variety of elements that contribute to the flow of the article. Again, as you are dealing with a longer-than-average article, you might want to use more quotes, anecdotes, and opinions from you and other experts, as well as statistics and other facts. Check if the newspaper will allow you to include images, diagrams, or tables, as they are also useful in breaking down information and keeping the reader engaged.

If you find that you are veering away from the main topic during your feature, consider adding a sidebar, assuming the newspaper allows them. A sidebar is an element in itself that contains related but separate information on your topic. It is usually short and is located alongside the feature. The sidebar could include a list of important elements of your topics, a quiz, poll, or additional resources. Check the paper's guidelines and speak to the editor about the appropriateness of including a sidebar.

Conclude your article as you would an op-ed. Be sure to summarize your points, and if there is a directional recommendation or a final thought, you should leave the reader with that before ending your piece.

Magazines and newspapers present your ideas to people both within and outside of the academy. It is important to take advantage of the opportunity to contribute to one, as you can not only share your expertise with those who have not had access to it but also broaden your circle of contacts and colleagues. Often, this can lead to opportunities to write within other spheres, such as public policy.

POLICY BRIEF

Writing policy differs from so much of the other writing you do as a sociologist because it adds an extra step to sociological analysis and understanding. While the beginning steps are the same, once you have collected data or completed research, you must apply this information. As you are expected to use your expertise to recommend some kind of action, policy briefs are also different from much of the other writing in this book (but similar to other writing for the public), because you take a particular perspective and steer your readers in that direction.

A policy brief is often written because of a specific request by a decision maker but might also be created because of the importance of an issue or problem. For advocates, the request may be for one particular method of dealing with a particular issue. For someone who falls into the category of consultant, a policy brief might present several options so decision makers can choose a path of action.

The brief will usually be between six and eight pages in length and should, like much of the writing we have discussed in this chapter, use well-researched evidence to support the perspective(s) of the author. The argument should be clear, and each point should be easy to find and strengthened with research and examples. The use of subheadings can often help direct readers to your point and onto the path you want them to walk, but, again, do not use it as a way to avoid transitions from paragraph to paragraph or section to section.

A policy brief should begin with a title. As with a newspaper article, you want to select a title that is both catchy and informative to lead someone to the document and encourage them to read further. As a policy brief has a directed purpose, a title that shares that purpose is the most useful to potential decision makers.

An executive summary should be the first substantive part of the document (although it may be the last part you write). Here, you want to summarize the important aspects of the brief. An executive summary acts as a mini proposal or a long abstract, as it presents all the information in the brief with minimal details. For many, the decision whether to read the document or not comes after reading the executive summary. The executive summary should be a few paragraphs and include a description of the problem, reasons why the current approach is not working, and suggestions for an alternative approach. Sometimes this is written in short paragraphs or in a bulleted list.

The next three sections should take the executive summary and expand on it. This should begin with a detailed description of the problem, including its history and causes and how those have led to the current policy responses. In describing the current problem, you are providing evidence that this is something decision makers should consider and address. Include any information or predictions you might have about what will happen if the problem is not taken care of. You should also make sure to explain who the stakeholders are. Who is most affected by the problem? Who benefits from a change in policy?

This section should be followed by a detailed description of the policies as they are currently situated and what the problem with them is. Here is where you make the argument that something needs to change. You must have an understanding of both the current policy and the problems with it to suggest an alternative direction. The readers want to know that you have that knowledge before they can trust you to make an appropriate suggestion for change.

Finally, you need to present your alternative. You have explained to the reader what the problem is and why it has not been adequately addressed. Now you must provide your audience with a new direction. This section should be an instruction manual for implementing your ideas. Your recommendation should be laid out, step-by-step, so that decision makers can follow your suggestions and move forward with your ideas. This should also include some potential alternatives to your ideas and why these alternatives would not be as effective as your initial suggestion. Adding ideas for monitoring the effectiveness of the policy or any budgetary information can enhance your presentation. If models of your solution exist in other areas or industries, they can provide illustrations of the usefulness of your ideas.

There is some debate about whether white papers should include images or diagrams. Generally, they are known for being "grey" and void of anything besides the white of the paper and the black of the text. However, diagrams, graphs, and charts, if they are helpful to your argument, can add something new to your presentation and clarify your point for readers. Remember that readers are not necessarily coming from academia, as you are, and therefore may benefit from the more friendly presentation a diagram provides. Do not include an image simply because you feel your report could use one. It should be necessary or supportive of your argument or not used at all.

The brief may also include an appendix and a works cited section. If you have referenced other documents, people, or locations, you may include information about them here. The appendix is usually not included in the word or page limit.

To some extent, a policy brief is a marketing document. The purpose is to convince others of the urgency or importance of an issue and then to present one or several important ways to deal with it. To accomplish this task, many of the rules of marketing can be useful.

Know Your Audience

The purpose of a policy brief is to present policy options to a target audience. This audience is most often made up of those in governmental positions but may also include journalists, donors, researchers, or local administrators. Through the brief, the author should attempt to sway the audience to his perspective. If the brief will be disseminated to larger groups beyond decision makers, it's important to speak in a language that will be understandable by both groups. This also means that while academic language is not necessarily appropriate, the document should still be written professionally. Make sure that your language is not only clear but also structured in a way that speaks to the strengths and interests of your audience.

Focus

The brief should be focused. If you have been working on a particular issue, the document should cover only that one issue of importance. It should also be short and direct. Remember that the purpose of writing the document is to convince and not to confuse. Make sure other points, purposes, or ideas do not bog down the document.

Be Realistic

While we all have fantasy lists of what we wish could happen to solve a particular issue, for a policy brief to be taken seriously, it must be feasible and include action that can be taken by the decision makers. The inclusion of a budget can often show the possibility of using a policy. You could also include a partial version of a policy in case complete and immediate implementation might be difficult.

This document may be submitted to decision makers or other individuals by you or by someone else on your behalf. Often, it will include a discussion or presentation. In that case, you might want to consider compiling some talking points.

TALKING POINTS

We will conclude our chapter on writing for the public with a discussion of talking points. These are mentioned here, briefly, because they are an important way to present your public persona. Also, while they are most similar to the type of writing done in creating an outline (see Chapter 3), they are unique in a few ways, and we thought it would benefit our readers to include them here. Talking points are also an important part of writing for the public, as well as a good exercise for any academic since they involve condensing your work into its essential elements.

In the business world, talking points are used to ensure that anyone who speaks on behalf of a company—on television, on the radio, or in a newspaper, for example—is consistent. In academia, talking points may be used differently. Your talking points are the pieces of information in your work that you want to make sure to highlight. Once you have talking points on a particular research project, paper, or article, you can use them for a presentation, interview, or simply your "elevator pitch"—the summary of your research in 5 minutes (the length of an elevator ride). Generally, if you are in academia, you are writing talking points for yourself. However, most of the advice in this section can also be used if you are writing for someone else.

In many ways, talking points are an outline of your work, and creating them can help you think about what is important in what you are doing and the points that would be of most interest to your audience. Talking points are neither intended to remain static nor will they include every aspect of your research. Like so much of the writing in this volume, your talking points will change to fit your audience—what is appropriate or relevant for one group may not have the same effect on another.

Talking points are also not intended to be recited word-for-word. They are usually written as bullet points to remind you (or others) of the points you need to hit during your presentation or interview. They should be short (ideally, only a sentence per point) and should be written without exclamation points or bold text. You don't need to add the emphasis. The whole point of the talking points is that they are your emphasis.

You should arrange your talking points in a hierarchy, starting with the most important and including the secondary points below it. An alternative is to organize them in the order you would like to reveal them. You may find that your work is arranged more by first point, second point than by most important point, secondary point. Additionally, if you find that some of your points break down into several smaller points, you can include sub-bullets that support your main point. The most important thing is to keep your talking points short, so it is better to break your main point into smaller points than to create one convoluted talking point.

In general, three is a good number of talking points. This is few enough that you could probably memorize them while still covering all your points for a particular audience. For a conference presentation, you may want to expand to five points, but keep in mind that you will likely need to include points for each of the sections of your paper (see Chapter 8), so it may be easier for you and your audience simply to expand on your three main points rather than adding two more.

Again, you should keep in mind your audience. While your research as a whole might include more than three important points, you likely have three that are most relevant to your audience. If you are presenting to a group interested in Latino issues, you should emphasize the points in your research that most speak to that community. It may make sense to you to create a master list of talking points from which you can select those that apply to your group of interest.

Your talking points should be clear and free of both jargon and derogatory or accusatory language. Remember that you are trying to make your point, not bring attention to someone else's. There are situations where your research is about a dialogue or even an argument with another person, but even in that situation, you can usually avoid attacking an individual and focus on critiquing her work.

Talking points are not just for politicians, pundits, companies, or organizations. Academics can also find them useful in presenting themselves and their work to others. Your talking points should travel with you so you will always be prepared to share your work with those you meet.

Not all sociologists believe that writing for the public is an important part of their role as academics. However, making your ideas, analysis, opinions, and suggestions clear to those outside of an academic sphere provides the opportunity to expand the realm of sociology and explore the depths of your knowledge. This chapter provides you with the information you need to do just that.

SUMMARY

This chapter examines the different types of writing a sociologist might participate in to speak to those outside of academia. The chapter covers the following topics:

- Guidelines for creating academic blogs
- The different types of writing one might submit to a newspaper or magazine
- Writing a policy brief that addresses an issue or problem
- Compiling talking points from your research

In this "Writing in Practice" piece, R. L'Heureux Lewis-McCoy describes his own experiences with speaking to the public through his appearances on television and writing for blogs and newspapers.

WRITING IN PRACTICE

by R. L'Heureux Lewis-McCoy

Would you rather "create a discourse that traverses multiple spheres, providing access to fields that the public are marginalized from" or "write pieces that audiences beyond the university read"? If you answered the latter, you are probably like me. You have been trained to read and write in "academicese" but also realize that academic jargon and publications rarely reach communities beyond the ivory tower.

While I have successfully passed through the ranks and earned a PhD and am currently toiling away on the tenure track, I am well aware that many of the academic articles I write will seldom reach masses of people. When I decided to go into sociology, my goal was to contribute to discussions about race, ethnicity, and education to generate social change. Soon after arriving in graduate school, I learned that it is rare for mainstream American sociologists to contribute actively to public discourse. While one of my professors told me, "My journal publications are my activism," I found myself wanting to tap into a different tradition. By reading about the Black sociological tradition—a tradition that prided itself on both scholarship and activism for the public good—I found a place where authors wrote across publications and audiences. Borrowing from this model, I forged my own path that serves the demands of academic publication (tenure is a necessity) while creating the opportunity for pushing public conversations via public sociology.

During graduate school, I began my first blog, "Black at Michigan," where I discussed what was happening with Black students on the University of Michigan campus, as well as with Black folks within the state of Michigan. Not long after this, I began to contribute editorials to local papers and was soon receiving calls from local media to talk and write about issues of race in the area. From this point forward, I had to work on making complex ideas accessible in a short space.

Writing for public audiences is very different from writing for academic journals and books. While academic audiences are often familiar with subtle nuances and research literatures that span decades, public audiences rarely come to a subject matter with that depth of background. This does not mean that public audiences are naïve—far from it. Rather, their background is usually linked to the experiential, not research based. This is an important point from which to begin, because while jargon is often seen as the major issue with academic writing, not clearly explaining terms and concepts is more often a central issue for the masses.

Public writing is more than "translation" or "boiling down" ideas; it involves connecting to the needs and worldviews of one's audience. Each publication, be it print or web based, has a different target audience. Knowing one's readership is key to determining the length, tone, and approach to a piece. Doing research on the place you intend to publish is essential, because both print- and web-based publications have desired lengths and formats and shy away from duplicate topics—choose wisely, because public conversations often move quickly. In academia, we are often told to write narrowly on a slice of our expertise without discussing other portions. In public writing, you are often asked to write on your expertise (or, in a number of cases, to write outside of your area of expertise—to break that down would take an entirely different essay) but to place it in greater context. You are asked to step away from the minutia of your data and connect them to an issue that concerns the public eye in the moment. On rare occasion, your expertise and project may be a perfect fit for a media outlet where no extrapolation is needed, but more often than not, you will have to make the connections between what you study and what is being discussed in this week's media hopper.

Choose the number of ideas you present wisely. Most times, when I begin to write on a topic, I feel I should unload a full literature review so the reader knows I'm qualified to speak on the topic and to provide the reader with a common vocabulary. This may make for good thesis writing, but it makes for very poor public writing. Instead, I try to think of two, at most, central points that I want the readers to take away from the piece. Within the first two lines, I have to make my points clear and then unpack them in the few remaining paragraphs. Think about your opening as if it contains the two most important lines of your abstract. For me, this tends to mean

(Continued)

(Continued)

(1) what people think they know (null hypothesis) and (2) what I found that counters that (alternative hypothesis). Just like an academic article, I try to make sure each of my pieces makes a distinct contribution to the dialogue around a subject matter; if it doesn't, I'm not sure why I would write it.

There are many theories on what the role of an intellectual who does public work is, but I tend to believe a central role is exchanging ideas with those beyond the confines of academia. This, at the same time, carries challenges, the least of which is that as I write this, public writing is rarely considered in a tenure evaluation—though there is evidence of changes to that at some universities.

Writing for public audiences is a practice that is reemerging and continues to be redefined by each author's initiatives. Ultimately, you will have to find your own public voice, preferred writing venues, and topic range—which is part of the fun of doing it. Public sociological writing inevitably should point readers to deeper revelations than does reporting or opinion sharing and should facilitate unlikely, yet attainable, connections for readers. Doing public writing in company with academic writing helps me bring my original goals nearly full circle.

—Dr. R. L'Heureux Lewis-McCoy, PhD, is an assistant professor of sociology and Black studies at The City College of New York, City University of New York.

NOTES

1. Sang-Hun, Choe. 2011. "Help Wanted: Busybodies With Cameras." *New York Times*, September 29, p. A6. Retrieved August 4, 2012 (http://www.nytimes .com/2011/09/29/world/asia/in-south-korea-where-digital-tattling-is-a-growth-industry .html?pagewanted=all).

2. Joseph, Joel D. 2011. "We don't want an America 'made in China'" *USA Today*, September 28. Retrieved August 4, 2012 (http://www.usatoday.com/news/opinion/ forum/story/2011-09-28/depression-stimulus-public-works/50590552/1).

3. Raasch, Chuck. 2011. "Are unpaid internships office entree or free labor?" *USA Today*, September 1. Retrieved August 4, 2012 (http://www.usatoday.com/news/ opinion/forum/story/2011-09-01/Column-Are-unpaid-internships-office-entree-or -free-labor/50222800/1).

4. Joseph, Joel D. 2011. "We don't want an America 'made in China'" *USA Today*, September 28. Retrieved August 4, 2012 (http://www.usatoday.com/news/opinion/ forum/story/2011-09-28/depression-stimulus-public-works/50590552/1).

5. Raasch, Chuck. 2011. "Are unpaid internships office entree or free labor?" *USA Today*, September 1. Retrieved August 4, 2012 (http://www.usatoday.com/news/ opinion/forum/story/2011-09-01/Column-Are-unpaid-internships-office-entree-or -free-labor/50222800/1).

CHAPTER 11

WRITING IN GRADUATE SCHOOL AND BEYOND

Not only is sociology a fun and fascinating area of study, but students of sociology also have many excellent graduate school and career options. Sociology provides scholars with an array of insights into human behavior, group dynamics, community involvement, and social relations. Sociology also provides unique theoretical perspectives and research skills that will aid in one's understanding of social and cultural interactions. As a result, sociology—and the skills sociology majors and graduates learn and develop—is an asset to a number of career fields, as well as to master's and doctoral programs. There are so many different career options for sociology majors, and we cannot begin to cover all the types of writing you may encounter in the careers that attract sociology majors, as the career determines the writing style. This chapter does not focus on career or graduate school guidance but, rather, reviews the typical writing types and styles involved in preparing for careers where your sociological training can be applied, as well as the writing needed in preparation for advanced studies in sociology. First, since graduate studies are often the next step for sociology undergraduate majors, we will examine the different types of writing that often confront both master's and doctoral students.

GRADUATE SCHOOL: MASTER'S AND DOCTORAL PROGRAMS

In 2010, a record number of students applied to colleges and universities.[1] The number of students who applied to graduate programs also substantially increased. Many students who major in the social sciences in college intend to continue their education with graduate school and doctoral studies. Since sociology covers so many different areas of study, sociology students often apply to a wide array of graduate and professional studies programs, such as the following:

- Sociology
- Applied sociology
- Anthropology
- Social work
- International relations
- Law school
- Political science
- Public policy
- Urban studies
- Education
- Public health
- Criminology

This section will begin with a brief discussion of the differences between master's and doctoral programs in sociology, as well as the writing assignments students are likely to encounter in these programs. It is important to first note that students do not necessarily need to major or even minor in sociology to apply for master's or doctoral studies in sociology. Having an undergraduate major in sociology certainly helps, but most master's and doctoral programs supply their students with the necessary skills in theory and research methods for their respective programs.

Master's Programs

A master's degree signifies that the scholar has mastered the material in a particular area of study. This mastery may include an advanced understanding of readings, research, or theories in the scholar's field. Those interested in pursuing a master's degree in sociology can choose between two different types of sociology master's programs: sociology and applied sociology.

A master's degree in sociology, typically a Master of Arts (MA) or a Master of Science (MS), requires that students develop an advanced understanding of sociological theory and research methods. Ideally, the student should be able to apply what she learns in class and discovers through her research to real-world situations.

Applied sociology master's programs have become a lot more popular as career opportunities for social science majors have increased with the rise of research institutes, think tanks, and academic institutions. These master's programs spend substantially more time on research methods, quantitative in particular, and on the application of theory to real-world settings and programs. Those with a master's degree in applied sociology often go on to work in research and evaluation offices or programs. These sociology programs do not simply focus on studying and understanding the social world but, importantly, on how sociology can be used to advance the social world.

Master's programs in sociology typically require that full-time students complete about 2 years of coursework, or 36 units, as well as some kind of concluding project, such as a thesis, exam, or capstone project. Unlike undergraduate programs, master's programs in sociology have few required courses beyond theory, research methods, and possibly an internship or co-op course. One of the great benefits of both master's and doctoral programs is that students have not only the opportunity to select their courses but also ample opportunity for independent and advanced scholarship.

A master's degree in sociology provides numerous career opportunities, such as teaching at a community college or part-time teaching at a 4-year university (doctoral degrees are most often required for teaching full-time in a 4-year university). Sociology master's degrees can also lead to careers in research and evaluation institutes. Full-time master's students often complete programs in about 2 years. Master's programs also can help gauge one's interest in sociology and in advancing to a doctoral program.

Doctoral Programs

Although a bachelor's degree in sociology is not needed to be considered a successful candidate for many sociology doctoral programs, the more experience one has with sociology, such as a sociology major/minor, or even employment in a setting that utilizes sociological skills, the more prepared he is for advanced studies.

Doctoral degrees are the highest degree a person with a focus in sociology can attain. The PhD, or Doctor of Philosophy, signifies that the scholar is able to apply theoretical concepts and thinking to a particular area of research, with the ability not only to master the material but also to produce work that advances the particular area of study. Doctoral programs consist of coursework (typically around 60 units) and qualifying exams to advance in the program. These exams include oral examinations where students must demonstrate an understanding of sociological terms and concepts, as well as written exams that test theory and its applications. Doctoral programs culminate in the most well-known and often-feared part of every doctoral program: the dissertation. Dissertations will be discussed in more detail later in this chapter.

A master's degree is not needed to apply to a doctoral program. While in a doctoral program, after a certain number of credits in coursework are completed and often a large paper or exam, students will be eligible for an "en route" degree. This means that the required amount of coursework or exams has been completed to qualify for a master's degree. This helps doctoral students who need to have a master's degree for employment while still in school.

Doctoral programs in the United States are typically housed within larger colleges and universities. These programs often provide ample opportunities, both funded and unfunded, for doctoral students, such as experience with research or serving as teaching assistants.

It takes the average sociology doctoral student between 7 and 8 years to complete her program. Some students complete the program much more quickly; however, they often come in with a master's degree and transfer their credits into the doctoral program, reducing the amount of classes they have to take while in the program. Those who finish more quickly are often also funded, so they can focus on their studies and not work.

WRITING TO GET INTO GRADUATE SCHOOL

For most scholars, the first introduction to sociological writing begins when they are undergraduate students; however, those same skills develop and take shape among graduate students. Writing is integral to graduate studies, as students learn about advanced theory and research methods through their writing. Many graduate students have often remarked that writing is much more enjoyable in graduate school than in their undergraduate experiences. Graduate students select their own courses and research interests, and, therefore, graduate studies provide more options for studying topics independently. The first major hurdle in the writing process for someone wanting to pursue advanced studies in sociology is the writing involved in the application process for master's and doctoral programs.

Application Process

The graduate school application packet typically contains letters of recommendation, a statement of purpose, transcripts, a writing sample, and Graduate Record Examination (GRE) test scores. Between researching programs and funding opportunities and preparing your application packet, you will likely spend a year preparing to apply and applying to graduate school, particularly if you are interested in doctoral programs. The more time you give yourself, the more likely you will be successful in the application process. We will briefly examine what is often required in graduate program application packets as well as provide advice on preparing them. For additional information on applying to graduate programs, you should make appointments with your sociology professors and advisors.

Letters of Recommendation

Of course you don't write your own letters of recommendation, but you can take steps to ensure that you receive good letters from your recommenders. Seek out faculty members, employers, mentors, and other people who know you very well personally, academically, or professionally. You want to find someone who not only *can* write you excellent letters of recommendation or provide you with great references but *will*. It is useless to spend all your time trying to get someone to write you a letter when you know that person is unreliable or will not do it.

Most programs require three letters of recommendation or the names and contact information of three people who can provide you with a reference. Even though those writing you letters of recommendation always have great intentions, you should be certain to have at least five people in mind who you are certain will be able to write you a letter, in case one person backs out or cannot write the letter for a particular reason. This also gives you the option of selecting an appropriate person to write a letter for a specific school.

To ensure good letters of recommendation, you want to make sure you spend some time with the person writing you the letter. If you are seeking a letter from a professor, you should be certain to visit her office hours so she can write a letter that focuses on you as a whole and not only on your classroom experience. If you can, try to get a teaching or research assistantship as an undergraduate student. This provides valuable experience you can put on your curriculum vitae (discussed in more detail later in this chapter) and provides the writer of your letter with something to write about. As an undergraduate student, if you find a professor you like, you should also try to take multiple courses with this professor, as many will write letters only for students they have gotten to know over several courses. This may go without saying, but you should try participating in this class and presenting the professor with quality work. Also, make sure you give all your recommenders time to write your letters. The rule of thumb is to give at least a month.

You should make sure that each recommender has as much information about you as possible and all the information he needs to write your letter. This may include a highlight sheet (see the Appendix), which underscores you, your interests, and the program (or job if you need a reference for an employment opportunity) you are interested in. It can be as simple as a bulleted list. If the recommender is your professor, tell him what aspects of the course you have done well in, what is important to you about the school or program you are interested in, and how you fit those elements. You may also have recommendation sheets to give your recommenders, as well as the address, e-mail address, or website where the letter should be submitted.

Although you do have the right to view your letter of recommendation, as it is part of your academic file, master's and doctoral program applications always offer applicants the option to waive their right to view the letter. Whether or not you decide to do this is a personal choice, but our advice is to waive your right to view the letter. If you do so, chances are that the person writing you the letter of recommendation will be more honest and forthcoming in her description and analysis of your work.

Graduate Record Examination (GRE): Standard GRE and Sociology GRE

In the United States, almost all sociology doctoral programs and many sociology master's programs use the GRE to gauge an applicant's potential for success in graduate education. This 4-hour, computer-based exam measures quantitative and verbal reasoning, as well as critical thinking and analytical writing skills. Despite the controversy over using this test as a measurement of a student's success in graduate school, the GRE is widely used by many graduate programs. As such, prospective graduate students should spend an ample amount of time studying and preparing for the GRE by focusing on their analytical writing, verbal reasoning, and quantitative reasoning skills. The GRE is created and administered by the Educational Testing Service (ETS), the same nonprofit testing service that conducts the Scholastic Assessment Test (SAT). It is important to note that the GRE changes its format every few years, so you may want to confirm this information with ETS. However, the GRE tends to consist of the following three sections:

1. The *analytical section* includes two timed essays where test takers evaluate a logical argument and express their views on a critical issue. Responses are measured to ensure the test takers' ability to apply critical thinking and writing skills to the response.

2. The *verbal reasoning section* measures a test taker's reading comprehension skills and her ability to apply her reasoning skills. This section no longer includes antonyms and analogies. This section also consists of text-completion questions, which test the student's ability to interpret and evaluate what she has read.

3. The *quantitative reasoning section* examines math skills such as algebra, statistics, geometry, probability, arithmetic, and data analysis. It also focuses on reasoning skills and provides real-life scenarios. This section of the exam includes a number of multiple-choice questions. No writing is involved in the quantitative reasoning section.

A vast majority of sociology graduate/doctoral programs that require the GRE require only that students take the standard GRE; however, some programs require the Sociology GRE. The Sociology GRE consists of 140 multiple-choice questions that evaluate the test taker's knowledge of sociological concepts, terms, and theories—such as deviance and social stratification—along with statistics, data, and methods.

Statement of Purpose

With the increase in students applying to graduate school, it is imperative that you write a well-organized and well-prepared statement of purpose to separate you from the rest of the applicants. Most graduate program applications require that students write about themselves as well as their career and research interests. Examples of statements of purpose essay prompts are provided in the Appendix.

Graduate programs use a variety of different essay prompts and instructions. In addition, the way each applicant approaches and responds to the prompt will vary based on the individual student, program, research interest, career interest, etc. As a result, the best advice we can offer is to be honest and forthcoming in your essay. This is the most personal piece of writing—and, for many of you, the only piece of writing—you will write as part of your application packet. Be honest in your description of your research interests and career intentions. You are applying to be at this institution for, some of you, several years. It is important that you and the program are a good match.

Spend time writing your personal statement, and do not rush the writing process. Think about your research/career interests, why you chose sociology, why you want to attend this particular program. We would suggest seeking out help from a career or study center on campus, as well as from a sociology department advisor and/or professor, on composing and revising your statement of purpose. The key to a good statement of purpose is the same for any piece of writing: spending time researching the program, creating a draft, reviewing, editing, and rewriting. The more time you spend on your essay, the better it will be.

Writing Sample

Graduate program application packets routinely require writing samples as an example of your level of writing. Look through the different papers you wrote in your previous program of study or some of the professional papers you may have written as part of your employment. The paper you select should show that you are an effective writer with strong critical thinking and analytical skills. The writing sample should, ideally, be a social science paper or at least something the admissions committee or panel will understand. For example, a paper written for an anatomy course would not serve as an appropriate writing sample for most graduate or doctoral sociology program application packets.

Make sure you edit the writing sample before turning it in. Even if an application requires that you submit a writing sample that was a course paper, you can still edit it before turning it in. While you are still in college, you should keep in mind that you may need a writing sample for graduate school, so try to produce work while you are an undergraduate student that could serve as a writing sample in the future. You should not submit a paper with edits, a grade, or your professor's comments marked on it. Remember, it is a writing sample, not a sample of a graded course paper. Ideally, you will have a digital version of the paper saved, but if you do not, either choose another paper or retype it so you are submitting a clean copy to the admissions committee.

Transcripts

Graduate programs require a record of the courses you took as part of your undergraduate study, as well as the grades earned in said courses. Importantly, your transcripts contain your grade point average, or GPA. Graduate programs routinely set minimum GPA requirements for their applicants. The GPA requirement for admissions into a doctoral program (3.5 or B+/A−) is typically higher than for master's programs (3.0 or B). The higher your GPA, the more likely you will not only get into school but obtain funding as well.

WRITING IN GRADUATE SCHOOL

Students undertake a variety of writing projects while in sociology master's and doctoral programs. The type of writing project will be determined by the nature of the program, professor/instructor, and student's interest. Once you are in graduate school, you will do two major types of writing: course papers/projects and culmination papers/projects, such as a thesis or dissertation.

Course Papers

The most common papers you will write while in a graduate program are research papers and annotated bibliographies.

Research Papers

The research papers you will write as a sociology graduate student will likely be more thorough and in depth than the papers you wrote as an undergraduate student. These papers will typically require the analysis of theory or its application to a social issue. As a graduate student, you will often be required to reference or cite readings from scholarly journals and books. Ideally, the references you use to write these papers will also be used in your thesis or dissertation. The manuscript writing guidelines in Chapter 8 can help you complete research papers, although you will probably not be expected to conduct original research before producing such a paper. Your professor may ask that you concentrate more on one aspect of the paper than on others. For example, a professor may ask you to produce something that is closer to a literature review than to a completed manuscript.

Annotated Bibliographies

When writing annotated bibliographies while in graduate school, you should make sure to include the most prominent literature in the course's subfield to increase your general knowledge of the area and develop the literature review for your thesis or project. For a more detailed discussion on annotated bibliographies, see Chapters 3 and 4.

Culmination Projects

Graduate programs in sociology require that students complete a project that demonstrates that the student has mastered and can contribute to the field of sociology. This project is presented to a committee of sociology and social science faculty (in some cases, faculty members outside of your university can be included on these committees). Doctoral programs in sociology in the United States require that students complete a dissertation and, typically, at least one exam. Master's programs generally require a thesis, exam, or project/capstone.

Thesis

A thesis is a large research paper that contains an original idea or proposed theory that you expound on, test, or analyze in the paper. Many undergraduate programs also require students to write a thesis, usually for honors or specialized programs. A thesis is typically written as the culminating project in a master's program but not in a doctoral program. They can be written and formatted in a variety of different ways, which will greatly depend on the specifications of your committee. Once you have gathered the guidelines, Chapter 8 can help you formulate the required sections of a typical master's thesis.

Project/Capstone

Projects are increasingly becoming popular as the final assignment in a number of master's programs, most often in applied sociology graduate programs. All the research and courses you took while in your program culminate in a project that serves as the capstone of your education. Projects vary based on program requirements and student research interest. Projects are typically the application of theory to fix or provide advice on a problem or issue within an organization, institution, community, or some other social setting. Depending on the program requirements, you may find the policy paper in Chapter 10 to be a framework you can use to write up your project.

Comprehensive Exam

Often, both master's and doctoral programs have a variety of qualifying exams. Some exams require that you sit in a room and answer an essay question, while others require a paper written in the format of a journal article. You should take as much time as possible to answer the essay question. Make sure that you read the question carefully and take notes as to how you will answer it. Then follow the steps we have provided in this book: Put your notes into an outline, write a first draft, revise, and then write your second/final draft. Before you hand it in, check again to make sure you have answered the question. If your program allows, you should read previous versions of the exam so you have an idea of the types of questions your school asks.

Dissertation

In essence, a dissertation is a large paper, often book length, written based on the research interests of the scholar as well as the specifications of the researcher's committee. We have seen dissertations that range in length from 50 to 1,000 pages. Dissertations are designed not only to prove your knowledge of the field of study but also to demonstrate your ability to help advance the discipline through the examination of various theories and research methods. Generally, dissertations come in two types: an expanded version of an empirical paper or a book-formatted project, where each chapter covers a different aspect of the research. For both types, our chapter on research manuscripts will direct you in completing the writing required.

This discussion in no way encompasses all the writing you will do while in graduate school. You should also try to seek out faculty in your department who are actively engaged in your area of research. See if you can work with them on their projects. These faculty members may coauthor a publication with you, or you may be able to use some of the data being researched in your thesis or final project. Use graduate school to begin to develop and build up your curriculum vitae by presenting at conferences, obtaining research experience, and seeking out publications. Do not forget that while you want to have an enriching and well-rounded experience in graduate school, the reason students enroll in a graduate program is to complete the program and jump-start their careers.

CAREERS

Sociology is a fascinating area of study that provides skills applicable to many career choices. You will have different career options depending on whether you hold a bachelor's (BA), MA/MS, or PhD in sociology. Even an undergraduate major in sociology will provide you with a wide array of sociological insights and opportunities. Sociology offers skills in research methods, problem solving, editing, advising, and critical and analytical thinking.

Before you decide to pursue a degree in sociology—or in any field, for that matter—you should first ask yourself what you want to do with the degree.

Although many students take sociology courses or select the major because it addresses many interesting issues and topics such as religion, sexuality, disease, crime, etc., we advise students first to decide what they are interested in doing in their lives after school and then to determine if a sociology degree will help advance that particular career choice.

The American Sociological Association (ASA) website (www.asanet.org) is a great resource for students looking to pursue a career where they get to apply the skills they learned in their sociology courses. ASA provides the following career areas where a degree in sociology is helpful:

Figure 11.1

- *Social services* → in rehabilitation, case management, group work with youth or the elderly, recreation, or administration
- *Community work* → in fundraising for social service organizations, nonprofits, child-care or community development agencies, or environmental groups
- *Corrections* → in probation, parole, or other criminal justice work
- *Business* → in advertising, marketing and consumer research, insurance, real estate, personnel work, training, or sales
- *College settings* → in admissions, alumni relations, or placement offices
- *Health services* → in family planning, substance abuse, rehabilitation counseling, health planning, hospital admissions, and insurance companies
- *Publishing, journalism, and public relations* → in writing, research, and editing
- *Government services* → in federal, state, and local government jobs in such areas as transportation, housing, agriculture, and labor
- *Teaching* → in elementary and secondary schools, in conjunction with appropriate teacher certification

(http://asanet.org/employment/careers.cfm)

Since there are so many career choices for sociology majors, it is futile even to attempt to explain the different types of writing one may encounter as part of a particular career. The important thing is to use the lessons you have learned in this book to create the types of writing that are appropriate for the career you have chosen. Additionally, to apply to these career choices, you will be required to have at least a letter of interest/statement of intent/cover letter and a curriculum vitae, which will all be discussed in the following sections.

Curriculum Vitae

A curriculum vitae, or CV, is an academic résumé. CVs are used similarly to résumés in Europe, although in the United States, they are primarily used within academic and research institutions. In American academic institutions, we are much more likely to use a CV as opposed to a traditional résumé; as such, we will focus more in this chapter on writing CVs than on writing résumés.

While the traditional résumé primarily focuses on your previous work experience in the area in which you are applying, CVs focus on your research and teaching experience within academia or in an applicable area. Unlike résumés, which usually have the few subsections of contact information, education, work experience, and references, CVs provide much more information. CVs can contain the following subheadings: address/contact information, current employment, education, papers published, conference presentations, courses taught, research experience, grants, awards, fellowships, professional memberships, research/teaching areas of interest, languages spoken, specialized skills, and references. Keep in mind that there is no one right or wrong way to structure the CV, so you may find yourself experimenting with different formats to find one which most highlights your strengths.

First, list all information in chronological order, with the most recent information first. We suggest putting the month and year the CV was last updated at the top or bottom of your CV, possibly under your name or in a footer, so that you and the reviewer know that the CV is updated and, if the reviewer holds on to it, when it was last updated. Keeping track of dates is very important since you will need to provide timelines for attendance in educational programs and dates of publications and conference presentations. You should add items to your CV immediately after they happen. Many job applications will also ask you for this information.

In constructing your CV, you want to make sure it looks both professional and well organized. We suggest first laying out the various headings for each section of your CV and then using a formatting tool, such as a table, to organize the various headings. Once you have completed constructing your CV, you should hide the borders. You can do this in any edition of Microsoft Office Word, as well as in most other word-processing programs. As previously mentioned, CVs contain the following information and typically in the following order.

Name/Contact Information

Begin with your name, in larger font than the rest of the font sizes, in bold, and centered or at least separate from the other text on the line. Beneath your name, include your current address. If you are a current graduate student or affiliated with a university and can receive mail there, you should include your sociology department address. You can also include your home address if you like. Separate the university address from your home address by placing them on opposite sides of your name or on different rows. You should include your home or mobile phone number, as well as your e-mail address. It goes without saying that you should use your university e-mail address or your professional e-mail address. If you plan on posting your CV online, you may want to reconsider including your home address/personal telephone number. For example, it is unlikely that you will see the home addresses and personal telephone numbers of faculty on their CVs; however, home contact information may be the primary contact for people who do not have an office. Make sure it is clear whether you are providing your personal information or university information.

Employment

Typically, those with academic appointments or research-related positions include employment experience within academic or research institutions before educational experience. The title and name of the institution will be listed, as well as the dates the position was held. Some people with academic appointments will also include a section titled "Current Position" if they want to highlight a current experience. However, most students will skip over this section and begin with education.

Education

Provide your educational background, and for graduate students, begin by listing all undergraduate institutions attended as well as major and year of attendance and degrees completed. Also, note whether or not you graduated from these institutions and list the degrees earned and majors. List each institution, from your first undergraduate institution to the present. If you earned any special honors, such as Magna Cum Laude or a particularly high GPA, you may want to make note of that. Include any degrees you may have earned from certificate programs.

Publications

We realize that, as students, you may not have publications yet; however, we will briefly cover this section of the CV. Published articles and books listed on the CV should be written in ASA or American Psychological Association format. Publications are listed in chronological order from the most recent to the earliest. Some separate peer-reviewed publications found within scholarly journals from non-peer-reviewed publications. If an article, book, or some other work has been accepted for publication and is scheduled to be released or is forthcoming, list that publication first and write "forthcoming" where the date would appear.

Some opt to include separate headings for manuscripts under contract, manuscripts under review, and manuscripts in preparation. These sections are particularly important for graduate students, as they will likely have items to list under these headings but few or no publications. Provide references—without the date of publication and volume number, if applicable—for each manuscript that is under contract with a publisher.

Under the review section, list only those articles, books, or other writings that have been submitted and are still under review. There is some small debate over whether you should list the name of the journal while the manuscript is still under review, in the unlikely event that the reviewer may see your CV and recognize your work or because of the possibility that the journal may not accept your manuscript, which would then force you to continually change the name of the journal. However, many people do opt to include the place the manuscript is being reviewed, as it adds legitimacy to your "under review" claim.

In listing your manuscripts under preparation, make sure to include only those manuscripts you plan on submitting to journals or presses within the next few months.

Professional Presentations

List all your panel and roundtable presentations, including those you conducted at conferences and at your own institution. Provide your name, the year of the presentation, and the title of the work being presented, along with the institution and location where the presentation was held. This information should be provided in chronological order. Most professional sociology organizations allow students to present.

Teaching Experience

This section usually appears under a separate subheading from work experience, as CVs highlight your academic experience, teaching included. Again, you may not have information to include in this section; however, with more students working as teaching assistants and graduate students teaching courses, many of you will be including this in your CVs. Under teaching experience, list your official title, the name of the course, and the year and semester it was taught. If you served as a teaching assistant, also include the name of the instructor, and you may want to briefly list some of the responsibilities you held in the course.

Fellowships, Grants, Honors, Awards

List all your fellowships, grants, honors, and awards in chronological order, beginning with the most recent award given. List the name of the award, the year of the award, and who distributed the award. In the case of large monetary awards, such as grants, you also may want to include the amount awarded.

Previous Work Experience

List all the different positions you have held in academia and relevant non-academic and volunteer work. These include any research experience, paid or nonpaid; conference work; editing work; committee work; and internship or co-op work. Provide your title, making sure it is clear what role you performed and the date you performed it. These should be listed in chronological order from most recent to earliest. Again, unless you accomplished some amazing task while in high school and you are currently an undergraduate student, focus on work you have done since you entered college. You should also avoid listing any work that does not support your academic goals. While you might be proud of the time you spent working retail in the Adidas Originals or Disney Store, it is not relevant to your academic experiences.

Professional Memberships

If you have any active memberships in professional organizations, such as ASA, list the name of the organization as well as any special sections or organization committees you may serve on. All professional sociology organizations encourage student involvement and allow students to present their research and papers on special panels during conferences. Again, these organizations offer discount prices for membership and conferences for students.

Languages/Special Skills

If you know or are fluent in any other languages besides English, list the language and the level of fluency you have in writing, reading, and speaking that language. Also, list any statistical or qualitative programs or software packages you may be well versed in, such as SPSS and ATLAS.ti.

Areas of Interest

List your areas of research and teaching interest in sociology. In Chapter 3, we discussed and listed the different sociology sections and areas of study within sociology. Look through this list and select the areas that interest you most, and include any other areas of study within sociology that are not included in the list of sections.

References

You should have professional associations with at least three people who can provide you with a reference. Provide each reference's name, title, institution, institutional address, telephone number, and e-mail address. Those who act as references are typically professors or professional colleagues, mentors, supervisors, or employers. These should be the same people you have approached for letters of recommendation. Some people list up to four references on their CVs. These references should be able to speak to your research and career interests. Each person does not necessarily need to be aware of all aspects of your experiences, but you should make sure that, as a whole, they provide a complete picture of you. If you are not applying for a particular position and plan on posting your CV online, you may want to avoid including the names and contact information of your references and should simply write, "References furnished on request."

As students, you are not likely to have a very long CV, as you won't have much research or teaching experience yet. However, it is important to begin developing a CV while in school and to make sure you keep it updated.

There are two types of CVs: the abridged CV and the regular CV. A regular CV covers all your research and any teaching experience you may have participated in since you began your academic career—typically, this starts with college. Be certain to list all panel presentations, papers presented, publications, and relevant volunteer experience. You should keep track of everything you will include on your CV so you do not forget to include it all later. Some seasoned academics have CVs that are dozens of pages long.

An abridged CV, on the other hand, is a shortened version of your regular CV. For this, you should include information from your two most recent institutions. Abridged CVs are often tailored for the particular position, omitting all nonrelated positions and experience, and are typically only a few pages in length. When writing an abridged CV, it is important to let the reader know it is abridged. The reader will assume it is not abridged if not explicitly indicated. If the CV is abridged, write "abridged" in small font under your name or in the header, along with the month and year when the CV was last updated.

Focus your CV on your current and most recent educational experiences. If you have attended only undergraduate school, you should include on your CV any appropriate work you performed in high school. For example, if a sophomore in college won an award for a psychology paper she wrote in high school, she would include that on her CV. However, once she enters a doctoral program, she should no longer include what she did in high school, or even mention her high school under education on her CV. If she were to become an assistant professor, she would list information that goes only as far back as the start of her doctoral study. She would list her undergraduate degree but would no longer include her undergraduate work (unless this work included a major grant, fellowship award, or publication).

Since space is such an issue in constructing and organizing your CV, the font style should be Arial, Times New Roman, or some other standard font. With the exception of your name, the font size should be between 10 point and 12 point (for readability). Try to keep the margins about 1 inch all around.

Résumé

Unlike a CV, a résumé focuses more on professional, non-academic work experience. There are typically three different types of résumés: those written in chronological order (chronological), those based on skills (functional), and those that are more of a hybrid model—a combination of the two. You may want to do a search for résumés in the career you are interested in to make sure you create one that fits the position for which you are applying (see the sample résumé in the Appendix).

Chronological Résumé

In your chronological résumé, you should cover your relevant work experience for the position to which you are applying. For example, if you are applying for a job at a research institute and have a lot of work experience as a paid research assistant but spent a summer working at a fast-food restaurant, you can leave off your fast-food job. The résumé should generally be limited to one page, should be one-sided, and should cover all relevant work experience over the previous 10 years. Résumés provide similar information as CVs but in a much more condensed fashion. Even though space is typically an issue in constructing and organizing a résumé, you still need to make sure your résumé looks professional. The font style should be similar to that of a CV—Arial, Times New Roman, or some other standard font style—with the font size generally between 10 point and 12 point.

Name/Contact Information. Center your name, and be sure to make the font larger than the rest of the font sizes in the résumé. The idea is to make sure your name stands out. Below your name, provide your address, e-mail address, and telephone number. Since this is a résumé and not a CV, you should include your personal address; you will not necessarily need your university-affiliated information.

Objective. Your objective is the reason why you are applying for the position—in essence, the goal of the résumé. In fact, it is becoming increasingly popular to leave this objective section off of the résumé. However, choosing to include this in the résumé and referring to the position to which you are applying shows the employer that the résumé was especially tailored for that position. The decision on whether or not to include an objective is up to you. You may want to check what other people who have applied to a similar position have done.

If you plan to include an objective, it should be a short sentence describing to your potential employer your objective for pursuing this position. You will likely need to tailor your objective for the different jobs to which you are applying. Is your objective to find a position that will let you utilize your research analysis skills? Are you looking for an internship or co-op opportunity? This section shows the employer not only that you are interested in the position but how you fit the position. The objective describes a little about you to the employer.

Education. The education section comes after the objective statement or, if an objective is not included, below your name and contact information. Potential employers need to know your educational experience. Provide your degree, program/major, minor (if you have one), and the month and year you graduated or expect to graduate. Also list the name of the academic institution. List all the colleges or academic institutions you have attended since high school. If you attended several different colleges, you may want to limit your list to those from which you have obtained degrees or certificates. Your educational experience should be listed in chronological order, starting with your most recent educational experience or your most recently earned degree.

If you are applying for an academic position or a position that requires specialized training or a degree, you may want to highlight any educational qualifications and added experience you have. For example, you may want to include a short blurb in this section if you have earned a high GPA or graduated with honors.

Related Experience. As résumés are rather short, you want to focus this section only on your related experience. If you do not have a lot of experience, you can call it simply "experience." List your relevant work, volunteer, internship, and co-op experiences. Provide your title/position, making sure it is clear what role you performed and the date you performed this work. These experiences should be listed in chronological order from most recent to earliest.

Honors/Awards. List any honors, awards, or fellowships you may have received that relate to the position to which you are applying.

Skills. Here, list any skills and certifications you may have. If you know or are fluent in any other languages besides English, list them here along with the level of fluency you have in writing, reading, and speaking each one. If you know any particular software programs or are well versed in Microsoft Office, for example, inform the potential reviewer what this skill set is and how advanced you are in it.

Functional Résumé

A functional résumé is generally used for someone who has limited experience or is attempting to move into a position she has not worked in previously. Rather than focusing on the position, a functional résumé focuses on the relevant skills you may have gained over several different positions. Functional résumés are compiled in different ways, but they typically include the following sections.

Contact Information. Your name should be centered, in bold and in a slightly larger font, at the top of your résumé. Your personal contact information, including your address, e-mail, and telephone number, should follow.

Objective. Explain why you are applying for this position. What is the purpose of this résumé? How do you fit this position?

Summary of Qualifications/Profile. In this section, either called summary of qualifications or profile, you should include a quick summary of your skills. What stands out in your experience that you think a potential employer would be interested in? Write in quick, short sentences. This should not be any longer than two paragraphs.

Professional Skills. Without necessarily naming the particular positions, describe in detail the skills you gathered during your work experience. If you are interested in finding a job in a nonprofit office and you've worked as a record keeper in several different retail locations, you can talk about your skill with word processing, strict record keeping, and communication with clients. You should include three or four categories of skills, detailing beneath each one how it applies to you.

Skills Summary. If there are additional skills you think are important, you can include them in a list of bullet points.

Education. Finally, you can include your educational information, beginning with your most recent school.

References. Try not to include your list of references on the résumé itself; instead, you should include the phrase, "References will be furnished on request." An interested potential employer will contact you for a list of references. If you do want to or are required to include references on your résumé, provide each reference's name, title, institution, institutional address, telephone number, and e-mail address. Those listed as references are typically professors or professional colleagues, mentors, supervisors, or employers. Your reference list should consist of people who will provide a positive evaluation to a potential employer.

Hybrid Résumé

A hybrid résumé begins the same way as the functional résumé but, above the education, includes a related experience section and lists the few positions you have worked where the experience is relevant to the position to which you are applying. You might also include volunteer and community service experiences.

Letter of Interest/Intent

Letters of interest, sometimes referred to as letters of intent, consist of four major parts: your introduction, a description of your experience, reasons why you would be a good match for the position, and your appreciation for having your letter reviewed (letter writing is discussed in detail in Chapter 2).

Letters of interest are usually broken down into four sections:

The *first section* serves as an introduction to the employer and states the position to which you are applying. You also state here why you are writing the letter.

The *second section* describes your relevant work experience and how it applies to the current position.

In the *third section*, describe your character traits and any special skills you may have.

The *fourth section* concludes the letter and thanks the potential employer for her or his time.

As you can see, writing plays an integral role within sociology—it helps us become sociologists. A couple of very helpful books can get you started on the variety of career options sociology students have. *Great Jobs for Sociology Majors* by Stephen Lambert and *Careers in Sociology* by W. Richard Stephens, Jr. both provide useful resources that will help you if you are interested in a career where you can apply the skills you developed as an emerging sociologist.

SUMMARY

This chapter examines professional as well as graduate school writing. We focused not only on the major writing assignments found within most sociology graduate programs but also on the writing involved in the graduate school application process. Additionally, this chapter examines the writing necessary in the beginning stages of a sociology career. More specifically, this chapter reviews the following areas:

- Master's and doctoral sociology programs, as well as the types of writing usually performed within these programs
- Letters of recommendation, letters of intent, the GRE, and other aspects of the application process
- Course papers and culmination papers, such as dissertations
- How to write a CV and résumé, as well as the differences between the two

This chapter contains two "Writing in Practice" essays. In the first piece, Rutgers University sociology doctoral student Shatima J. Jones explains how she used course papers to help inform her dissertation research. The other piece was written by Dr. Martine Hackett, a sociologist formally employed by the New York Department of Health and Human Hygiene. Dr. Hackett explains how she "translates" sociology for those in professional settings who are not sociologists. She also explains the value of sociology methods and theories for those outside of the academy.

WRITING IN PRACTICE

by Shatima J. Jones

When I began my graduate career 4 years ago, the task of writing three 20-page final course papers was daunting. I'd entered grad school knowing that I was interested in questioning the existence of a "Black community." But after my first semester of writing three course papers, I became frustrated about spending so much time completing the assignments without feeling even one step closer to a thesis or dissertation. I couldn't imagine any immediate or future usefulness of the papers to my research interest. I soon figured out two key strategies to help me successfully write final course papers and make progress toward a thesis. First, I chose classes that related to my research interest versus classes I was interested in. Second, I conceptualized and wrote final course papers as possible sections of my thesis or dissertation. These strategies have enabled me to write a master's thesis and three complete dissertation chapter drafts to date.

As soon as I was able to take elective courses, which was at the beginning of my second year, I signed up for courses that related to my research interest rather than course topics I was generally interested in. By this time, I'd figured out that I wanted to begin research in a place that has been historically recognized as a significant institution to the "Black community"—the barbershop—to find out if and how Black men express a sense of relatedness to one another. I took an ethnography course in the fall in hopes of getting started with research connected to my thesis. This course allowed me to pick a research site, collect data, and write fieldnotes daily. Though writing throughout the course was intense at times, writing the 50-page final paper was not arduous since it consisted of the raw fieldnotes loosely grouped together by themes. There was no theory, literature review, or analytic frame to the paper.

I knew I was on to some interesting dynamics in the barbershop. The following semester, I registered for a qualitative methods course so I would be able to stay in the field and continue to collect data. The final paper for this class, however, required the inclusion of theory and a literature review in addition to my empirical findings. I mostly read classic ethnographies on race and place and on Black barbershops, in particular, as an analytic frame. I had a sharper gauge of what was happening in the barbershop given the considerable amount of data collected and the time I'd spent in the field. My final paper for the qualitative methods course was the first draft of my master's thesis.

I then shared my paper with several people. I sent the paper to my former ethnography professor, in whose class I initially began my fieldwork. I also had my qualitative

(Continued)

(Continued)

methods professor's comments to take into consideration. I asked a couple of peers who are interested in race and ethnography to read my draft as well. The next step was to take all the comments given to me and figure out which suggestions I would include in my next round of revisions. I generally revised based on critiques that were consistent among the readers, regarding the need to clarify my writing, definition of key terms, and warnings about making claims not proven by the data I provided. I thought more carefully about incorporating comments I felt weren't in line with my intended goal for the paper. I also read and incorporated recommended literature.

After a couple more rounds of revisions, the paper was a good enough draft to set up a proposal meeting with three professors forming a qualifying paper committee. I sent the paper draft to them, and we met to discuss the next round of revisions. I revised the paper based on comments from the committee members and from a couple of peers before it was passed as my master's thesis. It had taken about a year for me to craft this master's thesis.

Notably, I managed full-time coursework as I was writing and revising drafts of my master's thesis. I followed the rule of picking classes that related to my research interests. For instance, I took a class titled "Ghettos, Communities, and Urban Enclaves" during the same semester as the qualitative methods course. I wrote a final paper that discussed several leading theories and conceptualizations of community formation. A substantial portion of the final course paper for the community class was included in my dissertation proposal—which is an expansion of my research on the existence of a "Black community." Likewise, I took Sociology of Culture the same semester that I defended my master's thesis. I wrote a final paper that links the history of the Black barbershop as a cultural institution to its current media representations in pop culture. The paper is now a dissertation chapter draft.

I want to clarify that picking courses based on your research interest doesn't require having an established dissertation topic prior to course selection. On the contrary, taking courses related to my broad research interests introduced me to literatures and existing findings in the field—so much so that it helped me transform my interests into a topic and narrow the scope of my proposed research agenda. The courses allowed me to study projects that had already been conducted in the areas of my research interest. I could then begin to think about how I could build on the existing works with my thesis or dissertation research. This is also the phase when I felt as though whatever research topic I came up with had already been carried out and published. And it was actually during that time of taking classes, trying to think of a final paper topic, and feeling as though every topic that interested me had already been done that I began to hone in on what my thesis and dissertation research might involve.

In closing, writing in graduate school can seem intimidating at first. The selection of courses related to my research interest was an invaluable tool that helped me organize and transform my approach to writing as a student. I would ask myself the following questions when choosing electives: Can I think of one way this class may contribute to the development of my thesis or dissertation research interest either theoretically, empirically, or methodologically? Can I think of a final paper topic that incorporates material from the course and could also serve as the basis of a thesis section or a chapter draft in my dissertation? Plus, when it came time to write the final papers, I was excited instead of anxious. I knew that I would revisit the paper as a part of my thesis or chapter in the dissertation. In the end, writing in grad school became a pleasant step toward making progress with my thesis and dissertation.

—Shatima J. Jones is a doctoral student in the
Sociology Department at Rutgers University.

WRITING IN PRACTICE

by Martine Hackett

I can speak and write "sociology," but I don't get to use it much anymore. Having spent the past 4 years as a public health professional in the largest health department in the country, I am in a place where sociology is considered somewhat of a foreign language. Successfully translating sociology in my writing in a non-academic setting resembles navigating a language in a new locale. It means using the right terms at the right times, all with an awareness of how the audience is absorbing it all. The link between sociology and public health makes sense on the surface. Public health is the study and solving of a range of health issues—from disease outbreaks to smoking bans to condom distribution—for the entire population served. Those in the population who are disadvantaged often have worse health outcomes, and many of the key issues sociologists are concerned with are present when looking at the health and well-being of the public. However, public health folks have their own language that they are very fond of using. This language is based in epidemiology and has a strong bureaucratic accent. Writing in public health is practical, describing conditions in a direct manner.

(Continued)

(Continued)

Translating sociological terms and concepts for those who are not familiar with them adds an additional element to communication. In my work, I connect sociological concepts such as inequality by race, ethnicity, gender, and class to poor health outcomes and present it both to my colleagues in public health and to the general public. For example, when describing the conditions for infant mortality, it has proven invaluable to possess the language that can describe the larger piece of the puzzle and explain how structural inequalities influence the health of communities and, ultimately, individuals. Providing the statistics of morbidity and mortality is an important and necessary work in public health. Often, a sociological perspective is useful to answer the public questions about why the numbers are the way they are. The ability to translate those concepts in an understandable manner through writing is essential.

Making this translation often means struggling for the right words. Recently, I contributed to a report on child fatalities and the changes in how the causes of infant deaths are coded by the medical examiner. Traditionally, when an infant was found dead at home after going to sleep, the cause of death was designated as Sudden Infant Death Syndrome (SIDS). Though the exact cause was unknown, when the authority (the medical examiner) declared SIDS the cause of death, parents were somewhat comforted by being told there was nothing they could have done to prevent the death. However, in recent years, medical examiners have increasingly classified the cause of death for infants found dead in bed as suffocation. This decision changed the statistics and had a different effect on parents, who were now guilty of putting their infants at risk. What I was witnessing was the social construction of a cause of death and the creation of a new social problem. But how do I write that without the jargon so the audience can understand this relevant sociological concept? I focus on choosing words that precisely describe the concept and include only information that contributes to the audience's overall understanding of the situation.

Different audiences also must be considered. In fact, with all my writing at work, I am aware of the different audiences. When writing to colleagues, it is usually more important to be accurate, clear, and, most important, concise. When writing materials for the public, translating numbers (rates, ratios, prevalence, significance, etc.) into plain language is necessary to make those numbers mean something to people. Overall, I have found that just bringing a sociological imagination to work is helpful in most social service–type jobs, since the reasons so many of these issues exist are rooted in inequalities.

In my experience with navigating the terrain of public health, I have learned a few helpful tips. Translating sociology means this:

- Connect what you are writing about to contemporary, real-world issues and how these concepts are currently playing out.
- Feel comfortable with the sociological concepts you are discussing, but avoid going too deep. As long as it is accurate, no one will be testing to see if you know the fine, deeper points of sociological theories.
- Beware of politics! Very little is value-free, and what you are writing does not just represent you; it represents the place that pays you, and you need to be cautious. I have found that getting approval from multiple sources along the chain of command may be time-consuming but is ultimately a time saver. Pay attention to what your boss and, particularly, what your boss's boss suggest, and make their revisions. Yes, changing what you write is the norm.
- Write clearly and get to the point.
- Skip the references. People are not interested in references unless they are in a research report or grant proposal.

Ultimately, sociology is the study of the social world, and since we all live in that world, we can all understand these concepts on some level. I have found that writing for nonsociologists means finding that place where we all share a deeper human connection and explaining it in a way people understand is a worthy endeavor. If what you are writing about is a social fact, a true concept, then it can be explained so everyone understands it. What you are doing is simply giving a name to something people are most likely already familiar with in their own lives. These are the issues that appeal to a universal language of human nature. Some things need little translation at all.

—Dr. Martine Hackett, PhD, is a special assistant professor
at Hofstra University in Long Island, New York.

NOTE

1. Schmidt, Peter. 2010. "Graduate-School Applications Spiked After Economy's Plunge." *The Chronicle of Higher Education*, September 14. Retrieved April 23, 2011 (http://chronicle.com/article/Graduate-School-Applications/124387).

ASSIGNMENTS

The following assignments are designed to help students learn about the writing discussed in the corresponding chapters.

CHAPTER 2

Paragraphs

Read several paragraphs from a journal article.

- Can you identify an introduction, a main point, any elaboration, and the conclusion or transition?
- What words are used to signal each type of paragraph?

Subsections

Read a journal article.

- How far do you have to read before you discover a connection to any of the main propositions?
- How does the writer indicate the main propositions?

Read a journal article.

- Identify the different types of paragraphs.
- Classify each paragraph as main point, elaboration, or conclusion.
- Classify elaborations as affirmative or contradictory.

Voice

Find a paragraph from an article or something you have written.

- Can you rewrite it for an audience of students?
- What about for professors?
- What about for educators or politicians?

Letters

Reread an e-mail you have written to someone.

- Does it have all the pieces we discussed?
- If you read it out loud in an angry tone, does the meaning of the letter change?
- What about if you read it out loud in a sad tone?

CHAPTER 3

Propositions: Developing a Thesis Statement

Select one subject of interest within sociology based on the American Sociological Association sociology sections described in the chapter.

- Develop one **topic** for this subject.
- Create one **research question** for this topic.
- Create one **thesis statement** for this topic.

CHAPTER 4

Book Reviews: Writing Book Reviews

- Write a 900-word book review in 12-point Times New Roman font, with 1-inch margins all around.
- This book review should be double spaced.
- You must provide a title, a citation of the book, and your contact information.

Book Reviews: Book Review Comparison

- Read a book review from *The New York Times* (http://www.nytimes.com/pages/books/index.html).
- Then read a book review from a scholarly journal. You can also go to your campus library website and type in the name of an academic book in the keyword search and type "review" or select "books reviewed." You can also select *Contemporary Sociology,* which is a journal of book reviews.

- Write a short, 300- to 400-word essay comparing and contrasting book reviews (showing how they are similar and different). What could be done to the *New York Times* review to make it look similar to an academic book review and vice versa?

CHAPTER 5

Institutional Review Board: IRB Review Essay

Imagine you are conducting a qualitative or quantitative research study that requires human participants.

- Identify a sample population, research methodology, and research question and hypothesis.
- Look up your institution's IRB office, also commonly known as the office of research compliance.
- In a short essay, describe what you would need to do to complete the IRB approval process for your institution.
- Identify the IRB forms you would have to submit to your institution's IRB office for this project. Would your project likely be exempt, expedited, or go for a full review?

CHAPTER 6

Grants: Writing Grant Proposals

*To conduct research, sociologists often have to write grants for supplies, to pay respondents, and for travel. Imagine that you have **1 year** to complete a research project and you are applying for a grant for **$10,000**. Write a grant proposal for a research project. Your grant proposal should contain the following information (as you would with any grant, pay particular attention to formatting instructions and the word count):*

- A creative title (not "Grant Proposal")
- Introduction to the problem (200–300 words)
- Literature review (500–600 words)

- o Must contain at least **five** scholarly journal articles
- o Must contain at least **one** book
- o Make sure to note in your literature review: What does the literature on the topic say about your problem? Where is the literature lacking?

- Research methods (300–350 words)
  - o Will you be using qualitative or quantitative methods (be specific about which one and how you will go about you data collection)? Who will your subjects be? Where will they be located? Try to be as detailed as possible.

- References
  - o Provide a complete American Sociological Association citation for **each** article, book, or any other source **cited** in the literature review or introduction (you cannot provide the citation to an article/book that you did not reference in the literature review or introduction sections).

- Budget
  - o The grant you are applying for is for $10,000. You cannot request more than $10,000. Try to budget as close to $10,000 without going over. In your budget, you must include a justification for **every** purchase. You may want to consider the following costs: travel (flight, hotel, per diem [cost of food]); payment for your research subjects (cash, gift certificates) or for items you may want to purchase for your subjects in exchange for the interview/survey/focus group; cost of photocopying; pens; pencils; computer software (most grants don't cover the cost of computers); pay for research assistants to conduct interviews or transcribe.

- Budget tables
  - o Create tables breaking down the budget. Create a separate table for each topic (for example, do not list the cost of transcriptions and cost of hotel rooms in the same table).

- Format
  - o Times New Roman, 13-point font; single spaced, with 1 1/2-inch margins all around. Include **page numbers (page x of y)** and **your last name** in the header of each page (see examples at the top of this page); each word count should come at the end of each of these sections. Be sure to include a cover sheet.

CHAPTER 7

Qualitative Research: Writing Fieldnotes

*Immerse yourself in a public environment, such as a park, mall, or some other public space, for **4 hours.***

- Write a set of detailed fieldnotes describing what you see and the conversations you overhear.
- This could be written as a narrative or as a set of bullet points.
- These fieldnotes should be between 7 and 8 pages in length.

CHAPTER 8

Manuscripts: Scholarly Journal Submission Essay

- Select two of the scholarly journals from the list of sociology journals in the chapter.
- Write a brief essay in which you compare and contrast the submission requirements of the two journals.

CHAPTER 9

Editing: Introductions and Conclusions

- Take an old course paper and read only the introduction and conclusion.
- Where do you say you are taking your reader?
- Where do you actually take your reader?
- Try to write a quick outline of your paper based on the introduction and conclusion.
- How does your outline compare with what your paper is really about?

Editing: Reading Introductions

- Read the introduction of a journal article.
- Can you outline the article from the introduction?
- Read and outline the article.
- What is missing or unclear when you compare the two documents?

CHAPTER 10

Research: Newspapers and Magazines

- Pick up several different newspapers from the area you want to publish in.
- What kind of language do they use?
- How are they similar or different?
- What can you conclude about their audiences from their language, structure, or distribution?

Research: Blogs

- Choose a topic of interest to you, and search popular blogging software for blogs that cover it.
- What do you like about the blogs? What do you think could be done better?
- Is there an angle you want to take on the topics that hasn't been done (or done well)?

Writing: Op-Ed

- Read your favorite newspaper in your city.
- Save the articles that speak to you the most.
- Make a list of the things in the articles that speak to you.
- Keep note of the things you disagree with. Be sure to include why you disagree and what, if any, additional information you can provide.

Writing: Policy Documents

- Consider a problem in your city, state, or country, and ask yourself the following questions:

  o Why is it a problem?
  o Who does it affect?
  o What has been done to try to change it?
  o What should be done to change it?

CHAPTER 11

Career: Creating a Curriculum Vitae

Write a CV. Make sure to list the following information:

- Education
- Papers you have written for classes (instead of publications—that is, unless you have publications)
- Class presentations (instead of conference presentations—again, unless you have presented at a conference)
- Research experience
- Volunteer/real-world work experience
- Grants/scholarships/awards
- Professional memberships (most sociology organizations allow, and encourage, student membership)
- Research interests
- Three references (at least two must be professors)
- Format: 10- to 12-point, Times New Roman font, with 1-inch margins all around (See the sample CV in the Appendix.)

Appendix

CHAPTER 2

Often Mistaken Words

These are a few examples of words that are commonly mistaken for each other. We have not included every example, nor have we included every definition of each word. Our intention is to provide you these samples with the hope that they can assist you to become better writers. You should follow up with a dictionary or thesaurus for further information.

Then	vs.	Than
adv. At that time OR soon after that		*prep.* In comparison with
He remembered that he had jumped the turnstile and then run into the train.		She hoped to make him jealous by being more beautiful than he remembered.

Advice	vs.	Advise
n. A suggestion meant to assist		*vb.* To give advice
My sister's advice convinced me not to see him anymore.		Please advise me on these investments.

Affect	vs.	Effect
vb. To produce a material influence on or alteration in		*n.* Something that inevitably follows an antecedent (a preceding event, condition, or cause)
The paralysis affected his limbs.		The effect of the change in food on the animals was lethargy.

Your   vs.   **You're**

Adj. Possessed by yourself   Contraction of "you are"

This is your mail.   You're missing my point!

Accept   vs.   **Except**

vb. To receive willingly   *prep.* With the exclusion or
                                                 exemption of

I'll accept the box for my   I'll eat anything except eggs.
neighbor.

Desert   vs.   **Dessert**

n. An area of land with no or   *n.* A food served after a meal
little water

Being in the desert is like standing   Orange sherbet was my favorite
behind a bus.   dessert as a kid.

Its   vs.   **It's**

Adj. Possessed by itself   Contraction of "it is"

The house looks great. Its door   It's too late for dinner.
frames are solid oak.

Lay   vs.   **Lie**

vb. To put down   *vb.* To be in a horizontal position

Please lay your coat down on the   Just lie quietly until nap time is over.
bed.

Past   vs.   **Passed**

adj. Occurring in a time before   *vb.* To have moved by
this

My childhood is all in the past.   The car quickly passed us.

Their	vs.	They're	vs.	There
adj. Possessed by them		Contraction of "they are"		*adv.* A position away
Scarlett and Carlos are their friends.		They're going to head over to the party soon.		You don't have to come here; just stay there.

To	vs.	Too	vs.	Two
prep. Movement toward		*adv.* Also or excessively		*adj.* One more than one
Please move to the right.		I made too many cookies.		There are two of us.

Lose	vs.	Loose
vb. To miss or fail to win		*adj.* Not tight
I tied it on so I wouldn't lose it.		The screw was too loose.

Cite	vs.	Site	vs.	Sight
vb. To quote or refer to		*n.* A location		*n.* Ability or something to see
Don't forget to cite your references.		I visited the site of the new school.		The bird was a beautiful sight.

Sentences

At a very basic level, a sentence is something doing something. "A man walked" is an example of this. It begins with a capital letter. There is a noun, and there is a verb. The sentence ends with a period, exclamation point, or question mark. If you look back at the previous five sentences, you can see the same basic elements. A noun is a person, place, thing, animal, or abstract idea. The world is filled with nouns: *Chair, television, cat, turtle,* and *dog* are all examples of nouns. A verb expresses an existence, action, or occurrence. *Run, jump, sleep,* and *live* are all examples of verbs.

If we look back at the original sentence, we know several things. There existed a man, and he walked. However, there is a lot missing from this sentence. Who is this man? Why is he walking? How is he walking? Where is he walking? Some of the questions may be answered by the sentence that precedes or follows this one, but there is still space within the sentence if you wish to elaborate. For example, an adjective is a word that modifies or describes a noun or pronoun. In our original sentence, the man could be tall or smart, young or terrified. In academic writing, these kinds of adjectives are less likely except when describing individuals in qualitative research. Instead, you might use adjectives such as *alternative, consistent, decreasing, different, important, innovative, hierarchical, high, necessary, possible, primary*, and *significant*. Adverbs modify or describe verbs or adjectives. An adverb might be added to the sample sentence and lead to the man walking quickly or crazily. Again, some of the adverbs you might use in academia are *also, even, extremely, further, generally, only, particularly, perhaps, probably*, and *relatively*.

A sentence can also include other parts of speech, such as pronouns, which replicate or replace a noun. Often, we use the last name of an author to refer to that author later in a sentence or paragraph, but pronouns such as *he* and *she* are also used. There are also prepositions, which show the relationship between or among words in terms of direction, place, time, cause, manner, and amount. Examples of prepositions are *to, under, on, at, after*, and *by*. Finally, conjunctions connect words, sentences, or clauses. The conjunctions used in academia do not differ significantly from those used outside of an academic sphere. These are words such as *and, or, but, if, after, unless*, and *although*.

In academia, many of our sentences are compound sentences. When we talk about changing the length of your sentences to adjust the flow of your work, you can often accomplish that by creating or destroying compound sentences, which use conjunctions or transitions to connect clauses or sentences.

A clause is a group of words containing a subject and a verb. An independent clause has a subject and a verb, and can stand alone or be part of a larger compound sentence. A dependent clause cannot function as a sentence by itself. Usually, dependent clauses are preceded by a comma or a conjunction.

A more complicated version of the compound sentence is a complex sentence. This is a combination of several independent and dependent clauses. These are also very common in academic texts.

If students internalize school cultures as well as what is said in a lesson or textbook, then it makes sense to foster learning environments marked by habits of risk taking, generosity, and understanding of self and others. (DiPardo 2000:307)[1]

Active Words[2]

These are some examples of words that present you as someone who is actively engaged in whichever behaviors you are participating in. These may be helpful for cover letters, résumés, or curriculum vitae.

–A–

Accelerated	Administered	Assembled
Accomplished	Advised	Assumed responsibility
Achieved	Analyzed	
Adapted	Arranged	

–B–

Balanced	Blazed
Billed	Built

–C–

Carried out	Completed	Coordinated
Channeled	Conceived	Counseled
Collected	Conducted	Created
Communicated	Contracted	Cut
Compiled	Controlled	

–D–

Delegated	Determined	Dispatched
Demonstrated	Developed	Distributed
Designed	Directed	Documented

–E–

Edited	Enabled	Evaluated
Effected	Energized	Expanded
Eliminated	Established	Expedited

–F–

Facilitated	Found	Functioned as

–G–

Gained	Generated	Graduated
Gathered	Graded	

–H–

Handled	Hired

–I–

Implemented	Innovated	Interpreted
Improved	Inspected	Interviewed
Increased	Installed	Introduced
Influenced	Instituted	Invented
Initiated	Instructed	Issued

–L–

Launched	Lectured	Led

–M–

Maintained	Mastered	Modernized
Managed	Met with	Motivated

–N–

Negotiated

–O–

Operated	Ordered	Oversaw
Optimized	Originated	
Orchestrated	Organized	

–P–

Participated	Prepared	Proved
Performed	Presented	Provided
Pinpointed	Produced	Published
Planned	Programmed	Purchased

–R–

Recommended	Referred	Revamped
Recorded	Reinforced	Reviewed
Recruited	Represented	Revised
Reduced	Researched	Revitalized

–S–

Saved	Sold	Suggested
Scheduled	Solved	Supervised
Screened	Spearheaded	Supported
Served	Standardized	Surpassed
Set up	Steered	
Simplified	Structured	

–T–

Taught	Trained	Tripled
Tested	Translated	Typed

–U–

Underwrote	Updated	Used

–W–

Won	Wrote

Sample Job Cover Letter

123 Electric St.
New York, NY 10023
September 18, 2012

Dr. Christopher McCoy
6000 West End Ave.
New York, NY 12345

Dear Professor McCoy,

I am writing to apply for the position of statistical consultant at The College of the State of New York. I currently hold a master's degree in sociology and have spent the past year as a consultant for New York College. I am confident that my experiences in the application of mathematical concepts will serve me well in your school.

My research has focused on the effect of inclusion versus isolated classrooms for gifted children. I have found that while inclusion allows the entire class to move forward, it can impede the advancement of children who have moved beyond the standard curriculum.

I have also taught several courses in statistics at both the undergraduate and graduate levels. In my classes, I allow students to make connections to their lives through a selection of variables of importance to the students for their analyses.

During my time in graduate school and this past year, I have also had the opportunity to participate in several community-based organizations. I have worked closely with gifted children and their families to ensure the best educational environments could be found for the children.

I want again to express my interest in a position at The College of the State of New York. I have enclosed a copy of my résumé and several references you may contact. I look forward to speaking to you further.

Sincerely,
Adrian Garcia

Sample Submission Letter

Sunday, August 5, 2012

Dr. Nick R. Bocker
Journal of Sport in America
1 Penn Plaza
New York, NY 10119

Dear Dr. Bocker,

Enclosed, please find the paper titled "Sports at the Forefront of Culture," which I am submitting to *Journal of Sport in America*.

"Sports at the Forefront of Culture" examines the place of sports in contemporary American society. Using examples from the NBA, NFL, NHL, and MLB, the paper analyzes the ways culture influences sport as sport influences culture. This paper presents an important debate about what our interest in and following of sport teams says about our society, how we see ourselves, and how others see us.

I am currently a graduate student at The College of New York and am working on my dissertation on the impact of sports. I look forward to the opportunity to publish this article in *Journal of Sport in America* and to share my research with an audience interested in issues in sports. Please contact me if you have any further questions.

Sincerely,
J. Jenkins, Jr.

Sample Request Letter

123 Electric St.
New York, NY 10023
September 18, 2012

Dr. Joey Amaya Milan
6000 West End Ave.
New York, NY 12345

Dear Dr. Milan,

I hope you are doing well and that the summer has been enjoyable for you. I am writing this letter to let you know that I am applying for a position at New York College and to ask if you are available to write a letter of recommendation for me for this position. I recognize that this is a busy time of year, and, as such, I have attached a copy of my résumé, my cover letter, and a brief note highlighting my recent experiences. I can also meet with you if you need to speak with me. Please let me know if you require further information from me before beginning. Thank you again for your help.

Sincerely,
Zoe Robin

Sample Thank-You Letter

Dear Mr. James,

It was really great to meet you yesterday. I am writing to thank you for the opportunity to interview with you. It was wonderful to hear more about New York College and to speak to you about how I might become a part of it. I hope to have the opportunity to work with you in the future.

Sincerely,
Anthony Summer

CHAPTER 3

American Anthropological Association

The style of the American Anthropological Association (AAA) is most often used within the field of anthropology and its journals. However, as there can be a lot of overlap in the topics and research of interest to those within the social sciences, we have included AAA guidelines in addition to the APA and ASA styles, which are more likely to be found in sociology.

Short direct quotes should be incorporated into the text of your paper and enclosed in double quotation marks. Citations should be written in this format: ([author's last name] [year]:[page number]). If the quote is indirect or you are referring to the entire book, you need not include the page number. Insert a space between the author's last name and the year but not between the year and the page number. Again, you need not put the author's last name in parentheses if you include it as you discuss the quotation, and, if the year of publication is included with the author's name, you need not include it in the parentheses. Finally, if there is more than one author of one volume, include each person's last name (up to three authors) with commas between them and an *and* before the last author's name. If a work has three or more authors, include only the first author's name and use *et al.* for the other authors. If you are citing multiple works by the same author and date, they should be ordered alphabetically by the title of the book. If they are from different dates, they should be ordered chronologically, with each item separated by a semicolon.

Block quotations—those of more than four manuscript lines—should be indented, with a space before and after the quote. Most journals will also allow them to be single spaced. You should introduce the quotation with either a comma or a colon. The in-text citation should follow the ending punctuation and be placed in brackets rather than parentheses.

Examples

Citing the entire book:

Garcia (2003) strongly agrees.

Citing one author—name not in text:

"the issue with public health" (Garcia 2003:29)

Citing one author—name in text:

As Julio Garcia [**write the author's first and last name on first mention; afterward, write only the LAST name**] suggests, "the issue with public health is that time and again funding is often denied to the groups and organizations most in need" (2003:29).

Citing two authors—names not in text:

(Lopez and Best 2010)

Citing three or more authors—names not in text:

(Leblanc, et al. 2010)

Citing multiple works by the same author—same year:

(McGruder 2009a; 2009b)

Citing multiple works by the same author—different years:

(Pugh 2008; 2009)

Citing multiple works by different authors—chronological order:

(Carrillo 2000; Torres 1999; Bartley 1982)

If you are using a later edition of a volume than its original, include only the date you are citing from in the in-text citation. In the reference section, first place the date you referenced and then follow it with other dates in brackets.

Works in production or near production:

Tyner (in press)

Works without a date:

Tyner (N.d.)

Electronic resources:

(Powell 1999, Chapter 1, Section 3, Paragraph 5)

In the reference section, the heading should be a first-level heading. Each item should be single spaced and, after the second line, formatted as a hanging indent and in title case. References should be in alphabetical order by author's last name. Like American Sociological Association format, authors' full first and last names should be included in the reference section (no *et al.* or initials unless that is how they have referred to themselves in their document). If you have multiple works by the same author, list them in chronological order from oldest to newest. If an author has completed both solo work and multiauthored work, include the solo work first, followed by the multiauthored work.

Books, one author:

Anyon, Jean. 1997 Ghetto Schooling: A Political Economy of Urban Educational Reform. New York: Teacher's College Press.

Books, multiple authors:

Attewell, Paul, and David E. Lavin. 2007 Passing the Torch: Does Higher Education for the Disadvantaged Pay Off Across the Generations? New York: Russell Sage Foundation.

Bryk, Anthony S., Valerie E. Lee, and Peter B. Holland. 1993 Catholic Schools and the Common Good. Cambridge, Massachusetts: Harvard University Press.

Edited volumes (entire):

If there is a volume number, it should go after the name of the book, following a comma: "vol. 2." If there is an edition number, it should go after the name of the book, following a period: "3rd edition."

Arum, Richard, Irenee Beattie and Karly Ford eds. 2011 The Structure of Schooling. 2nd edition. Mountain View: Mayfield Publishing Company.

Edited volumes (chapter):

Coleman, James, Ernest Campbell, Carol Hobson, James McPartland, Alexander Mood, Frederick Weinfeld and Robert York, eds. 1966 Equality of Educational Opportunity. *In* The Structure of Schooling. Richard Arum, Irenee Beattie, and Karly Ford, eds. Pp. 231–267. Mountain View: Mayfield Publishing Company.

Journal articles:

Battle, Juan. 1997 The Relative Effects of Married Versus Divorced Family Configuration and Socioeconomic Status on the Educational Achievement of African American Middle-Grade Students. The Journal of Negro Education 66(1):29–42.

Aguirre, B. E., Dennis Wenger and Gabriela Vigo. 1998 A Test of the Emergent Norm Theory of Collective Behavior. Sociological Forum 13(2):301–320.

Articles from magazines or newspapers:

Berger, Joseph. 2007 Some Wonder if Cash for Good Test Scores Is the Wrong Kind of Lesson. New York Times, August 8: B7.

Information posted on a website:

Botsch, Carol Sears. 2000 Septima Poinsette Clark. USC Aiken. http://www.usca.edu/aasc/clark.htm accessed August 5, 2012.

For other online information, cite exactly as you would for the print version of the article. If it is available only online, also include the URL.

Chicago Style

As a social scientist, you will rarely be required to cite in Chicago style, particularly for a course paper in sociology. However, some journals do require their authors to write and submit their work in this style, so it is important to recognize and understand how to cite in this format. Chicago and Modern Language Association (MLA) are similar styles, but in college, MLA is emphasized within the humanities and liberal arts, while Chicago is intended to be a more general format. For these reasons, we will use Chicago here rather than MLA.

In-Text Citations (Notes)

Chicago does not use in-text citations. Instead, references are usually placed within an endnote or footnote in the text. The first note should include all information needed for referencing. The following notes need only include the author's last name, a short title, and page numbers. If you cite the same pages directly following each other, you should use "Ibid." If the rest of the source is the same but the page numbers are different, follow "Ibid." with a comma and then the page numbers.

Examples

Books, one author:

If there is a volume or edition, it should be placed after the title and not italicized.

Jean Anyon, *Ghetto Schooling: A Political Economy of Urban Educational Reform* (New York: Teacher's College Press, 1997).

Books, multiple authors:

Paul Attewell and David E. Lavin, *Passing the Torch: Does Higher Education for the Disadvantaged Pay Off Across the Generations?* (New York: Russell Sage Foundation, 2007).

Anthony S. Bryk, Valerie E. Lee, and Peter B. Holland, *Catholic Schools and the Common Good.* (Cambridge, Massachusetts: Harvard University Press, 1993).

Edited volumes (entire):

Richard Arum, Irenee Beattie, and Karly Ford, eds. *The Structure of Schooling*, 2nd ed. (Los Angeles: Pine Forge Press, 2011).

Edited volume (chapter), more than three authors:

James Coleman and others, "Equality of Educational Opportunity," in *The Structure of Schooling*, 2nd ed., ed. Richard Arum, Irenee Beattie, and Karly Ford (Los Angeles: Pine Forge Press, 2011), 120–136.

Journal articles:

Juan Battle, "The Relative Effects of Married Versus Divorced Family Configuration and Socioeconomic Status on the Educational Achievement of African American Middle-Grade Students," *Journal of Negro Education* 66, no. 1 (1997): 29–42.

B. E. Aguirre, Dennis Wenger, and Gabriela Vigo, "A Test of the Emergent Norm Theory of Collective Behavior," *Sociological Forum* 13, no. 2 (1998): 301–320.

Articles from magazines or newspapers:

Lauran Neergaard, "Use of Condoms Stalls: CDC Issues Report on Teens' Sexual Behavior," *Milwaukee Journal Sentinel*, July 25, 2007, 3A.

Information posted on a website:

Carol Sears Botsch, "Septima Poinsette Clark," USC Aiken, http://www.usca.edu/aasc/clark.htm (accessed July 15, 2012).

For other online information, cite exactly as you would for the print version of the article. If it is available only online, also include the URL.

The references header should be centered at the top of the page and should begin on a new page. Each item should be double spaced and formatted as a hanging indent. All major words should be capitalized in journal titles, but chapters, articles, books, and web pages should be set in sentence case. References should be in alphabetical order by author's last name. You should use authors' last names and first initials for all authors up to seven. If there are more than seven, follow the last name with ellipses. If you have multiple works by the same author, list them in chronological order from oldest to newest. If an author has completed both solo work and multiauthored works, include the solo work first, followed by the multiauthored work. Be sure that the letters that follow the dates of works by the same author in the same year match up with those used in the in-text citations. Books and journal titles should be italicized.

CHAPTER 5

Sample Consent Form

UNIVERSITY OF NORTH AMERICA
AGREEMENT OF CONSENT FOR RESEARCH PARTICIPANTS

[Title of project]

[Principal investigator's name]

[Academic department]

   You have been invited to participate in this research study. Before you agree to participate, it is important that you read and understand the following information. Participation is completely voluntary. Please ask questions about anything you do not understand before deciding whether or not to participate.

PURPOSE: The purpose of this research study is [**This should be a short, concise statement that can be clearly understood by individuals with no knowledge of the researcher's field—avoid all jargon.**] You will be one of approximately X participants in this research study.

PROCEDURES: [**This should be a step-by-step account of procedures as observed/experienced by the participant. For audio- or video-taping, include a statement such as, "You will be audio-taped during the interview portion of the study to ensure accuracy. The tapes will later be transcribed and will be destroyed after X years beyond the completion of the study. For confidentiality purposes, your name will not be recorded."**]

DURATION: Your participation will consist of [**This should inform the potential participant of the number of sessions, minutes, hours, days, etc. they will be actively engaged in the research.**]

RISKS: The risks associated with participation in this study include [**No study is without risk. If the risks are minimal, please state that the risks are no more than the participant would encounter in everyday life. If there are identifiable risks, list the risks and describe the safeguards in place to avoid these risks. Depending on the type of research you are conducting, you may become privy to information that triggers the mandatory reporting requirements for child abuse, child neglect, elder abuse, or intent to harm self or others. In these types of research, this must be disclosed as a risk to participants.**]

BENEFITS: The benefits associated with participation in this study include [**Benefits refer to direct benefits. Research sometimes provides subjects with treatment, diagnosis, or examination for an illness or condition. In these cases, the research involves evaluations that may benefit the subjects by improving their condition or providing a better understanding of their condition. Investigators should clearly detail these potential benefits in the consent form, while not overstating these benefits. Additionally, benefits cannot be guaranteed. Not every study has direct benefits to subjects. If the study does not have direct benefits to subjects, state this. You can also include a statement that participation may help provide a better understanding of the topic you are researching.**]

CONFIDENTIALITY: All information you reveal in this study will be kept confidential. All your data will be assigned an arbitrary code number rather than using your name or other information that could identify you as an individual. When the results of the study are published, you will not be identified by name. The data will be destroyed by shredding paper documents and deleting electronic files [**number of years or months, etc.**] after the completion of the study. [**A statement describing procedures taken to protect the privacy and confidentiality of the participant. Describe how, where, and for how long data will be stored, plus how the data will be disposed of and any anticipated use of the data in the future. In addition, describe how tapes (if used) will be maintained and when they will be erased. Also, discuss the limits of the confidentiality. For example, if focus groups are used, you cannot ensure that other participants will maintain the subject's confidentiality and privacy (such as "All focus group participants are instructed to keep discussions confidential; however, the researcher(s) cannot guarantee that all focus group participants will respect everyone's confidentiality"). For research regulated by the Food and Drug Administration (FDA), please include a statement that indicates research records may be inspected by the FDA.**] Your research records may be inspected by the University of North America Institutional Review Board or its designees [**insert study sponsor if sponsored by a funding agency, and the FDA for research regulated by the FDA] and (as allowable by law) state and federal agencies.

COMPENSATION: [Delete this section if not applicable. If applicable, describe the amount of compensation, how and when it will be distributed, and in what form. The key issue the Institutional Review Board will evaluate is the potential for compensation to be coercive. If prorated payments will be paid to subjects for early withdrawal or another purpose, that information needs to be clearly stated.]

EXTRA COSTS TO PARTICIPATE: [Research sometimes requires subjects to pay out of pocket for certain aspects of the research study. This can include, but is not limited to, transportation costs to and from the study site, costs related to medicines or other treatments, costs of study-related supplies, etc. If there are no extra costs to subjects, delete this section.]

INJURY OR ILLNESS: [This section is not required unless this project involves more than minimal risk.] University of North America will not provide medical treatment or financial compensation if you are injured or become ill as a result of participating in this research project. This does not waive any of your legal rights or release any claim you might have based on negligence.

VOLUNTARY NATURE OF PARTICIPATION: Participating in this study is completely voluntary, and you may withdraw from the study and stop participating at any time without penalty or loss of benefits to which you are otherwise entitled. [Indicate the procedure for a participant to withdraw her/his data. Although participants should be able to withdraw their participation at any time, situations do occur during the research process that make that difficult or even impossible. For example, if at some point during the research project the data will be de-identified, it may not be reasonable to find and extract a particular person's data from the data set. In this section, also indicate what will happen to the data if participants withdraw.]

CONTACT INFORMATION: If you have any questions about this research project, you can contact [insert principal investigator's name and contact information, plus the name and contact information for any additional research personnel who also serve as a contact for participants.] If you have questions or concerns about your rights as a research participant, you can contact University of North America Office of Research Compliance at (296) 555-2443.

I HAVE HAD THE OPPORTUNITY TO READ THIS CONSENT FORM, ASK QUESTIONS ABOUT THE RESEARCH PROJECT AND AM PREPARED TO PARTICIPATE IN THIS PROJECT.

Participant's Signature _____ Date _____

Participant's Name _____

Researcher's Signature _____ Date _____

Sample Assent Form

UNIVERSITY OF NORTH AMERICA
ASSENT FORM FOR RESEARCH PARTICIPANTS

[Title of project]

Investigator(s): [List all individuals (names and degrees) who will obtain assent from subjects]

We are doing a research study. A research study is a special way to find out about something. We want to find out [purpose of study in simple language].

You can be in this study if you want to. If you want to be in this study, you will be asked to [Describe procedures simply].

We want to tell you about some things that might happen to you if you are in this study. [Describe risks—e.g., painful procedures, other discomforts, things that take a long time.]

If you decide to be in this study, some good things might happen for you. [Describe possible direct benefits, or state that there is no direct benefit from being in the study.] But we don't know for sure that these things will happen. We might also find out things that will help other children someday.

[For medical treatment studies only; please delete if this does not apply to your project.] If you don't want to be in this study, we will tell you about the other things we can do for you.

When we are done with the study, we will write a report about what we found out. We won't use your name in the report. All the information you provide will be kept private. No one except the research team will know that you are in the study unless you and your parents decide to tell them. The only time we would break this rule is if you tell us information we think your parents need to know to be able to keep you or other people safe. For example, if you have been having serious thoughts about hurting yourself in some way, we would inform your parents.

Even if your parent/guardian agrees to your participation in this study, it is still your decision whether or not to be in the study. You do not have to be in this study if you don't want to. You can say "no," and nothing bad will happen. If you say "yes" now but you want to stop later, that's okay too. If something about the study bothers you, you can stop being in the study. All you have to do is tell the researcher you want to stop. If there is anything you don't like about being in the study, you should tell us, and if we can, we will try to change it for you.

If you have any questions about the study, you can ask the researcher. We will try to explain everything being done and why. Please ask us about anything you want to know.

If you want to be in this study, please sign and print your name.

I, _____, want to be in this research study.

Signature _____ Date _____

Investigator Signature _____ Date _____

Sample Parent Permission Form

UNIVERSITY OF NORTH AMERICA
PARENT PERMISSION FORM

[Title of project]

[Principal investigator's name]

[Academic department]

Your child has been invited to participate in this research study. Before you agree to allow your child to participate, it is important that you read and understand the following information. Participation is completely voluntary. Please ask questions about anything you do not understand before deciding whether or not to give permission for your child to participate.

PURPOSE: The purpose of this research study is [**This should be a short, concise statement that can be clearly understood by individuals with no knowledge** of the researcher's field—avoid all jargon.] Your child will be one of approximately X participants in this research study.

PROCEDURES: [This should be a step-by-step account of procedures as observed/experienced by the child participant. For audio- or video-taping, include a statement such as, "Your child will be audio-taped during the interview portion of the study to ensure accuracy. The tapes will later be transcribed and will be destroyed after X years beyond the completion of the study. For confidentiality purposes, your child's name will not be recorded."]

DURATION: Your child's participation will consist of [This should inform the parent of the number of sessions, minutes, hours, days, etc. that the child will be actively engaged in the research].

RISKS: The risks associated with participation in this study include [No study is without risk. If the risks are minimal, please state that the risks are no more than the child would encounter in everyday life. If there are identifiable risks, list the risks and describe the safeguards in place to avoid these risks. Depending on the type of research you are conducting, you may become privy to information that triggers the mandatory reporting requirements for child abuse, child neglect, elder abuse, or intent to harm self or others. In these types of research, this must be disclosed as a risk to participants.]

BENEFITS: The benefits associated with participation in this study include [Benefits refer to direct benefits. Research sometimes provides subjects with treatment, diagnosis, or examination for an illness or condition. In these cases, the research involves evaluations that may benefit the subjects by improving their condition or provide a better understanding of their condition. Investigators should clearly detail these potential benefits in the consent form, while not overstating these benefits. Additionally, benefits cannot be guaranteed. Not every study has direct benefits to subjects. If the study does not have direct benefits to subjects, state this. You can also include a statement that participation may help provide a better understanding of the topic you are researching.]

CONFIDENTIALITY: All information your child reveals in this study will be kept confidential. All your child's data will be assigned an arbitrary code number rather than using your child's name or other information that could identify your child as an individual. When the results of the study are published, your child will not be identified by name. The data will be destroyed by shredding paper documents and deleting electronic files [**number of years or months, etc.**] after the completion of the study. [**A statement describing procedures taken to protect the privacy and confidentiality of the child participant. Describe how, where, and for how long data will be stored plus how the data will be disposed of and any anticipated use of the data in the future. In addition, describe how tapes (if used) will be maintained and when they will be erased. Also, discuss the limits of the confidentiality. For example, if focus groups are used, you cannot ensure that other participants will maintain the subject's confidentiality and privacy (such as "All focus group participants are instructed to keep discussions confidential; however, the researcher(s) cannot guarantee that all focus group participants will respect everyone's confidentiality"). For research that is regulated by the FDA, please include a statement that indicates the research records may be inspected by the FDA.**] Your child's research records may be inspected by the University of North America Institutional Review Board or its designees [**insert study sponsor if sponsored by a funding agency, and the FDA for research regulated by the FDA**] and (as allowable by law) state and federal agencies.

COMPENSATION: [Delete this section if not applicable. If applicable, describe the amount of compensation, how and when it will be distributed, and in what form. The key issue the Institutional Review Board will evaluate is the potential for compensation to be coercive. If prorated payments will be paid to subjects for early withdrawal or another purpose, that information needs to be clearly stated.]

EXTRA COSTS TO PARTICIPATE: [Research sometimes requires subjects to pay out of pocket for certain aspects of the research study. This can include, but is not limited to, transportation costs to and from the study site, costs related to medicines or other treatments, costs of study-related supplies, etc. If there are no extra costs to subjects, delete this section.]

INJURY OR ILLNESS: [This section is not required unless this project involves more than minimal risk.] University of North America will not provide medical treatment or financial compensation if your child is injured or becomes ill as a result of participating in this research project. This does not waive any legal rights or release any claim based on negligence.

VOLUNTARY NATURE OF PARTICIPATION: Your child's participation in this study is completely voluntary, and your child may withdraw from the study and stop participating at any time without penalty or loss of benefits to which your child is otherwise entitled. [Indicate the procedure for a participant to withdraw her/his data. Although participants should be able to withdraw their participation at any time, situations do occur during the research process that make that difficult or even impossible. For example, if at some point during the research project the data will be de-identified, it may not be reasonable to find and extract a particular person's data from the data set. In this section, also indicate what will happen to the data if participants withdraw.]

CONTACT INFORMATION: If you have any questions about this research project, you can contact [insert principal investigator's name and contact information, plus the names and contact information for any additional research personnel who also serve as contacts for participants.] If you have questions or concerns about your child's rights as a research participant, you can contact University of North America's Office of Research Compliance at (296) 555-2443.

I HAVE HAD THE OPPORTUNITY TO READ THIS PARENT PERMISSION FORM, ASK QUESTIONS ABOUT THE RESEARCH PROJECT, AND AM PREPARED TO GIVE MY PERMISSION FOR MY CHILD TO PARTICIPATE IN THIS PROJECT.

Parent's Signature(s) _____ Date _____

Parent's Name(s) _____

Researcher's Signature _____ Date _____

Verbal Script

My name is David Stein. I am a student in the Sociology Department at Maine State University. I am working with Dr. Stephanie Rosario, my thesis advisor in the Sociology Department, on this project.

I am conducting research on television viewing habits and their influence on the voting habits of college students. I am recruiting participants to take part in short interviews, which will require approximately 15 to 20 minutes of your time.

Your participation is voluntary. If you choose not to participate or to withdraw from participation at any time, you will not be penalized in any way. The results of this study may be published, but your name will be kept confidential to the extent allowed by law.

If you have any questions, please contact me at david.stein@mainestate.edu.

May I interview you, and do you agree to be a part of this study?

I would like to audio-tape your responses so that I can record the details of our conversation accurately. I will be the only one listening to the audio tape. All information gathered will be kept strictly confidential and will be stored in a password-protected computer file.

May I audio-record our phone conversation?

CHAPTER 11

Sample Statements of Purpose

The University of Chicago

A candidate's statement of academic purpose should discuss your academic and career objectives in a concise, sharply focused, and well-crafted essay. This statement must be completed online as part of the Online Graduate Student Application. Admissions committees are particularly interested in this statement, so it is considered a vital part of your application. Therefore, you should be as specific as possible in discussing your academic objectives and research interest. There is a 2,500-word limit for the statement of purpose on our online application.

Stanford University

The statement of purpose should describe succinctly your reasons for applying to the Doctoral Program in Sociology at Stanford, your preparation, study and research interests, future career plans, and other aspects of your background and interests which may aid our admissions committee in evaluating your aptitude and motivation for pursuing a Ph.D. in Sociology.

The University of North Carolina, Chapel Hill

Please provide a personal statement that describes your reasons for seeking a PhD in Sociology at UNC, your major intellectual interests and career goals, the sort of research and scholarship you hope to pursue, and the most important aspects in your background that have prepared you for graduate study in Sociology. The statement should be not more than three pages long.

University of Illinois at Chicago

The **Personal Statement** is a short statement (2–3 pages) detailing how and why you decided to pursue a PhD in sociology, including personal, work, and research experiences. Applicant should indicate their present research interests as well as any information they want the graduate committee to consider in their deliberations. The personal statement should be sent directly to the department.

The Ohio State University

A statement of purpose, which should outline the applicant's relevant training, research experience, academic goals, plan of study, career objectives, and reasons for choosing sociology at Ohio State. Any special circumstances that need explaining should be noted as well.

The University of Wisconsin–Madison

We'd like to know the kinds of topics and approaches that interest you. The statement should make us understand that you are really interested in a scholarly life as a sociologist. Why sociology? Why Wisconsin? Are there particular faculty or program areas of special interest to you? Do you see your research interests as well-defined or fairly open at this point? Based on your knowledge and thinking now, what research problem(s) would you hope to pursue while here.

University of California, Los Angeles

A statement of purpose, not to exceed three typewritten double-spaced pages outlining reasons for pursuing graduate work, interests within sociology, and any pertinent intellectual and career experiences and interests. The Admissions Committee considers a strong applicant to have well-conceived research interests, past research accomplishment, and intellectual biography.

Sample Curriculum Vitae

Betty A. Deas

Work Address
Sociology Department
University of North America
New York, NY 10036
bdeas618@unorthamerica.edu

Home Address
77 W. Monticello Ave. #3931
New York, NY 10023
(212) 555-7270 (home)
(626) 555-8245 (cell)

Education

PhD	2014 (expected)	Sociology	The University of North America
MS	2007	Applied Sociology	Stand College
BA	2003	Sociology, magna cum laude, honors in sociology	Port Charles University

Doctoral Dissertation

Title: An Intersectional Analysis of State-Funded Welfare Programs

Committee: Chair: Rajaun Rodriguez
             Members: Arielle Rasmussen, Roberto Sanchez, Nikisha Welcome

Research Interests

Historical Sociology; Sociology of Science; Race/Ethnicity; Sex and Gender; Sexualities; Immigration; Class; Quantitative Research Methods

Fellowships, Grants, and Awards

2012   Dissertation Fellowship, The University of North America

2010   Graduate Research Grant, The University of North America

2007   The University of North America Teaching Fellowship

2007   Stand College Master's Thesis Award

2002   Port Charles Student Leadership Award

Teaching Experience

2010   Instructor, The University of North America, "Historical Sociology"

2009   Teaching Assistant, The University of North America, "Introduction to Sociology," under Anisa Cribb

2008   Teaching Assistant, The University of North America, "Statistics," under Richard Hahn

Publications

Adams, Roxsan and Betty A. Deas. 2010. "Challenges in Qualitative Research: Meeting Respondents."

Deas, Betty A. 2008. "Review of *The Housing Crisis: A Social Problem*." *Journal of Social Issues,* 42(4): 371.

Manuscripts Under Preparation

MacEachern, Conrad and Betty A. Deas. "Mexican Nationalism and Racial Perceptions in the United States." Revise and resubmit.

"'Show Me the Money': Funding Non-Profit Organizations." In progress.

Professional Presentations

2011   "'Show Me the Money': Funding Non-Profit Organizations." American Sociological Association, Las Vegas, NV.

2009   "Mexican Nationalism and Racial Perceptions in the United States." Society for the Study of Social Problems, San Francisco, CA.

Related Experience

Research Assistant, The University of North America, Sociology Department, under Dr. Nikisha Welcome, 2009–Present

Research Consultant, Society of Religious Institutions, 2007–2009

Professional Organizations

The American Sociological Association

The Association of Black Sociologists

Sociologists for Women in Society

Society for the Study of Social Problems

The Society of the Study of Symbolic Interactionism

Association for Applied and Clinical Sociology

Eastern Sociological Society

References

Nikisha Welcome, PhD
Department of Sociology
The University of North America
299 W. 12th St., New York, NY 10012
(212) 555-2343
nikisha.welcome@unorthamerica.edu

Arielle Rasmussen
Department of Sociology
The University of North America
299 W. 12th St., New York, NY 10012
(212) 555-8462
arielle.peterson@unorthamerica.edu

Roberto Sanchez
Department of Sociology
The University of North America
299 W. 12th St., New York, NY 10012
(212) 555-2853
robert.williams@unorthamerica.edu

Sample Résumé

Louise Miller

27 W. 128th Street Apt. 2

New York, NY 10027

(917) 555-1142

louisemiller@gmail.com

Objective: To utilize my office skills, customer service experience, and academic knowledge in a library position at The University of North America

Experience: Kaplan, Inc.   New York, NY   January 2006–present

Technology Procurement

- Currently working in the Technology Procurement Department
- Utilizing Microsoft Outlook and BMC Magic Client Services software, fulfilling technology order requests by creating and updating service tickets, and tracking shipments through vendor websites

Anthropologie   New York, NY   May 2003–January 2006

Sales Associate, Loss Prevention Specialist

- Provided friendly, attentive customer service at the busiest location in an upscale clothing, furniture, and housewares retail chain
- Handled multiple-line phone system, cash register, multitasking in high-pressure environment
- Maintained and restocked two-story sales floor; rapidly carried, sorted, and replenished large volumes of clothing and merchandise

Cycle Count Specialist   March 2005–August 2005

- Improved accuracy of store's estimated merchandise loss due to theft or error ("shrink") from more than 4% previous year, meeting goal of 1.0% dollar loss
- Responsible for thoroughly searching sales floor and two separate Manhattan stockrooms for missing items; involved some heavy lifting/moving boxes
- Communicated updates to corporate office via telephone and Microsoft Outlook

New York City Ballet   New York, NY   June/July 2002

Telefundraiser

- Conducted persuasive telephone calls in high volume, encouraging Ballet attendees to contribute to the nonprofit Ballet Guild

Account Resource   Oak Brook, IL   2000–2001

Temporary Office Support Staff

- Worked for United Parcel Service, American Pharmaceutical, MTI Globetrotters
- Developed spreadsheets and documents using Excel, Word, IBM OnDemand
- Performed extensive data entry tasks, reorganized and maintained filing systems

Education:

City College of New York   New York, NY   2005–2007

- 3.89 GPA; BFA in studio art

School of Visual Arts   New York, NY   2002–2003

- Worked toward BFA in illustration

Beloit College   Beloit, WI   1998–2000

- Worked toward BFA in studio art with a minor in Asian studies
- Studied at Kansai-Gaidai University in Osaka during fall semester 2000
- Intensive summer Japanese course at University of Chicago, 1999
- 1998 National Merit Finalist, Beloit College Presidential Scholarship recipient

Skills:

- Adept in both PC and Macintosh platforms
- Microsoft Word, Outlook and Excel, Adobe Photoshop and Illustrator
- Familiar with PowerPoint and HTML
- Excellent math, grammar, and proofreading abilities
- Proficient in Japanese

References available on request.

Sample Highlight Sheet

Dear Dr. Fitzpatrick,

Here is a summary that highlights the work I have accomplished this year. In the past 8 months, I have done the following:

- Worked as a teaching assistant for three courses in the Sociology Department at New York State University in New York, New York, which were highly rated by the students and the faculty member I worked with:

- o Introduction to Sociology (1 section)
- o Race, Class and Gender (1 section)
- o Social Statistics (1 section)
- Worked with the faculty member to prepare a course for next semester
- o Sociology of Work
- Revised a paper previously submitted in your class on the ways racial tensions played out in a public park, for which I received an A
- o "Race in the Park"
- Had a paper accepted for a conference presentation
- o Duncan, Patrick. 2011 (forthcoming). "Race in the Park," to be presented at the American Sociological Association Annual Conference.
- Submitted my dissertation manuscript to Paradise Publishers for review

In my letter for the position at New York State College, I decided to highlight the following:

- My research experience and scholarly work on race
- My teaching experiences at the school
- My experiences with advising students

Please let me know if you have any questions or need any further information. Thank you again for all your help.

NOTES

1. DiPardo, Anne. 2000. "What a Little Hate Literature Will Do: 'Cultural Issues' and the Emotional Aspect of School Change." *Anthropology & Education Quarterly* 31(3):306–32.

2. Dowling, Tamara. 2010–12. "Career Article 110: Action Words." *SeekingSuccess.com*. Retrieved August 4, 2012 (http://www.seekingsuccess.com/articles/art110.php).

BIOGRAPHIES

Angelique Harris is assistant professor of sociology in the Department of Social and Cultural Sciences at Marquette University. Her research and teaching interests include the sociology of health and illness, race and ethnicity, gender and sexuality, media studies, religion, and social movements. Dr. Harris has written numerous articles, book chapters, book reviews, and encyclopedia entries. Her book, *AIDS, Sexuality, and the Black Church: Making the Wounded Whole*, explores the Black Church AIDS movement in New York City and examines how cultural constructions of AIDS influenced the mobilization efforts of the Black Church.

As a doctoral student, Dr. Harris served as a writing fellow for the Writing Across the Curriculum (WAC) program at Queens College, City University of New York (CUNY). WAC is a program that encourages colleges and universities to incorporate more writing into coursework to improve both student writing and learning. As a writing fellow, Dr. Harris aided faculty in developing writing assignments for social science students in writing-intensive courses. She also conducted workshops, worked one-on-one with students, and met with faculty to address the writing needs and concerns of their students. After earning her PhD from the Graduate School and University Center, CUNY, and before working at Marquette University, Dr. Harris worked in a tenure-track position for 4 years at California State University, Fullerton, where she regularly taught the Writing for Sociology Students course—a writing course geared toward sociology undergraduate students.

Alia R. Tyner-Mullings is an assistant professor of sociology and a founding faculty member at The New Community College at City University of New York (CUNY), the first new college to open in the CUNY system in 40 years. Her areas of interest are the sociology of education, the sociology of communities, the sociology of sports, and cultural studies. Dr. Tyner-Mullings's coedited volume, *Critical Small Schools: Beyond Privatization in New York City Urban Educational Reform*, includes 10 chapters describing the strengths and challenges of small public school education in New York City. A book based on her work in small schools is forthcoming.

As a writing fellow in the Writing Across the Curriculum program at Hunter College, CUNY, Dr. Tyner-Mullings worked with students from the social sciences and humanities on their course writing, as well as coordinating a statistical study on the ways writing is used in undergraduate courses on campus. Dr. Tyner-Mullings taught the writing component of CUNY's Pipeline Program, which prepared advanced undergraduate students for writing at the graduate level. Additionally, she has given multiple presentations on academic writing at the graduate level and has conducted several career workshops for undergraduates covering resume and cover-letter writing.

"WRITING IN PRACTICE" CONTRIBUTORS

Chapter 2

Barbara Katz Rothman is professor of sociology at Baruch College and the Graduate School and University Center, City University of New York (CUNY), and holds visiting professorships at the Charité Universitätsmedizin Medical School and Hospital International Masters in Health and Society in Berlin, the International Midwifery Preparation Program at Ryerson University in Toronto, Canada, and the Department of Sociology at Plymouth University in the United Kingdom. Her books include *In Labor*; *Laboring On*; *The Tentative Pregnancy*; *The Book of Life*; *Recreating Motherhood*; and *Weaving a Family*, and have been translated into German, Japanese, and Finnish. She has developed a course in writing for publication, which she teaches to doctoral students in sociology at the Graduate School and University Center, CUNY, and has led workshops on the topic for midwives in the United States and Canada.

Chapter 3

Cynthia W. Bruns is an instruction and reference librarian at the Pollak Library at California State University, Fullerton. She specializes in teaching research methods to sociology and criminal justice classes, as well as assisting individual students with their research questions and locating the materials the students need. Cynthia Bruns has a master's degree in library and information science and a master's degree in American studies. Her thesis for American studies was "Into the Wilderness: The Rise and Decline of Backpacking in America During the Years 1965–1977." This study reflects her long-term interest in backpacking and her love of exploring the wilderness. Cynthia Bruns wrote about the explosion of appreciation for backpacking in the United States that coincided with the development of the Environment Movement during the 1960s. During this period, backpacking became a vacation fad among Americans as concern over the deteriorating state of our environment grew. One of the advantages of working in a university library is the endless array of research possibilities continually being presented. She finds the research process fascinating and is currently exploring the topic of our changing attitudes toward the environment.

Chapter 4

Richard E. Ocejo earned his doctorate in sociology at the Graduate School and University Center, City University of New York (CUNY), and joined the Department of Sociology at John Jay College of Criminal Justice, CUNY, as an assistant professor in fall 2009. In his research, he has specifically used ethnographic and qualitative methods to examine the disparate definitions of, conflicts over, and uses of community among people who contest and construct a nightlife scene on the gentrified Lower East Side of Manhattan. Ocejo regularly teaches courses on sociological research methods, focusing on qualitative methods, urban sociology, and introductory sociology. He is currently working on a project that examines the meanings of work and craft among tradesmen. This ongoing research focuses on the attitudes and practices of people in several traditional, but reinvented, occupations to reveal the changing nature of work in the postindustrial economy. In addition to scholarly articles in *City & Community*; *City, Culture, and Society*; and *European Journal of Cultural Studies*, Ocejo has also published encyclopedia articles on "cultural capital" in the *Concise Blackwell Encyclopedia of Sociology* and on the "service economy" in the *Encyclopedia for the Study of Social Problems*, as well as book reviews in *City & Community*, *International Journal of Urban and Regional Research, Sociological Forum*, and *Contemporary Sociology*. He regularly publishes book reviews for the online journal *Metropolitics*. Ocejo edited a reader, titled *Ethnography and the City: Readings on Doing Urban Fieldwork* (Routledge, 2012), and a book on his Lower East Side research will be published through Princeton University Press in 2013.

Chapter 5

Carter Rakovski is an associate professor of sociology at California State University, Fullerton (CSUF). She holds a PhD in sociology and an MS in statistics from the University of Massachusetts at Amherst. She has worked as a statistical consultant for the Department of Veterans Affairs and Bentley University. She has been a member of the Institutional Review Board at both Bentley University and CSUF. Dr. Rakovski's research examines direct-care workers in long-term care, intersectional identities (race, gender, and citizenship), and worker satisfaction and safety. She is a member of the Fibromyalgia and Chronic Pain Center at the Health Promotion Research Institute, CSUF, where she studies employment and caregiving roles among people with fibromyalgia and chronic pain.

Chapter 6

Juan Battle is professor of sociology, public health, and urban education at the Graduate School and University Center, City University of New York. He is also the coordinator of the Africana Studies Certificate Program. With more than 60 grants and publications—including books, book chapters, academic articles, and encyclopedia entries—his research focuses on race, sexuality, and social justice. He received his PhD from the University of Michigan.

Chapter 7

Thurston Domina is assistant professor of education and sociology at the University of California, Irvine. Dr. Domina earned his PhD in sociology from the Graduate School and University Center, City University of New York, in 2006. A sociologist of education, his research focuses on the ways rising educational expectations have shaped the high school experiences of American youth. He has studied a wide range of educational policies and interventions, including secondary-school curricular reforms and detracking, college outreach programs for disadvantaged youth, affirmative action, and other policies related to college admissions and financial aid. His work has been published in *American Educational Research Journal, Educational Evaluation and Policy Analysis, Journal of Higher Education, Social Science Research,* and *Sociology of Education,* among others. Dr. Domina's research relies primarily on quantitative research methods, including distributional, quasi-experimental, and panel data approaches.

Randol Contreras is an assistant professor of sociology at the California State University, Fullerton. He received his doctorate from The Graduate Center of the City University of New York. As an urban ethnographer, he studies social inequality and crime while seeking to uncover the pain and suffering of marginal populations. His book entitled, *The Stickup Kids: Race, Drugs, Violence, and the American Dream*, (Berkeley: University of California Press, 2012) is based on field research in his old South Bronx neighborhood, where he followed the lives of Dominican Stickup Kids, or drug robbers, who robbed wealthy drug dealers who stored large amounts of drugs and cash. Currently, he has started exploratory field research on the "Black and Brown" racial tension that exists between African Americans and Latino/as in South Los Angeles and Compton.

Chapter 8

Colin Jerolmack received his PhD from the Graduate School and University Center, City of University of New York, and is assistant professor of sociology and environmental studies at New York University. His research and teaching interests include urban and community studies, environmental sociology, human–animal relations, and culture. He has published articles in a number of leading sociology journals and is the author of a forthcoming book about how relationships with animals and nature shape urban social life.

Chapter 9

James A. Holstein is professor of sociology in the Department of Social and Cultural Sciences at Marquette University. His research and writing projects have addressed social problems, deviance and social control, mental health and illness, family, and the self—all approached from an ethnomethodologically informed, constructionist perspective. He has authored or edited more than 40 published volumes, as well as dozens of journal articles. In collaboration with Jaber F. Gubrium, much of Holstein's work addresses the relation between theory and method in qualitative inquiry. Recently, his attention has focused on the interactional production of narrative realities. Holstein has served as editor of the journal *Social Problems* and the research annual *Perspectives on Social Problems*. He received his PhD from the University of Michigan.

Chapter 10

R. L'Heureux Lewis-McCoy is assistant professor of sociology and Black studies at The City College of New York, City University of New York. His research and advocacy focus on the areas of education, race, and gender justice. In the area of education, he studies how diverse school districts address equity and demographic change. He regularly comments in national media, including *Ebony*, *The Root*, and *The Grio*, and has been a guest on national television programs such as the *O'Reilly Factor* and *Our World With Black Enterprise*. He holds a PhD in public policy and sociology from the University of Michigan.

Chapter 11

Martine Hackett is a sociologist and public health professional whose research interests include maternal–child health, infant mortality, health communication, and health disparities. She previously worked as a deputy director at the New York City Department of Health and Mental Hygiene's Bureau of Maternal, Infant, and Reproductive Health, and as a television producer. She received her BFA in film and television from New York University, a master of public health from Hunter College, and a doctorate in sociology from the Graduate School and University Center, City University of New York. Currently, she is a special assistant professor at Hofstra University in Long Island, New York, and her work centers on public health issues in the suburbs and how social media can achieve health equity.

Shatima J. Jones is a PhD candidate at Rutgers University in the Department of Sociology, where she also received her master's degree. Her research interests are in urban ethnography, race, and community. Specifically, her dissertation research focuses on how Black men think about and perform race via everyday talk and interaction in the barbershop, and how these interactions shape community.

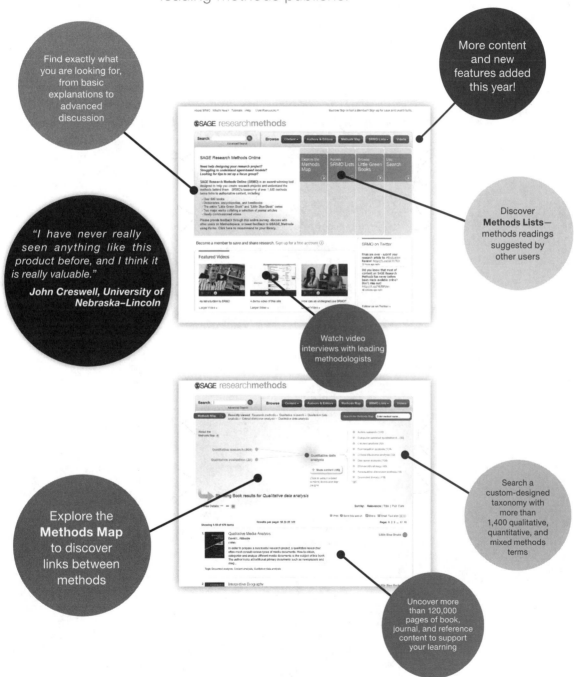

⑤SAGE research**methods**

The essential online tool for researchers from the world's leading methods publisher

Find exactly what you are looking for, from basic explanations to advanced discussion

More content and new features added this year!

Discover **Methods Lists**— methods readings suggested by other users

"I have never really seen anything like this product before, and I think it is really valuable."

John Creswell, University of Nebraska–Lincoln

Watch video interviews with leading methodologists

Explore the **Methods Map** to discover links between methods

Search a custom-designed taxonomy with more than 1,400 qualitative, quantitative, and mixed methods terms

Uncover more than 120,000 pages of book, journal, and reference content to support your learning

Find out more at
www.sageresearchmethods.com